THE WIVES OF
GEORGE IV

THE SECRET BRIDE AND THE
SCORNED PRINCESS

CATHERINE CURZON

PEN & SWORD
HISTORY

AN IMPRINT OF PEN & SWORD BOOKS LTD.
YORKSHIRE – PHILADELPHIA

First published in Great Britain in 2021 by
PEN AND SWORD HISTORY
An imprint of
Pen & Sword Books Ltd
Yorkshire – Philadelphia

ISBN 978 1 47389 749 6

Typeset in Times New Roman 11.5/14 by
SJmagic DESIGN SERVICES, India.

Printed and bound by CPI Group (UK) Ltd, Croydon, CR0 4YY

Pen & Sword Books Limited incorporates the imprints of Atlas, Archaeology,
Aviation, Discovery, Family History, Fiction, History, Maritime, Military, Military
Classics, Politics, Select, Transport, True Crime, Air World, Frontline Publishing,
Leo Cooper, Remember When, Seaforth Publishing, The Praetorian Press,
Wharncliffe Local History, Wharncliffe Transport, Wharncliffe True Crime and
White Owl.

For a complete list of Pen & Sword titles please contact
PEN & SWORD BOOKS LIMITED
47 Church Street, Barnsley, South Yorkshire, S70 2AS, England
E-mail: enquiries@pen-and-sword.co.uk
Website: www.pen-and-sword.co.uk

Or
PEN AND SWORD BOOKS
1950 Lawrence Rd, Havertown, PA 19083, USA
E-mail: Uspen-and-sword@casematepublishers.com
Website: www.penandswordbooks.com

Contents

Illustrations

1. Mrs Fitzherbert. John Condé, after Richard Cosway, 1792.
2. Caroline of Brunswick. Pierre François Ducarme, after an anonymous artist, 1820-1829.
3. His Royal Highness George, Prince of Wales. John Condé, after Richard Cosway, 1794.
4. George III and the Royal Family. Richard Earlom, after Johann Zoffany, 1771.
5. George III. William Wynne Ryland, after Allan Ramsay, 1794.
6. Charlotte of Mecklenburg-Strelitz. Richard Houston, after Johann Zoffany, 1772.
7. Princess Charlotte of Wales. Anonymous.
8. Bartolomo Bergami [sic]. Anonymous.
9. HRH Caroline, Princess of Wales, and the Princess Charlotte. Francesco Bartolozzi, after Richard Cosway, 1799.
10. Mrs Fitzherbert, *Journal des Luxus und der Moden 1786*. Anonymous, 1786.
11. William Austin, Her Majesty's Protege [sic]. Anonymous, 1820.
12. Their Royal Highnesses the Prince & Princess of Wales. Francesco Bartolozzi, after H de Janvry, 1797.
13. Princess Charlotte Augusta holding her deceased child. Anonymous, 1818.
14. James Harris, Lord Malmesbury. Franciscus Sansom, after Sir Joshua Reynolds, 1784-1790.
15. Baron Pergami. Anonymous, 1821.
16. *Ah! sure such a pair was never seen so justly form'd to meet by nature*. George Cruikshank, 1820.
17. *The Royal George Afloat; or, Tom Tough in High Glee*. J Lewis Marks, 1820.
18. *The Morning After Marriage, or, A Scene on the Continent*. James Gillray, 1788.

19. Henry Brougham, 1ˢᵗ Baron Brougham and Vaux. Henry Hoppner Meyer, after James Ramsay.
20. The Right Honourable Spencer Perceval. William Skelton, after Sir William Beechey, 1813.
21. *The Modern Paradise, or, Adam and Eve Regenerated.* Anonymous, 1786.
22. Sir William Sidney Smith. Edward Bell, after John Westbrooke Chandler, 1799.
23. *Installation of a Knight Companion of the Bath.* Theodore Lane, 1821.
24. Theodore Majocchi. Abraham Wivell, 1821.
25. Henry Brougham, 1ˢᵗ Baron Brougham and Vaux. Friedrich Rossmässler, 1833.
26. *Miss Endeavouring to Excite a Glow with her Dutch Play Thing.* George Cruikshank, 1814.
27. *A Late Arrival at Mother Wood's.* Workshop of Robert Isaac Cruikshank, 1820.
28. Carlton House. John Pye, after an anonymous artist.
29. Coronation of King George IV in Westminster Abbey. Charles Turner, after Frederick Nash.
30. View of the Coronation Procession of George IV. Anonymous, 1821.
31. The Right Honourable Sylvester Douglas, 1ˢᵗ Baron Glenbervie of Kincardine. Edward Harding, after Sir Thomas Lawrence, 1794.
32. *View of the Funeral Procession of Her Late Majesty, Taken on the Spot.* Anonymous, 1821.

Acknowledgements

A massive merci to everyone at Pen & Sword, especially Jon and Laura, and of course my fierce and fabulous editor, Lucy!

In times as strange as these we all need a bit of glorious Georgian glamour, so to everyone who likes to dip their toes into the long eighteenth, I say *rococo 'n' roll*. Adrian – for making *BMW* into something very special indeed – and Rob, Kathy, and Debra, for lists, laughter and loveliness, I send you the biggest of hugs. And Helen, HOW is it 1.00 am?

Pippa, Nelly, and the Rakish Colonial – keep on rocking!

The Royal Family

The fifty-seven year marriage of George III and Queen Charlotte was by far the most fruitful of any of the kings of Georgian Britain. From the birth of George IV in 1762, to that of Princess Amelia in 1783, Queen Charlotte was either carrying a child or recovering from a birth for more than twenty years. The royal children and their spouses are listed below.

George IV
    Maria Fitzherbert (m.1785)
    Princess Caroline of Brunswick-Wolfenbüttel (m.1795)

Prince Frederick, Duke of York and Albany
    Princess Frederica of Prussia (m.1791)

William IV
    Princess Adelaide of Saxe-Meiningen (m.1818)

Charlotte, Princess Royal
    King Frederick I of Württemberg (m.1797)

Prince Edward, Duke of Kent and Strathearn
    Princess Victoria of Saxe-Coburg-Saalfeld (m.1818)

Princess Augusta Sophia

Princess Elizabeth
    Frederick, Landgrave of Hesse-Homburg (m.1818)

Ernest Augustus, King of Hanover
    Princess Frederica of Mecklenburg-Strelitz (m.1815)

Prince Augustus Frederick, Duke of Sussex
  Lady Augusta Murray (m.1793)
  Lady Cecilia Underwood (m.1831)

Prince Adolphus, Duke of Cambridge
  Princess Augusta of Hesse-Kassel (m.1818)

Princess Mary, Duchess of Gloucester and Edinburgh
  Prince William Frederick, Duke of Gloucester and Edinburgh (m.1816)

Princess Sophia

Prince Octavius

Prince Alfred

Princess Amelia

Introduction

"I have this morning seen the Prince of Wales, who has acquainted me with his having broken off all connection with Mrs Fitzherbert, and his desire to entering into a more creditable line by marrying; expressing at the same time that my niece, the Princess of Brunswick, may be the person. Undoubtedly she is the person who naturally must be most agreeable to me. I expressed my approbation of the idea, provided his plan was to lead a life that would make him appear respectable, and consequently render the Princess happy. He assured me that he perfectly coincided with me in opinion."[1]

When King George III wrote to William Pitt on 24 August 1794, his words belied years of scandal, family feuding and anguish. Dealing with the entangled affairs of his eldest son never made for an easy life.

Throughout the centuries, lots of women have married princes. It is supposed to be the stuff that fairy tales are made of; a confection of dashing grooms and swooning brides and true love that conquers all. Needless to say, the reality was somewhat different. Marrying into royalty was always a delicate business, and business was often the operative word.

In the last years of the eighteenth century, no bachelor was more eligible than George, Prince of Wales. As the eldest son of King George III and Queen Charlotte of Mecklenburg-Strelitz, the young prince was the heir to one of the most powerful thrones in the world. He was as dashing as he was pretty, and he was eminently well-connected. The heir

---

1. Stanhope, Philip Henry, 4th Earl Stanhope (1879). *Life of the Right Honourable William Pitt, With Extracts from His Papers, Vol II*. London: John Murray, p.432.

to the throne was also deep in debt, at constant odds with his parents, and dogged by a string of messy and very public break-ups. By the time the Prince of Wales finally stumbled drunkenly to the altar to wed his cousin, Caroline of Brunswick, he was nursing a badly kept secret: his other wife.

This is a book about two women who never met, but who had one very big thing in common. Maria Fitzherbert and Caroline of Brunswick were the wives of the infamous Prinny, King George IV. One of them loved him, one did not. One bore him a child, the other did not. One union was legal, one was anything but. Between them, the two marriages spanned decades, and provided acres of newsprints and oceans of gossip. This is the story of the two wives of George IV.

Act One

Maria Fitzherbert
(26 July 1756 – 27 March 1837)

"Mrs Fitzherbert lived for several years with great openness, as the wife of the Prince of Wales, and in the enjoyment of the entire respect of society. [...] The case is a very peculiar one, from its standing in so dubious a position both with respect to law and morality."[1]

A Catholic Girl

When Mary Anne Smythe was born in 1756, it was into a Georgian world. The Hanoverian kings had been on the throne for more than forty years thanks to the Act of Succession, which guaranteed them the British crown and knocked out more than fifty Roman Catholic candidates who stood in line ahead of them. The Glorious Revolution ended the reign of James II in 1688 and ushered in a new era for the British monarchy, one in which no Roman Catholic could ever reign. Twenty-six years later, the Protestant King George I arrived with his German entourage and assumed his place on the throne.

Life for a Catholic in eighteenth century England was not easy. Catholics were forbidden from holding Crown offices or from sitting in the House of Commons or the House of Lords. They could not serve as officers in the forces or even be employed as schoolteachers and should they marry in a Catholic ceremony, that marriage was not recognised as legal. The Marriage Act of 1753 ruled that all weddings other than those of Quakers and Jews must be held in a Protestant church, and heavy penalties awaited those who disobeyed. It was in this world that the little

---

1. *Dundee Courier*. 4 August 1862; issue 2802.

girl who would become known as *Mrs Fitzherbert* grew up, and she was born a Catholic.

Maria was the daughter of Mary Ann Errington and Walter Smythe, the fourth son of Sir John Smythe, 3rd Baronet. The family motto, *Regi Semper Fidelis* – to the king ever faithful – would prove prophetic for young Mary Anne. The Smythes had always been loyal to the Crown and had received their Baronetcy in 1660 from Charles II. The eldest daughter of Walter Smythe would certainly remain true to the family motto.

Thanks to an enormous inheritance, Walter Smythe managed to combine two vital ingredients of Georgian social climbing: money and breeding. He was also a respected soldier who served with the Austrian army, marrying Mary Ann Errington on his return to England. In keeping with their impressive lifestyle, the couple made their home at Tong Castle in Shropshire, which they rented from the Duke of Kingston. It was in the castle's Red Room that Mary Anne Smythe was born. Or perhaps it wasn't, for a popular local story tells that the Smythes left Tong for London as Mary's due date approached. When she went into labour on the road, some claim that the mother-to-be was offered shelter in a local farmhouse and it was there that Mary Anne was born. Wherever she came into the world, we can be certain that she was the eldest of nine children born to the couple.

Mary Anne's early life was spent at a comfortable estate at Brambridge near Winchester, which her father bought soon after her birth. Here the family created a Catholic chapel, where they could welcome a visiting priest to say mass. It was a quietly privileged upbringing.

Though it was actually against the law for children to be educated abroad, those born into Catholic families would only be educated in their own faith if they were schooled away from England. It was a law that few observed and the Smythes were no different. In 1769, when Mary Anne was 13, she left Shropshire for France and a Catholic convent education.

There has long been debate over which convent housed the teenage Mary Anne, with popular legend connecting her to the so-called Blue Nuns[2] in the Faubourg St Antoine, but no record of the young Miss Smythe exists in their papers. Though the location remains a

---

2. This English order, actually the Order of the Conception of the Blessed Virgin Mary, was given its nickname due to the nuns' blue habits,

mystery, Mary Anne was what is known as a *pensioner*, or a student who lodged at the convent. It was a far from remarkable life, but one of discipline and learning which was intended to sculpt a respectable, intelligent and obedient Catholic wife.

Mary Anne, however, was anything but unremarkable, and it was during her educational stay in France that she met her very first monarch. Later in life she described the unique encounter to Lord Stourton.

> "Attentions from Royalty, as I have heard Mrs. Fitzherbert say, as if to prognosticate her future destinies, commenced with her at a very early age. Having accompanied her parents, while yet a child, to see the King of France at his solitary dinner at Versailles, and seeing Louis the Fifteenth pull a chicken to pieces with his fingers, the novelty of the exhibition struck her fancy so forcibly that, regardless of Royal etiquette, she burst into a fit of laughter, which attracted the Royal notice, and His Majesty sent her a dish of sugarplums by one of his courtiers. The bearer of this Royal present was the Duke de Soubise, as she afterwards heard from himself, who well remembered the circumstance; and it is rather a curious coincidence, in her connection with Royalty that the last dregs of bitterness were presented to her from a Royal table connected with a French Sovereign, Louis the Eighteenth."[3]

What an experience it must have been for the adolescent girl not only to join her parents to watch the king of France dine, but to see him tearing apart his supper with such ferocity that it reduced her to laughter. No doubt Mr and Mrs Smythe were less than amused when the monarch's gaze settled on their little girl, but Louis was far from offended by her cheek. Instead, he sent her a gift of sugarplums not via a servant, but via a duke. Just as Mary Anne's first brush with a king took place at a dinner table, so too did a dinner table mark the end of her very own royal affair many decades later. Prophetic indeed.

---

3. Langdale, Charles (1856). *Memoirs of Mrs Fitzherbert*. London: Richard Bentley, pp.113-114.

Marriage and Mourning

When 18-year-old Mary Anne returned to Brambridge, she was "in the first blush of her loveliness. Her abundant hair, which she wore naturally, in defiance of the fashion of the day, was of a pale gold, her eyes hazel-brown, her complexion that of the wild rose and hawthorn, her features exquisitely chiselled, her figure full of grace. Even more attractive than her beauty was her sunny disposition, her vivacity, her natural unaffected manner"[4]. For a world in which women were measured by their marriage prospects, it was a heady mix indeed.

> "Friday last was married by Special Licence, Edward Weld, Esq; of Lulworth Castle, to Miss Smythe, daughter of Walter Smythe, of Brambridge, in Hampshire."[5]

Edward Weld, the Roman Catholic master of Lulworth Castle, was twice Mary Anne's age when he was introduced to the sheltered young lady by a member of her family. He was instantly smitten and Mary Anne became Mrs Weld of Lulworth in 1775. Edward marked the occasion by adding his second wife to a portrait of him with the first, late Mrs Weld. It was an unusual way to celebrate, but the union was a happy if painfully short one despite the eccentricities of the groom. Mary Anne Weld became a widow within three months of her marriage.

Upon his marriage, Edward drafted a new version of his will, leaving the bulk of his estate and fortune to his new bride. According to Mary Anne, he was preparing to sign the document one morning when the newlyweds decided to go out for a ride together instead. Fatefully, Edward fell from his mount during their hack and returned home to Lulworth Castle badly shaken, but apparently uninjured. The will was still unsigned when Edward went to bed to sleep off the shock. Instead, his condition worsened and he died soon after.

Mary Anne was heartbroken. She fled her home to stay with neighbours as her brother-in-law and Edward's sole heir, Thomas Weld, travelled to Lulworth Castle to organise the family's affairs. Despite consulting

---

4. Wilkins, William Henry (1905). *Mrs Fitzherbert and George IV*. London: Longmans, Green, and Co, p.8.
5. *Public Advertiser.* 18 July 1775; issue 14287.

his late brother's legal representative, Thomas found no evidence of the new will and instead decided that Mary Anne would receive what she was legally due according to her marriage contract. The widow was to receive £800 per year, more than enough to keep an eligible 18-year-old in comfort until she could marry again.

The teenage widow left Lulworth Castle to Thomas and his family and returned once more to Brambridge. Here she entered into mourning. Mary Anne found little in the family home to cheer her as her father, once so vital and active, was paralysed by a stroke soon after her return. She spent her early widowhood in peaceful contemplation and, as the months passed, her intense grief began to fade until she was looking more like her old self again. When Mary Anne looked more like her old self, men had a tendency to notice.

> "On Wednesday morning in St. George's Church. Hanover-Square, Thomas Fitzherbert, Esq; jun. of Swinnerton, in Staffordshire, was married to Mrs. Weld, Relict of the late Edward Weld, Esq of Lullworth Castle, Dorsetshire."[6]

Three years after Edward Weld's untimely death, Thomas Fitzherbert, "a tall and powerful man with a tendency to corpulency which he endeavoured to counteract by great abstemiousness in diet and by the most astonishing efforts of bodily activity and violent exercise"[7] came to visit the Smythes. Ten years Mary Anne's senior, Thomas was a respectable Catholic landowner who resided in a sprawling country home at Swynnerton in Staffordshire, as well as a house on Park Street in London's fashionable Mayfair. He was also a sociable, wealthy and highly eligible man who could trace his lineage back to the twelfth century. For Mary Anne, he was heaven-sent. The couple were married in 1778. It had become fashionable to Latinise one's Christian name and the young widow reinvented herself as Mrs Maria Fitzherbert. Her widow's weeds were replaced by fashionable gowns once more.

Maria's second marriage set her up for life. Included in the contract was a settlement of £400 per year, plus £600 a year to be paid in the

---

6. *General Advertiser and Morning Intelligencer*. 26 June 1778; issue 413.
7. Leslie, Shane (1939). *Mrs Fitzherbert: A Life Chiefly from Unpublished Sources*. New York: Benziger Brothers, p.12.

event of Thomas' predeceasing his wife. Little did he know it at the time, but it was to prove a very wise move indeed. Life at Swynnerton was comfortable and Maria developed a lifelong friendship with the neighbouring Jervis family, but she especially loved her frequent trips to London, where Thomas hosted gatherings of influential Catholics at his Mayfair home. It was during the short marriage to Thomas Fitzherbert that Maria was presented at court to her future mother-in-law, Queen Charlotte. It was also during her second marriage that Maria first saw the 16-year-old gadabout who would become her third and final husband. Even at this young age, the Prince of Wales thought nothing of openly pursuing a pretty woman, but there's a fine line between complimentary and creepy.

> "Mrs. Fitzherbert told us this evening that the first time she ever saw the Prince was when she was driving with her husband Mr. Fitzherbert. They were in Park Lane when he turned round and said "Look. There is the Prince." The second time was a few days subsequently when she was going with her husband to a Breakfast given by Mrs. Townley at Corney House, Chiswick, As they were turning down the Lane she perceived that the Prince had followed her, and had stopped to look at her."[8]

Thomas Fitzherbert was a man of deep religious beliefs and strongly supported calls for the restrictions on Catholics to be lifted. In 1778 the Papists Act, the first act for Roman Catholic Relief, eased the strictures on Roman Catholics in Great Britain on condition that they agreed to take an oath of allegiance to the crown. Because of the long-standing connections between Catholics and the Stuart claimants to the throne, it was of vital importance that they now make a binding vow to the Protestant monarchy. Crucially, the Act also allowed Roman Catholics to serve in the armed forces and at a time when Britain was fighting a losing battle in the American War of Independence, increased manpower was the government's primary concern.

Those who opposed reform were worried by the implications of the changes, specifically the possibility that opening the armed forces

---

8. Leslie, Anita (1960). *Mrs Fitzherbert: A Biography*. York: Scribner, p.21.

up to Catholics would give them the perfect hiding place in which to plot treason against the crown. Lord George Gordon[9], head of the Protestant Association, stoked up these fears and led a march of around 50,000 people to Westminster on 2 June 1780, demanding that Parliament repeal the Act. Wearing blue cockades as a symbol of the Protestant Association, the crowd cheered Gordon as he delivered a petition against Roman Catholic Relief. News reports offer an insight into just how tense the situation became.

> "In consequence of an advertisement from Lord G. Gordon for those persons who had signed the petition for a repeal of the bill past [sic] last session in favour of the Roman Catholics, to assemble in St. George's-fields, an incredible number attended with cockades in their hats. [...] About half past two o'clock the whole body arrived near the Houses of Parliament, and gave a general cheer. Notwithstanding the great concourse of people, there seemed not, at three o'clock, the least appearance of a riot. But we are sorry to add, from another correspondent, that afterwards some of the company behaved with some indiscretion towards those whom they deemed enemies to the petition. Lord M[ansfield] was rudely treated, and the glasses of his carriage broke; a certain Bishop (who has been a strenuous supporter of the bill in favour of the Papists) was not suffered to enter the House of Lords; and [others] were extremely ill-used, having their bags pulled off, and their hair flowing on their shoulders. [...] it was expected that the mob every minute would force [t]heir way into the House of Commons."[10]

Though the crowd didn't succeed in entering Parliament, tempers flared outside the Palace of Westminster. When evening fell, the march

---

9. Lord George Gordon was later charged with high treason and held in the Tower of London, where he occupied very comfortable rooms as he awaited trial. He was acquitted thanks to a robust defence by the future Lord Erskine in a trial that made Erskine's legal name.
10. *Gazetteer and New Daily Advertiser*. 3 June 1780; issue 16009.

became a mob as Catholic homes, embassies and places of worship were ransacked and burned. The Gordon Riots continued for days and even spread as far as Newgate Prison, which was breached by the mob in an effort to release imprisoned rioters. When the crowds turned their attention to the Bank of England, King George III ordered soldiers onto the streets, resulting in a pitched battle in which many were injured. At the end of the riots a week later, nearly 300 people were dead, and hundreds were placed under arrest.

As anti-Catholic violence and arson spread across the city, Thomas Fitzherbert and others sympathetic to the cause gathered to defend the homes of Roman Catholics. They battled through the crowds and smoke, fighting exhaustion to keep their friends and property safe. Despite his physical strength, the effort left Thomas exhausted. He returned home to Park Street, took a bath and went to bed, just as Edward Weld had five years earlier. Just like Edward Weld, it was to prove the undoing of him.

As the night wore on, Thomas was gripped by a violent fever. Maria became his devoted nursemaid and tended to his every need, but nothing seemed to bring her ailing husband any respite. When physicians visited his bedside they told Maria he had caught a chill, but the chill ran deeper than any she had known before. In fact, given his exposure to the acrid smoke as he fought to extinguish fires and shore up buildings, it seems more likely that Thomas sustained some sort of lung damage from the flames, or even contracted a serious pulmonary or respiratory disease as he mingled with the vast crowds. Whatever the cause, his condition grew worse by the day until Maria decided that drastic measures were called for.

What Maria had seen in London terrified her, and her husband's condition was living proof of the horror of the riots. With his health growing weaker, they packed up their things and travelled to Nice in France, where Maria hoped that the warm weather and gentle pace of life would pull her husband back from the brink. Instead, the once strapping Thomas grew ever more frail. He died in May 1781, leaving Mrs Fitzherbert a widow for the second time. This time, however, he had signed his will. Swynnerton went to Thomas' brother but virtually everything else was bequeathed to Maria, including a payment of £1,000 per year. The widow Fitzherbert was made for life.

The Prince of Wales

> "It is something remarkable, that [the Prince of Wales] was
> born on the anniversary of his illustrious family's accession
> to the imperial throne of these kingdoms, and about the hour
> of the day on which that succession took place."[11]

Though Maria and Caroline never met, they were linked by one man.
In order to understand what later transpired, it's important to see what
circumstances forged King George IV. Capricious, selfish and often
hysterical, he was not what his parents had been hoping for.

The Prince of Wales was born on 12 August 1762. He was the first
child of George III and Queen Charlotte, who had been married for just
eleven months when the heir to the throne was born. The king and queen
were famously devoted to one another and as befit their son and heir,
little George wanted for nothing. Queen Charlotte had suffered through
a painful and difficult labour to deliver her first child and as the Tower of
London's cannons fired to announce his birth, the little prince slumbered
in his velvet and satin-lined cradle. This was no low-key entry into the
world, and it set the tone for the rest of the prince's life. As he slept in
that opulent cradle, surrounded by nurses and rockers, female admirers
were admitted forty at a time to gaze on him. Perhaps this is where the
prince's love of the limelight was born, because in his glory days there
was little he loved more than being admired by ladies.

As the eldest of fifteen royal siblings, the Prince of Wales was the
first child of Charlotte and George to be entrusted to the care of Lady
Charlotte Finch, who would become a fixture in the royal household[12].
Though the intention was to raise a pious and humble boy, George was
naturally intelligent and wilful, with a hot temper that would only grow
worse as the years passed. Raising the little Prince of Wales would prove
to be a more challenging job than anyone might have anticipated.

George's education was taken care of by Lord Holderness and a
handpicked team of tutors who embodied all of the qualities that the king
hoped his son would learn to mirror. Alongside his younger brother and

---

11. *Gazetteer and London Daily Advertiser*. 13 August 1762; issue 10392.
12. Lady Charlotte retired in 1793. She died twenty years later at the age of 88.

best friend, Frederick, Duke of York[13], George was subject to an intensive and highly disciplined educational regime from dawn until dusk. Meals were humble and the food was simple, a stark contrast to the feasts that George would enjoy when he reached adulthood, and even fun was timetabled. Along with lessons in the schoolroom each little boy was entrusted with his own plot of earth, where the king hoped they would learn to share his love of working the land. The joys of learning and piety were encouraged and the pleasures of the flesh strictly forbidden. George, however, had more interest in earthly delights than his father ever did.

As far as Charlotte and George were concerned, chief among the skills required for a future king was discipline. If George stepped out of line he was soundly thrashed, but instead of beating good behaviour into him, all the punishment did was foster a spirit of rebellion. Governed with an iron fist in his early years, as a man, George would be determined that nobody would ever tell him what to do again.

The prince longed to join the military but as heir to the throne that was an impossibility. Instead, he was rewarded with his own regiment, which was strictly for show, and he took to dressing in elaborate and stately military uniforms even though he never had any hope of seeing active service. Denied the opportunity to embrace his dream, the Prince of Wales sought to employ his excess of energy elsewhere. And where better for a pretty, rich and highly eligible young heir to a powerful throne to find a distraction, than in the arms of the beauties of London?

After his sisters' governess rejected his advances, in 1779 George finally met a woman who was as interested in him as he was in her. She was Mary Darby Robinson, a married actress whose road to stardom had been rocky at best. She gave up her career to become the prince's first mistress and it cost her dear. When he moved out of his parents' home into his own establishment at the age of 18, George threw Mary aside. Her career and reputation were left in tatters and her prince couldn't care less. It was a salutary lesson that any would-be lover would do well to learn.

Surrounded by willing women, spending money as though it was going out of fashion, and casting off the piety and discipline of childhood, the young royal really went to town. He befriended senior Whigs and developed political allegiances that went against everything his traditionalist Tory father stood for. When young George wasn't

---

13. Frederick was born on 16 August 1763.

politicking he was partying and his love life was the talk not just of the town, but of the chattering classes across Europe.

The Prince of Wales fell in love easily and he fell out of love even faster, so the ladies came and went from his pleasure palace at Carlton House with worrying speed. When he met a twice-widowed Roman Catholic however, all of that was set to change. For the first time but certainly not the last, the starry-eyed Prince of Wales fell head over heels in love. Whether Maria liked it or not, he was determined to capture her heart.

The Widow Fitzherbert

Thomas' death left Maria bereft. She dressed herself in her widow's weeds once more and went into deep mourning. This was no show either, for Maria and Thomas' marriage had been one of love, not duty. At first she remained in France, splitting her time between Nice and Paris, but in 1782, Maria returned to England. After months of mourning she began to emerge from her seclusion and once again the house on Park Street became a gathering place for her society circle. It was a fateful move.

Maria Fitzherbert was not a lady of the grandest birth, but nor was she exactly lowly. Her father's half-brother, Lord Sefton, took Maria under his wing and his wife became the young widow's constant companion. In the care of the Seftons, Maria embarked on a tentative round of social calls to the most glittering personalities of the day, and it wasn't long before the attractive young widow was the talk of the town.

> "A new *constellation* has lately made an appearance in the *fashionable hemisphere* that engages the attention of those whose hearts are susceptible to the power of beauty. The widow of the late Mr. F[itz]h[erbert] has in her train half our young Nobility; as the Lady has not as yet discovered a partiality for any of her admirers; they are all animated with hopes of success."[14]

According to popular rumour, Maria received plenty of marriage proposals on her return to the capital. At just 25, the day would surely come when she would take a third husband but for now, Maria was in

---

14. *Morning Herald.* 27 July 1784; issue 1170.

no rush to do anything drastic. George, of course, did drastic better than anyone. It's a measure of just how fascinating the wealthy young widow was to London society that the *Public Advertiser* later printed the following, extraordinarily precise record of her movements.

> "YESTERDAY Mrs. Fitzherbert took an airing in Hyde-Park for one hour, twenty minutes, and forty-two seconds, attended by her coachman and one footman."[15]

When the Prince of Wales caught sight of the attractive young lady who had only recently arrived in town, he was instantly besotted, as he had been with so many other attractive young ladies before her. Through their mutual circle of friends, he lost no time in finding out who she was and when he heard of Maria's connections to Lord and Lady Sefton, contriving a meeting was easy. The Seftons kept a box at the Italian Opera, where the prince was a regular attendee. All he needed to do was to visit when Maria was in attendance and ask for an introduction. George was used to women falling at his feet and despite being six years Maria's junior, he expected her to follow suit, but he had reckoned without this good Catholic girl. A respectable widow like Maria had no intention of becoming a mistress, royal or otherwise, but George couldn't resist the *White Rose*, as some of her more florid admirers termed her. He was determined to win Maria's affections.

At their first meeting, George should have been alerted to Maria's character not only by her veiled face, but by the fact that she still wore her widow's cap and bonnet. Nevertheless, he wasn't deterred. The prince chose his moment with care, waiting until Maria was leaving on the arm of her uncle, Henry Errington, to make his move. He approached the party on the opera steps and requested an introduction to the lady behind the veil. From then on, whenever Maria was at the opera, so was George. The chase was on.

Maria was of an altogether different stripe than the courtesans and actresses that George had been so used to romancing. Not only was she a respectable Catholic, she was also in the final throes of mourning for the beloved husband she had lost before his time. To become entangled with a man who enjoyed a reputation like that of the Prince of Wales would

---

15. *Public Advertiser*. 12 May 1786; issue 16216.

be foolhardy to say the least. Maria's future was secure; she was well taken care of, moved in expensive circles and would doubtless make a good third marriage in time. A dalliance with the womanising Prince of Wales could prove catastrophic. He had already destroyed the reputation and fortune of Mary Robinson and Maria would certainly have known, because the stories of *Florizel and Perdita* were splashed across the newspapers every day. Maria would not capitulate, no matter how hard the prince tried. And make no mistake, the prince certainly did try.

The vast majority of the letters that passed between Maria and George were burned by the late king's executor, the Duke of Wellington, during a visit to Mrs Fitzherbert's London home on 24 August 1833. This was done to save the royal family from any embarrassment. So voluminous was the incinerated correspondence that Wellington eventually declared that, "we had better hold our hand for a while, or we shall set the old woman's chimney on fire"[16], but some pieces remained. Maria stored her marriage certificate and a small selection of papers at Coutts Bank, determined to keep hold of the paperwork that would protect her reputation, and even with their most intimate correspondence forever lost to us, there should be no doubt that Maria would have been flattered by George's interest. As the most fashionable and eligible man in England, the Prince of Wales was difficult to resist, but Maria was determined to try.

When George invited the widow Fitzherbert to a series of glittering events at Carlton House, she attended more out of a sense of flattered duty than anything else. She certainly didn't use George's interest to leverage influence or power as some of his mistresses did, but preferred to attend merely as a guest, rebuffing any notions that the prince might have of making her the star attraction.

Yet the more Maria resisted, the more the Prince of Wales pressed. In fact, what might have once flattered Maria eventually began to oppress her. George appeared wherever she went, bullying his way into getting the seat beside hers at banquets or into monopolising her in the ballrooms of London. He threw enormous and showy occasions at Carlton House to impress Maria and when she dared decline the occasional invitation, he went to her home and hammered at the door, loudly wailing of

---

16. Anonymous (1876). *The Edinburgh Review: Vol CXLIII*. Edinburgh: Longman, Green, Reader, and Dyer, p.473.

his love for her. It must have been mortifying. At 21, the impetuous royal believed that he would die if he could not have Maria. Maria, a respectable Catholic widow with everything to lose if she capitulated to life as a mistress, was determined to resist. She wasn't playing hard to get, she was protecting her honour at all costs.

Though Maria initially revelled in their exchanges of banter, George's passion took her by surprise. In fact, the prince had fallen madly in love again and that spelled potential disaster for Maria. As good company and witty banter gave way to something that looks to modern eyes uncomfortably like harassment, she began to seek a way to escape the attentions of the Prince of Wales. Her only option would be to leave the city midway through the season, but after spending so long in mourning and seclusion, Maria didn't want to compromise her own enjoyment simply to escape an unwanted suitor. Yet the longer she stayed in London, the greater the possible damage. As Mrs Fitzherbert told her memoirist, "She resisted with the utmost anxiety and firmness the flattering assiduities of the most accomplished Prince of his age. She was well aware of the gulf that yawned beneath those flattering demonstrations of Royal adulation."[17]

At the end of the season, Maria headed for the peaceful sanctuary of a house in fashionable Twickenham, where she hoped to be free of George's constant harassment. Instead he followed her there and gossip began to swirl around the couple again. Faced with the possible ruin of her reputation, Maria opted to cut George out her life altogether. When he called to see her she sent word that she wasn't at home and his letters went unanswered. In practical terms, it really didn't matter whether society believed they were intimate or not, because what mattered to Maria was the eye of the Almighty. If she behaved in a manner that was above reproach, she believed that the Lord would see that too, and would know that she had committed no sin.

George didn't see things that way. All he saw was the woman he loved but who would not consent to be his mistress, even though she knew that there was no chance she could be his wife. Any legal marriage between Maria Fitzherbert and the Prince of Wales was prevented by the Royal Marriages Act, which predated their romance by more than a decade.

17. Langdale, Charles (1856). *Memoirs of Mrs Fitzherbert*. London: Richard Bentley, pp.117-118.

Despite public protests about its draconian measures the Act had been pushed through Parliament by Lord North and George III in response to the marriage of the king's brother, Prince Henry, Duke of Cumberland and Strathearn, to Mrs Anne Horton, a widowed commoner. For a prince to marry so far beneath himself without first seeking the permission of the sovereign was beyond the pale, but Cumberland had known that there was no point in even asking. The pious and sober George III would never have approved a match between his brother and Mrs Horton but would instead have considered it an affront to the dignity and station of the royal family. When Cumberland went ahead with the wedding in secret and told George about it later, the monarch was furious. He banished his brother and resolved to introduce a new legal barrier to any further unions. The resultant Royal Marriages Act 1772 ruled that:

> "[…] no descendant of the body of his late majesty King George the Second […] shall be capable of contracting matrimony without the previous consent of his Majesty, his heirs, or successors, signified under the great seal, and declared in council, […] (and that every marriage, or matrimonial contract, of any such descendant, without such consent first had and obtained, shall be null and void, to all intents and purposes whatsoever."

Queen Victoria found the apparent impact of the Royal Marriages Act particularly baffling, and commented to Lord Melbourne that it seemed strange that her pious grandparents had managed to produce a clutch of sons who didn't share a Godfearing bone between them. Melbourne agreed, commenting that, "Though that Marriage Act may have been a good thing in many ways, still, it sent them like so many wild beasts into society, making love everywhere they went, and then saying that they were very sorry they couldn't marry them."[18]

Under the terms of the new Act, the descendants of George II could only marry with the consent of the monarch. If consent was withheld, once the parties were over 25, they could inform the Privy Council of their intent to marry and would then have to wait for twelve months.

---

18. Aspinall, Arthur (ed.) (1963). *The Correspondence of George, Prince of Wales, Vol II*. London: Cassell, p.xxxviii.

If no objection was made by either of the Houses of Parliament, then the wedding could go ahead. In the case of George and the Catholic Maria, however, things weren't quite so simple. There was still the Act of Settlement to consider.

> "That all and every persons that is, are, or shall be reconciled to, or shall hold communion with the see or church of Rome, or shall profess the Popish religion, or shall marry a Papist, shall be excluded, and be for ever incapable to inherit, possess, or enjoy the crown and government of this realm and Ireland, and the dominions thereunto belonging, or any part of the same."

The Act of Settlement was passed by Parliament in 1701 and more than eight decades later, it was to have a significant impact on the romance of the Prince of Wales and the widow Fitzherbert. The Act ensured that no Roman Catholic could succeed to the throne and in doing so propelled the Protestant Hanoverians to the front of the line of succession. In addition, should a sovereign or their heir marry a Catholic, they would become ineligible to rule. Maria was already starting from the backfoot as a commoner, so George III would certainly have been resistant to granting the Prince of Wales permission to marry her regardless of her religion. Her Roman Catholic faith was the final and immovable nail in the coffin, and there was literally no chance that the king would agree to such a marriage. George didn't care what his father thought though. No act or law or lack of permission would stop the prince and the widow from making one of the most scandalous royal marriages that the country has ever seen.

A Royal Miracle

Happily for Maria, she wasn't alone in her battle against the overbearing attentions of the Prince of Wales. Her friend Georgiana, Duchess of Devonshire, had been pursued by George herself and had successfully avoided his bed with her reputation intact. Instead she had become the prince's close friend, but she knew exactly how difficult he could be to dissuade.

George's passion for Mrs Fitzherbert was the talk of Bath when Georgiana visited to take the waters, so it came as no surprise to hear that the prince was distraught at Maria's resistance. George "would not rest till he told me his passion for Mrs. F. and his design to marry her," wrote the duchess, "and any remonstrance from me was always followed by threats of killing himself."[19] Yet Georgiana was no innocent who could be suckered into the prince's fanciful threats, and she had known him long enough to know that the Prince of Wales fell in love easily and often. Against her better judgement, Georgiana agreed to speak to their mutual friend and ascertain whether his affections would ever be returned. Maria assured the duchess that she would never change her mind and Georgiana told George that, "her good sense & resolution seemed so strong that I own I felt secure of her never giving way."[20] On this occasion though, the Duchess of Devonshire had fatally misread the situation.

In early July 1784, Maria received a moonlit visit from royal surgeon Robert Keate, George's friend Edward Bouverie, and Lords Onslow and Southampton. The whey-faced men told her that the Prince of Wales had stabbed himself and was intent on suicide. Though his injuries had been dressed, the prince was threatening to reopen the wounds if Maria didn't immediately accompany the men to his Carlton House bedside.

Maria demurred, though the clearly distressed countenances of the party stopped her short of concluding that the whole plan was simply a ruse. She agreed to go to Carlton House if a respectable chaperone was permitted to accompany her and the parties agreed on the Duchess of Devonshire. The group travelled from Park Street to Devonshire House and, with Georgiana safely on board, continued onto Carlton House and the supposed deathbed of the Prince of Wales. Maria was shocked to discover that the report was apparently true. The young heir to the throne was as white as milk and his chest was wrapped in bloodied bandages, evidence of the injuries that looked likely to claim his life.

George summoned up the strength to ask Maria if she would take his ring in his final moments, so that he might die content in the knowledge that she had accepted his love. Maria agreed. Despite her suspicions, Georgiana agreed to lend the prince one of her rings and as George slipped it on to Maria's finger, he declared it was binding proof of their

---

19. Bessborough, Earl of (1955) (ed.). *Georgiana: Extracts from the Correspondence of Georgiana, Duchess of Devonshire*. London: John Murray, p.86.
20. Leslie, Shane (1939). *Mrs Fitzherbert: A Life Chiefly from Unpublished Sources*. New York: Benziger Brothers, p.22.

betrothal and that he had miraculously recovered. A horrified Maria and Georgiana fled for Devonshire House, where they wrote a statement documenting what had happened. Once Maria had safely sailed from Dover, the statement was delivered to Lord Southampton, who hosted George throughout his convalescence.

> "On Tuesday the 8th of July 1784 Mr. Bouverie and Mr. Onslow came to me and told me that the Prince of Wales had run himself thro' the body & declar'd he wd. tear open his bandages unless I wd. accompany Mrs. Fitzherbert to him. We went there & she promis'd to marry him at her return, but she conceives as well as myself that promises obtain'd in such a manner are entirely void – 9th of July 1784."[21]

As the lovestruck prince slumbered happily in Carlton House, Maria was in anguish. Before the next sunrise she had packed her bags and set off for Europe, determined to put some distance between herself and her unwanted Casanova. But was there really anything under those bloodstained bandages? Maria seemed to think so and later confided in friends that she had seen George's self-inflicted scars on multiple occasions during their relationship.

The germane question is whether George had truly self-harmed and if so, how serious the wounds really were. Maria swore that she had seen George's scars, but the Prince of Wales was addicted to drama, and bloodied bandages or a healed scar really would have proved nothing. His surgeon was present that night and he was certainly complicit in the plot to bring Maria to Carlton House and to subject her to the pantomime of a marriage. For that same surgeon to have bled his over-agitated patient isn't too much of a stretch of believability. George probably did have wounds on his body, but they likely posed no threat to his health or danger to his life.

In the days following Maria's departure for France, the Duchess of Devonshire wrote to Lord Onslow and asked if the prince would consent to a physical examination to prove whether his supposed suicide attempt had been genuine. Of course George refused. He played the wounded

---

21. Bessborough, Earl of (1955) (ed.). *Georgiana: Extracts from the Correspondence of Georgiana, Duchess of Devonshire*. London: John Murray, p.87.

innocent and replied not via Onslow but directly to Georgiana. The thought of submitting to a non-partisan physician was humiliating, said the prince, and he was cut to the quick that she would even suggest it.

> "[Though] it would be most exceedingly disagreable [sic] to me to put myself under the hands of a surgeon to whom I am perfectly unusued, [I] was still willing to do so, if your want of confidence in a man to whom you had expressed yourself as looking upon him as yr. best and dearest friend, could make you wish to subject him to so mortifying as well as degrading a situation. I do not therefore solicit my acquittal upon this subject as a favour, but I demand it as a justice due to me."[22]

The piqued prince resorted to ever more extravagant shows of despair, mourning the departure of "this most amiable of women [who] ever must be transcendently the dearest to me thro' life, whose character to all who knew her must be the most unblemished and respectable."[23] George's friend and former mistress, Elizabeth Armistead, painted a lurid picture of his behaviour when he visited the home that she shared with her husband and George's best friend, the Whig politician Charles James Fox.

> "[The Prince of Wales] cried by the hour, that he testified the sincerity and violence of his passion and his despair by the most extravagant expressions and actions, rolling on the floor, striking his forehead, tearing his hair, falling into hystericks [sic], and swearing that he would abandon the country, forego the crown, sell his jewels and plate, and scrape together a competence to fly with the object of his affections to America."[24]

Fox and Georgiana both urged George to think again, reminding him that marriage to Maria would disqualify him from the line of succession. The

---

22. Aspinall, Arthur (ed.) (1963). *The Correspondence of George, Prince of Wales, Vol I*. London: Cassell, pp.150-151.
23. Ibid., p.151.
24. Holland, Lord (1854). *Memoirs of the Whig Party During My Time: Vol II*. London: Longman, Brown, Green and Longmans, p.126.

Prince of Wales knew all that, but as far as he was concerned, no price was too great to pay for the love of Mrs Fitzherbert. Instead, George conceived an audacious plan that would allow him to follow Maria to the continent and woo her there. He sought his father's permission to move to France, where he promised to cut his spending and live a more frugal, pious life. The king wasn't taken in and rejected the request. George was devastated and told James Harris, 1st Earl of Malmesbury, "[my father] hates me; he always did, from seven years old."[25] It was a bitter pill to swallow.

Yet in his efforts to chase Maria across continents, George had unwittingly set in motion a chain of events that would eventually lead to the altar. The king was all too conscious of the need for an heir, and he knew that those lingering debts were the best leverage he would ever have over his wayward son. Years later, it would be Malmesbury himself who travelled to the continent, charged with the safe delivery of Caroline of Brunswick into her new life as the Princess of Wales.

To Europe

In the eighteenth century, few places were considered more restful or appropriate for a lady in need of some restorative relaxation than Aix-la-Chapelle, where Maria could enjoy the fabled hot springs and recuperate from the prince's smothering attentions. After several relaxing weeks in France she travelled on to The Hague as a guest of the Dutch Stadtholder, William V, himself a maternal grandson of George II. The Stadtholder loved any opportunity to improve his standing with the British side of his family and even hoped to secure the Prince of Wales' hand in marriage for his daughter. He was more than happy to welcome the celebrated and fascinating Maria Fitzherbert to his court.

In Maria the Stadtholder thought he'd found the perfect tutor for his daughter, Princess Louise, and he was quick to introduce them to one another. At just 15, Princess Louise had no idea that her new friend was being pursued by the man her father dearly hoped she would marry, but whether William V was aware of the intrigue between George and Maria is a matter of conjecture. Even if he was, her presence in The Hague presented too good an opportunity to introduce his daughter to British ways to pass up. For Maria it was a heaven-sent opportunity, for how

---

25. Malmesbury, 3rd Earl of (ed.) (1844). *Diaries and Correspondence of James Harris, First Earl of Malmesbury, Vol. II*. London: Richard Bentley, p.125.

better to rid herself of the unwanted affections of the prince than by doing all she could to encourage his possible marriage to Princess Louise? Sadly it didn't come off and the marriage plans never materialised. It's testament to the impression that Maria made that when the time came to leave Holland she did so aboard the royal barge. She travelled on through France and Switzerland, enjoying a leisurely trip with no prince peering over her shoulder to profess his undying love.

Maria was joined on her trip by her friend Lady Anne Lindsay and the bond that grew between the women on their voyage would last for decades. Anne enjoyed the company of Maria, whom she nicknamed *Fitz*, but she was rather less dazzled by her companion's charms than the gentlemen they met along the road. "She is a devilishly overbearing woman at times," she wrote of Maria, who she believed demonstrated "a haughty contempt [for men] which agrees with them as dogs but not as human creatures."[26] It is a marked departure from the swooning Mrs Fitzherbert who has been committed to the historical record

Whilst Maria and Anne were enjoying their sojourn in Holland, the Prince of Wales was pining for his lost love at home. Though he had been denied the chance to follow Maria, in truth, George didn't know where she was even if he *had* been granted permission to give chase. Determined to track her down, he sent spies and envoys including the ubiquitous Edward Bouverie to the continent and in no time at all they had found their quarry. Now George employed every weapon in his considerable arsenal to win back the widow Fitzherbert.

To give his efforts the stamp of respectability George employed the Duke of Orléans as his go-between and soon letters were going back and forth between England and France at a rate of knots. So numerous were they that some of the couriers who carried them were initially imprisoned on suspicion of espionage. Similarly, concerns were being voiced amongst the chattering classes about the frequency of the prince's visits to Devonshire House too. Though he had told Georgiana that he would not see her until she accepted that his suicide attempt was genuine, her supportive shoulder proved irresistible to George. Far from sending her to Coventry, the lovesick prince made daily pilgrimages to Georgiana's side to pour out his heart and woes. There were those who wondered if

---

26. Taylor, Stephen (2016). *Defiance: The Life and Choices of Lady Anne Barnard.* London: Faber & Faber, p.130.

he wasn't going to see the Duchess of Devonshire for a different sort of comfort altogether.

Eventually Georgiana agreed to write to Maria and ask if she had any plans to return to England. If she did, Fox was hopeful that he might be able to cobble together some sort of non-legal ceremony that wouldn't be a marriage, but would satisfy both parties. It was vital for his career that he retain the prince's favour, even if that involved going along with his most absurd flights of fancy. Maria's travels had given her some much needed clarity though, and she replied in no uncertain terms that she would not submit to a sham marriage.

"I cannot see the least good effect [coming to England] could possibly have," wrote Maria. "I am perfectly well acquainted with every Circumstance and why should I appear to give in to measures I can never consent to? Whatever Mr F[ox] or his friends say to [the Prince of Wales] they know in their own breasts they cannot approve off[sic], and I am confident there is not one of them that will take it upon themselves to say [the proposed marriage] is a legal proceeding."[27] Maria's escapades with the bloodied Prince of Wales in Carlton House had taught her a lesson: the word of princes and politicians could not always be believed. Pity the poor courier who was suspected of espionage thanks to the overzealous love life of the Prince of Wales.

Of course, Maria hadn't fled George because she felt nothing for him, but because he had succeeded in winning her heart, even though she knew any romance with the prince would be a hopeless cause. She wouldn't be his mistress no matter how much he or Fox begged, even when they argued that it was for the sake of the heir to the throne's physical and mental health. Eventually, George told Lord Malmesbury that he had resolved never to marry at all if he couldn't marry Maria, which she knew that he could never do without forfeiting his right to the crown. Maria decided that ultimately the only hope was to put their overheated intrigue aside and try and move on. The Prince of Wales and Maria Fitzherbert, however, were as bad at moving on as each other.

George wrote constantly to his "ever beloved Maria, wh. I am not only not ashamed of but must ever glory in"[28]. His letters ran to dozens

27. Bessborough, Earl of (1955) (ed.). *Georgiana: Extracts from the Correspondence of Georgiana, Duchess of Devonshire*. London: John Murray, p.88.
28. Aspinall, Arthur (ed.) (1963). *The Correspondence of George, Prince of Wales, Vol I*. London: Cassell, pp.150-152.

of pages and were filled with exclamations of undying love and threats of self-harm and suicide, claiming on the one hand to be the man of her dreams and on the other to be barely in control of his faculties at all. He sent her expensive bracelets "not as a Lover to his Mistress, but such as a husband has a right to send and a right to expect his wife will receive." Should there be any doubt about the motive of such gifts, George assured Maria that "I never presumed to make you any offer with a view to purchasing your Virtue. I know you too well." It was heady stuff and as he convalesced at Brighton under the watchful eye of Robert Keate, time to dwell on his beloved was one thing the prince had plenty of.

The king had heard of his son's attachment to Maria Fitzherbert though, and he was determined to end it once and for all. Should George wish to receive any further cash, he must consent to behave "like a rational being [and] he will find things much easier arranged than he may imagine; but if he acts otherwise he must remember these last words of a much distressed parent, he will in every sense be ruined and lose the affection and protection of him who as yet remains his very affectionate father." [29] But despite these warnings, the Prince of Wales lost all sight of rationality when it came to love.

On the continent, Lady Anne and Maria awaited each new letter from the man who signed himself "not only your most affectionate of lovers but the tenderest of husbands" with bated breath, with *Fitz* alternating between watching the road for the next courier and wishing that no courier would come at all. When Lady Anne returned to England, she left Maria in Europe alone to await the latest of the prince's epistles. Yet in all the time spent watching for her next letter, she hadn't anticipated meeting a brand new suitor instead.

A Lady Surrenders

Despite Maria's best efforts to avoid drawing any kind of attention to herself – other than cosying up to the Princess of Orange, of course – the comely, wealthy widow seemed able to attract attention with her mere presence. One of those who very definitely noticed her was the Marquis de Bellois, who was as celebrated for his good looks as he was for his

---

29. Georgian Papers Online (http://gpp.rct.uk, July 2020). RA GEO/MAIN/16460-16461 Letter from George III to George, Prince of Wales, 27 August 1784.

scandalous love life, and he fell for Maria just as hard as the Prince of Wales. They met at Plombières in Lorraine and Maria was utterly charmed by the dashing nobleman. Like George, Bellois had racked up a lot of debt and it's not too much of a reach to imagine that in the wealthy widow he saw the key to paying it off. He was determined to win Maria's hand.

The Marquis became Maria's shadow, but if she had refused a prince for whom she felt real affection, there was no chance at all that she would accept a marquis who she barely knew and whose scandalous reputation went before him. At first Maria put up with his constant presence but she soon began to find it wearisome, and she must have rued the jump that had taken from the frying pan into the fire. The longer she was associated with the notorious Bellois, the worse it would be for her.

When Bellois proposed marriage Maria categorically declined, leaving him with no hope that she was simply playing hard to get. He was furious and immediately began to spread a rumour that Maria, who had fled England to protect her name and reputation from scandal, had been his mistress. Soon there were those who believed that "she lived in the greatest familiarity"[30] with Bellois and that, when she fled to Paris by night to escape him, it was merely "the consequence of this intercourse."[31] Such an idea is patently absurd. Maria thought too much of her character and reputation to risk it all for a few nights of fun with a dashing nobleman who ought to have known better.

Yet when the story of the supposed affair reached the ears of the Prince of Wales, he was beside himself. Maria was out of his reach and far beyond his influence and he was faced with the very real possibility that she might well move on. The world was full of eligible men who would be free to marry a Roman Catholic widow and George wasn't one of them. In Europe, however, deprived of the company of Lady Anne or the circle she had left behind in London, Maria's resolve was weakening. George's letters became more frantic and were filled with threats of self-harm and abdication that left Maria reeling. They did the trick. "Wrought upon and fearful, from the past, of the desperation of the Prince, she consented, formally and deliberately, to promise she

---

30. Anonymous (1789). *The Universal Magazine of Knowledge and Pleasure, Vols 84-85*. London: Privately published, p.52.
31. Huish, Robert (1830). *Memoirs of George the Fourth, Vol I*. London: T Kelly, p.126.

would never marry any other person."[32] It was the first step in Maria's surrender.

Though romantic stories later claimed that George donned a disguise to travel to Paris and personally win back his lost love, these are sadly groundless. The prince was in England for the duration of his pursuit of Maria and he was a man who had trouble doing anything quietly. Besides, he was too busy beating his breast, tearing out his hair and wailing of his broken heart to Georgiana and Mrs Armistead to conceive and execute such an audacious and risky plan.

Once George had secured Maria's promise not to marry another, the die was cast and she began to consider the possibility of returning to England to become a bride for the third time. But what changed her mind? Maria was flattered by George's interest and during that heady season in London, there had been an undeniable spark between the two of them. He had simply come on too strong and scared her away.

The shock of the Bellois incident had a profound impact on the prince and he took up his pen and wrote Maria a mammoth letter of forty-two pages, begging her to return to him. If she did, he promised that they would be joined in a secret marriage that would be binding in the eyes of God.

This last desperate effort achieved what all those expensive gifts and threats of self-harm had not. Maria agreed to return to England before 1785 was out and marry her prince. George was ecstatic. He told Maria that though marriage to the Princess of Orange would guarantee a huge payday, all the money in the world would never tempt him away from the widow Fitzherbert. Time would prove that to be a lie.

> "[Had] I been without any attachment whatever, I shd. have risked the sacrificing of my happiness & liberty to any pecuniary or interested view, but being bound by all ye ties wh. love & honor can render forcible, wh. were confirm'd by the solemn vow I made unto you & unto Heaven in the most sacred manner & at the most aweful [sic] of moments, wh. was then register'd in the books of eternity [I] therefore immediately said yt. I was excessively sensible of my father's goodness but as I had frequently declar'd my

---

32. Langdale, Charles (1856). *Memoirs of Mrs Fitzherbert*. London: Richard Bentley, p.121.

sentiments yt. I never shd. marry unless it was the woman I cd. prefer to all the world (for I did not hold marriage in such slight estimation as some people did), he must excuse me if I declin'd his offer."[33]

George was sticking rigidly to the belief that the sham ring exchange in Carlton House had been a formal betrothal. He told Maria that "I have look'd upon myself as married for above this year & half, ever since I made to thee & thou madst to me in the face of Heaven, a vow mutually to regard one another as man & wife, & never to belong to anyone else but to each other."[34] George loved the chase and this was a chase unlike any other. He had to emerge victorious.

In fact, both the Royal Marriages Act and the Act of Settlement made marriage an impossibility. The king would never give his consent to a match between his son and a Catholic, knowing full well that it would result in George's removal from the line of succession, so the marriage wasn't legally binding. In the eyes of Maria and her God, however, it was. Thus, on the one hand, George retained his place in the line of succession, whilst on the other, Maria was free of any sin. It was a curious bit of manoeuvring and one that certainly took a lot of chutzpah on the part of the prince, but he never settled for an easy life if he could complicate it instead.

In his long letter George admitted that he had spoken to Maria's mother and her uncle about their marriage. This was probably true, and he gave Maria his sworn word that when he reached the age of 25, they would be able to marry without anyone stopping them. He suggested that they do this in Holland, where he would be happy to settle as a private citizen, away from the pomp and ceremony of royal life. Like so much else in the prince's letter and its confusion of empty promises and untruths, his take on the legal and moral implications of a marriage was grossly oversimplified. To make matters worse he compounded it with a lie, suggesting that the king himself would be willing to approve the marriage so long as it was done quickly, quietly and without any fuss. He even claimed that George III was happy to sanction the union as long

---

33. Aspinall, Arthur (ed.) (1963). *The Correspondence of George, Prince of Wales, Vol I*. London: Cassell, p194.
34. Ibid., p.196.

as the succession was settled on his favourite son, the Duke of York, instead.

> "[I asked the emissary, Hugh Elliot,] whether my father was very violent at ye. Idea of my being married [to Maria]. He said no, yt. he had said what was decreed in Heaven cd. not be subverted on earth; in short, yt. ye. only way for my father now to act was entirely to connive at it, wh. he believ'd was his intention. [...] If I will consent to give up *my* succession [and] transfer it to my brother [the king will] be ready to do anything I chuse respecting you, such as either acknowledging you as my wife or anything else I may please. [There] is no sacrifice, *my beloved wife*, yt. I have not & will not make for thee; thou art a treasure to me I can never part with, & I never can go too far to testify yt. love wh. never can end but with my life."[35]

The idea of George III, to whom rank and piety was everything, agreeing to accept Maria as George's wife if he surrendered his place in the line of succession to the Duke of York, is absurd. The king had pushed the Royal Marriages Act through Parliament against a tide of opposition from his subjects and there was no way that he would rescind it just a dozen or so years later. What's more surprising is that Maria apparently took George's claims at face value. Hopeful of a happy ending against the odds, she chose to believe what her lover told her, regardless of whether there was a grain of truth or reliability in it. George never thought in such concrete terms as legalities though. Ever the romantic, what he thought about was love.

When Maria set off for home, she knew that she would soon be a bride again. Clutched to her breast was a miniature of George's eye, that he had sent her as a romantic keepsake. At first George offered to meet her on the coast road but cold feet led to a change of plan and instead he promised to come to Park Street once night had fallen, even offering to slip in through the stables if necessary. It was the stuff of romantic fiction.

---

35. Ibid., pp.196-197.

Maria wrote to her friend, Lady Anne Lindsay, to pour out her heart. She was confused and uncertain, but she was willing to risk everything for a man who had, time and time again, proved himself to be a bad bet when it came to fidelity.

> "Could I banish from my idea the fatal consequences that may attend such a connexion I then might be happy in attaching myself for life to the man that has gone thro so much for my sake & to whom I feel myself very sincerely attached but also whenever I look upon it in a favourable light that idea vanishes in a moment & leaves such an oppression on my mind that I scarce know how to support myself. I shall make it the study of my life to make him happy.
>
> [...]
>
> What will become of me my dear friend I have nothing to trust to but his honour. It is in his power by having a proper conduct in the beginning to establish my reputation in the eyes of the world and if he does not do I must sink under him."[36]

So what are we to make of Maria Fitzherbert as she packed her bags and prepared to sail for home? What was she thinking during her journey back to England for the clandestine marriage service that even now the Prince of Wales was conniving? We have no way of knowing for sure, but Maria was a sensible and pragmatic woman, and it seems odd that she should fall for the prince's near-legendary charm after resisting it for so long. Perhaps she capitulated because of his repeated threats of suicide, but he'd made the threats so often that they'd lost all potency. Her motive was likely far more heady. Maria had spent all her life being respectable and a good deal of it in mourning. The romance with the tenacious, besotted Prince of Wales was everything that her existence so far had never been. It was exciting and forbidden and perhaps, for all her sensible respectability, exciting and forbidden were exactly what Maria Fitzherbert had been craving.

---

36. Taylor, Stephen (2016). *Defiance: The Life and Choices of Lady Anne Barnard.* London: Faber & Faber, p.144.

Marriage Plans

With the prince's promises and lies spurring her on to end what had been more than twelve months on the continent, Maria returned home to England in early December 1785. As far as she was aware, George really did adore her. He had forsaken his many other mistresses and dedicated more than a year to her pursuit, but with hindsight we now know something that Maria did not. There was nothing that excited the Prince of Wales more than the thrill of the chase. He was used to getting his own way and when his pleading and threats failed, he was capable of unleashing the most devastating charm offensive. This charm was enough to convince the prince himself that he was truly and devotedly in love. In truth, he was simply determined to get what he wanted, whatever the cost.

Ever since Maria had indicated that she was willing to come home and marry her prince, George had been busy trying to make the arrangements without attracting any suspicion. For a man who was such a favourite of the Georgian press this was easier said than done, but somehow he achieved it. One person who did have suspicions about the next chapter in the ongoing drama was his friend, Charles James Fox, who had once been willing to try and broker a deal between George and Maria himself. How he discovered the plans for a secret wedding is a mystery, but on 10 December 1785, he wrote to the prince and urged him not to do anything that might jeopardise his place in the line of succession. Fox played the part of concerned friend but he was really looking out for himself.

The prince was a devoted Whig and when he eventually succeeded to the throne, Fox envisioned that he would reap the rewards of his loyalty to the new monarch. George III was a dyed-in-the-wool Tory but his son was a Whig through-and-through. Should he be removed from the line of succession, then Fox's political ambitions would be dealt a swingeing blow. Fox had opposed the Royal Marriages Act from the start and now it was about to come back to bite them all.

> "I was told just before I left town yesterday […] that you were going to take the very desperate step (pardon the expression) of marrying [Maria] at this moment. If such an idea be really in your mind, and it be not now too late, for God's sake let me call to your attention some considerations

which my attachment to your Royal Highness, and the real concern which I take in whatever relates to your interest, have suggested to me, and which may possibly have the more weight with you when you perceive that Mrs. Fitzherbert is equally interested in most of them with yourself.

In the first place, you are aware that a marriage with a Catholic throws the Prince contracting such a marriage out of the succession of the Crown. Now, what change may have happened in Mrs. Fitzherbert's sentiments upon religious matters I know not; but I do not understand that any public profession of change has been made: and surely, Sir, this is not a matter to be trifled with [...]

If anything could add to the weight of these considerations, it is the impossibility of remedying the mischiefs I have alluded to; for if your Royal Highness should think proper, when you are twenty-five years old, to notify to Parliament your intention to marry (by which means alone a legal marriage can be contracted), in what manner can it be notified? If the previous marriage is mentioned or owned, will it not be said that you have set at defiance the laws of your country; and that you now come to Parliament for a sanction for what you have already done in contempt of it? If there are children, will it not be said that we must look for future applications to legitimate them, and consequently be liable to disputes for the succession between the eldest son, and the eldest son after the legal marriage? And will not the entire annulling of the whole marriage be suggested as the most secure way of preventing all such disputes?

[...]

It will be said, that a woman who has lived with you as your wife without being so, is not fit to be Queen of England; and thus the very thing that is done for the sake of her reputation will be used against it.

[...]

In the meanwhile, a mock marriage (for it can be no other) is neither honourable for any of the parties, nor, with respect to your Royal Highness, even safe. This appears so clear to me, that, if I were Mrs. Fitzherbert's father or brother, I would advise her not by any means to agree to it, and to prefer any other species of connection with you to one leading to so much misery and mischief.

[...]

Your Royal Highness knows, too, that I have not in my mind the same objection to intermarriages of princes with subjects which many have. But under the present circumstances a marriage at present appears to me to be the most desperate measure for all parties concerned that their worst enemies could have suggested."[37]

All of Fox's assertions were correct other than that of Maria being considered a poor choice for Queen of England, because that was never on the cards anyway. Regardless of what happened with the marriage, no Catholic could ever have become queen and Maria was certainly not about to renounce her faith for the sake of the Prince of Wales. The letter illustrated every negative of the proposed secret marriage, but George didn't want to know. In a response penned at 2.00 am on the morning after he received Fox's letter, he simply told another lie.

"Your letter of last night afforded me more true satisfaction than I can find words to express, as it is an additional proof to me, which I assure you I did not want, of your having that true regard and affection for me which it is not only the wish, but the ambition of my life to merit. Make yourself easy, my dear friend; believe me, the world will now soon be convinced that there not only is, but never was, any ground for these reports which of late have been so malevolently circulated."[38]

Whether Fox believed that nothing untoward was taking place, the prince's reply was evidence that Fox had played no part in the sorry business. It was enough for the wily politician, who made no effort to raise the matter again. When the Prince of Wales wrote to the Duke of

---

37. Russell, Lord John (1859). *The Life and Times of Charles James Fox: Volume II.* London: Richard Bentley, pp.179-182.
38. Ibid., pp.183-184.

York, it was to tell him placidly that "Things are very much in ye. state they have been for some time past, & London is as dull as anything can possibly be. Nothing new stirring."[39] In fact, George was feverishly busy arranging a marriage.

George lost no time in winning Maria's elder brothers Watt and Jack to his cause, for the siblings of royal favourites could often expect to benefit from the connection. What is more surprising is that he managed to convince her mother and her uncle, Henry Errington, of the wisdom of the plan too. As long as there was a marriage that bound the two together in the eyes of the Catholic church, that was enough to satisfy any moral objections, regardless of what the world might think. Maria was no innocent girl, but a woman who had been twice widowed and had travelled extensively. On the cusp of her thirtieth year she knew her own mind, and her own mind told her that she wanted to marry the Prince of Wales.

Satisfied that Errington and at least one of the bride's brothers would serve as witnesses, all that was left now was for the prince to find a willing cleric. This was no mean feat, given the unbending terms of the Royal Marriages Act, which promised punishment to any clergyman who officiated such a ceremony.

George wasn't about to let that stop him. He needed someone who was willing to assume the risks that came with officiating the wedding and could be trusted never to speak of it again. The prince entrusted the task of finding such a man to Colonel Gardiner, his private secretary, and Gardiner's first idea was to engage a military chaplain named Philip Rosenhagen, who wasn't noted for his particularly stringent morals. Surprisingly Rosenhagen declined, claiming that he could not be party to such deceit. It's more likely that he was driven to refuse by the prince's promise that he would be paid for his part in the ceremony, just not yet. No money, no Rosenhagen.

The next port of call was Reverend Johnes Knight, aka *Parson Johnes*, who had known the Prince of Wales since childhood. Forty-five years after the meeting to discuss the wedding, Parson Johnes recalled an audience with a dressing gown-clad George at Carlton House, where he was admitted to the conspiracy of silence.

---

39. Aspinall, Arthur (ed.) (1963). *The Correspondence of George, Prince of Wales, Vol I*. London: Cassell, p.205.

"[The Prince of Wales] detailed his long love for Mrs. Fitzherbert, the misery he had endured, the taunts he had received from the King in consequence of its having been suspected that the Prince, in the course of the last summer, had gone from Brighton to the French coast to visit Mrs. Fitzherbert. As a proof of his passion he then drew up his shirt, and showed a scar on his side, which the Prince said was caused by his falling on his sword that he might end his life with hopeless love. The Prince then spoke of his determination to repeal the Royal Marriage Act the instant he came to the Throne (which, by-the-bye, has never yet been done). The Prince in conclusion begged me, if I was really attached to him, to perform the marriage ceremony between him and Mrs. Fitzherbert. I used every argument I could think of to dissuade him from his purpose, but the more I argued against the marriage the more resolved the Prince seemed to become the husband of Mrs. Fitzherbert, and at last the Prince said, "If you refuse to marry me, I must find out another clergyman who will.""[40]

Touched by the prince's passion, Parson Johnes agreed to marry the couple. Only as he walked home did he begin to consider the possible repercussions, both legal and personal. He simply couldn't reconcile his conscience with the duty he had agreed to undertake. The parson wrote to the prince to explain and was released from his promise. It was back to the drawing board for Colonel Gardiner.

The third attempt to find a man of the cloth to officiate the ceremony was successful, and when Reverend Robert Burt was offered the job for a payment of £500 and the promise of future royal employment, he took it. Burt later became Chaplain in Ordinary to the Prince of Wales, but rumours that he was rescued from the Fleet Prison to perform the ceremony are untrue. No man by his name appears in the records of the infamous jail. Burt died just six years after the marriage, when he was still in his early thirties. If Lord Colchester was to be believed, the cleric cleared his conscience in his last moments.

---

40. Wilkins, William Henry (1905). *Mrs Fitzherbert and George IV*. London: Longmans, Green, and Co, pp.62-63.

"I learnt that the Rev. Mr. Burt, of Twickenham, actually married the Prince of Wales to Mrs. Fitzherbert," wrote Lord Colchester, "And received 500l. for doing it, as he himself declared to his family on his deathbed."[41] Burt's dying confession piqued the interest of royal watchers and the story of the Fleet Prison took hold. To some, he will forever and erroneously be the jailbird clergyman.

Royal Wedding

Just before 6.00 pm on the evening of 15 December 1785, the Prince of Wales stole from Carlton House on foot accompanied by his friend, Orlando Bridgeman. They were admitted without ceremony to Maria's home on Park Street, and once they were safely inside, Bridgeman took up watch with a drawn sword whilst George joined Maria and Reverend Burt in the drawing room. The couple were accompanied by her uncle, Henry Errington, who gave Maria away, and her brother, Jack Smythe, who served as witness. Before that tiny congregation, Maria and her prince were joined in matrimony.

George presented Maria with a handwritten marriage certificate which the couple and their witnesses signed. Maria kept the marriage certificate safe in her locked box at Coutts Bank, returning to it in her later years to snip out the names of the witnesses. Though it broke her heart to do so, she feared they might face prosecution otherwise. Legally, Maria Fitzherbert and the Prince of Wales were not married, because they had neither sought nor received the consent of the king. In the eyes of the Catholic church however, the ceremony that was performed at Park Street on that cold December evening was absolutely binding. Although Reverend Burt was not a Roman Catholic priest, that did not prevent the marriage from being recognised under the laws of the Church of Rome. Maria was not a mistress to the man she had fallen in love with and nor would she ever be. She was inarguably – in her faith and conscience at least – his wife.

Following the marriage of the prince to Caroline of Brunswick, there were those who argued "pretty loudly that Mrs. Fitzherbert is the lawful wife, and that the Prince of Wales is not lawfully married. One's blood

---

41. Abbot, Charles, Lord Colchester (1861). *The Diary and Correspondence of Charles Abbot, Lord Colchester: Vol I*. London: John Murray, p.68.

runs cold at such language"[42]. That was never the case. The requirements of the Royal Marriages Act were never met so the marriage was not legal, meaning that the terms of the Act of Settlement had not been breached. The heir to the throne had not legally married a Roman Catholic, so both his place in the line of succession and his subsequent marriage to the Princess of Wales remained valid.

Despite the prince's famously capricious ways, there's no reason to doubt that the couple was anything but truly in love. Yet they couldn't live openly together without it being assumed that Maria was George's mistress. The newlyweds spent a brief honeymoon in Richmond-Upon-Thames[43], then returned to their respective residences in order to lay to rest any gossip that might besmirch the bride's reputation. Before too long though the press had noticed the attachment between the duo. After one particularly starry-eyed visit to the theatre, it was reported that "The Prince was through the whole evening in that Box, where he who had eyes would most wish to be. Mrs. Fitzherbert never looked with more captivation."[44] Their devotion was mutual.

By the time Robert Hobart wrote to the Duke of Rutland on Christmas Eve 1785 to reflect that, "the lie of the day is that the Prince of Wales is to marry Mrs. Fitzherbert, but, I believe, totally without foundation,"[45] the deed was already done. The lie of the day had become the biggest secret in the kingdom. Secrets, however, were not so easy to keep when one of the parties involved happened to be the most famous man in the country.

> "[Lady Palmerston] says the report is that Mrs. Fitzherbert is, or is to be, at Carlton House; that she was married by a Roman Catholic priest; is to have 6,000*l.* a year, and is to be created a Duchess."[46]

---

42. Ibid., p.526.
43. Popular legend has it that the ballad, *Sweet Lass of Richmond Hill*, was written for Mrs Fitzherbert.
44. *The World*. 26 February 1787; issue 49.
45. Rutland, Charles Manners (1894). *The Manuscripts of His Grace the Duke of Rutland: Vol. III.* London: Her Majesty's Stationery Office, p.271.
46. Minto, Countess of (ed.) (1874). *Life and Letters of Sir Gilbert Elliot, First Earl of Minto, Vol I.* London: Longmans, Green and Co., p.98.

Despite the best efforts of all those involved, gossip about a secret wedding was spreading. Who started the ball rolling is a mystery, but it wasn't too much of a stretch for gossiping Georgians to recollect Maria's resistance to becoming George's mistress and wonder how in that case the couple had become so inseparable. Though Maria took a fashionable home in St James's Square and the prince remained at Carlton House, they came and went as a pair, maintaining their separate residences but hosting events and attending gatherings together. For the first time in years George was no longer pursuing ladies nor juggling mistresses. He was halfway to settling down.

"The town still talk of the Prince of Wales' marriage," wrote Robert Hobart to the Duke of Rutland. "He has taken a box for Mrs. Fitzherbert at the opera, and constantly passes the greater part of the night with her. [Her brother] Watt Smith [sic] appears already much elated with the honor that is intended, or rather the dishonor which has already attended his family."[47] It may seem odd that Mrs Fitzherbert was content to have such rumours attached to her name, but to her it wasn't what was said of her on earth that was the problem. Of far more import was her belief that in the eyes of heaven, she had committed no sin.

Money Troubles

In Georgian England, court gossip was the fuel that kept the engine of society running. Though the king and queen rarely indulged, it was only a matter of time before they heard whispers of their eldest son's rumoured marriage to Mrs Fitzherbert. Of course, they already knew all about his infatuation with her – that was impossible to miss – and there was no doubt that George III realised that George's wish to set up home on the continent had more to do with love than money, but they had never imagined he might go ahead and marry the lady contrary to the laws of the land.

In her gossipy memoirs of the Georgian court, Lady Anne Hamilton, a mischievous courtier and later, a friend of Caroline of Brunswick, imagined a fanciful scene between the Prince of Wales and his mother at a bitterly cold Windsor Castle. She wrongly placed a number of the prince's friends at the wedding, then went on to describe an audience between George and Queen Charlotte that supposedly followed. It is a

---

47. Rutland, Charles Manners (1894). *The Manuscripts of His Grace the Duke of Rutland: Vol. III*. London: Her Majesty's Stationery Office, p.271.

scene that bears mentioning if only for Lady Anne's claim that George had flung the unsubstantiated rumours of George III's own secret marriage to the Quaker Hannah Lightfoot[48] in his mother's horrified face.

> "The Queen insisted on being told if the news of his marriage were correct. "Yes, madam," replied he, "and not any force under heaven shall separate us. If his Majesty had been as firm in acknowledging *his* marriage, he might now have enjoyed life instead of being a misanthrope as he is. But I beg, further, that *my* wife be received at Court, and proportionately as your Majesty receives her and pays her attention from this time, so shall I render my attentions to your Majesty. The lady I have married is worthy of all homage; and my very confidential friends, with some of my wife's relations, only witnessed our marriage. Have you not always taught me to consider myself heir to the first sovereignty in the world? Where, then, will exist any risk of obtaining a ready concurrence from the House in my marriage? I hope, madam, a few hours' reflection will satisfy you that I have done my duty in following this impulse of my inclinations, and therefore I wait your Majesty's commands, feeling assured you would not wish to blast the happiness of your favourite Prince."[49]

Lady Anne concluded the scene, in her wildly inaccurate and tabloid style, with an assurance that the queen immediately granted her son all his wishes and never mentioned the matter again. That would certainly have suited the Prince of Wales, but nobody held rank and protocol in higher regard than Queen Charlotte, not even George III. She would never have sat quietly on her hands and accepted Maria Fitzherbert simply because George told her that she had to. Queen Charlotte was not a romantic, she was a realist. Confronted with rumours of the marriage, she would have known that the terms of the Royal Marriages Act had not been satisfied, meaning that the ceremony was a sham and rendering

---

48. For the full and rather fanciful story of George III and Hannah Lightfoot, see my own *The Scandal of George III's Court*.
49. Hamilton, Lady Anne (1832). *Secret History of the Court of England*. London: William Henry Stevenson, p.33.

Lady Anne's claims that she took it on the chin risible. With no approval from the king and queen, the Prince of Wales was still on the market, but Maria would never be presented at court again. Some things Queen Charlotte would simply never consent to, no matter how much and how mischievously the press needled.

> "*A Question.*- What is the reason that Mrs. FITZHERBERT, who is a lady of fortune and fashion, never appears at Court? She is visited by *some* ladies of high rank – has been in public with them – and yet never goes to the Drawing Room at St. James's. This Question is sent for publication by a person who pays no regards to the idle reports of the day, and wishes to have this mystery cleared up."[50]

As the Prince of Wales' life of luxury continued unabated, keeping up with his lifestyle was proving expensive even for a woman with an entail of close to £2,000 at her disposal. Soon Maria's finances were stretched to breaking point. George topped up her income to around £5,000 from his personal allowance, but it was mere pocket change compared to his other outgoings, particularly the ruinously expensive renovation of Carlton House. Though George enjoyed an annual allowance of £50,000, more than £30,000 was squandered on his stables alone and he loved to throw cash around whenever he and Maria went out on the town. To be this fabulous cost serious money.

> "Mrs. Fitzherbert wore an Italian tiffany petticoat, trimmed at the bottom with a broad black ribbon, embroidered with silver flowers, in a most tasteful and *nouvelle* manner. At the bottom of the ribbon was a broad silver fringe. The gown of the same tiffany as her petticoat, made in the stile of a *capot*, trimmed round in the same manner as her petticoat. A black stomacher, embroidered in a very superb manner with silver. The cap was peculiarly beautiful, made small and high, consisting chiefly of white crape, with a black ribbon, embroidered in the same manner as the trimming of her dress, twisted all round from bottom to top, in a most

---

50. *The Times*. 9 October 1788; issue 1140.

becoming style. At the left side, were three white ostrich feathers, and finished behind with two long lappets."[51]

Maria was the perfect hostess at fashionable Carlton House gatherings, but all of it came at a price. She might not have been a princess, but that didn't mean she couldn't live like one, and George happily shelled out more than £50,000 to ensure that her London home had the very best of everything. For a man whose entire allowance totalled that very sum, the books were soon more deeply into the red than ever.

Even George realised that things could not continue like that, and he summoned Fox and Richard Brinsley Sheridan to crisis talks at Carlton House. Together they ran through the royal accounts and came to the conclusion that an eye-watering £250,000 would steady the ship and satisfy all the prince's creditors. When they applied to the Prime Minister, William Pitt, for the sum, he understandably blanched. The matter was kicked across to Windsor, where George's plea for a financial handout landed on the king's desk like a hand grenade.

Faced with his son's predicament, George III replied that there would be no bailout without a full explanation of where the money had been spent. On top of that, he wanted his son to promise that he would never get into such dire financial straits again.

"From every thing which has passed between Me and the prince of Wales during these last two years, relative to His embarrassed situation, He must have seen that I held it impossible even to entertain the Consideration of any means to relieve Him, untill [sic] I should receive a sufficient Explanation of his past Expenses, and see a Prospect of reasonable Sexurity [sic] against a Continuation of his Extravagances.

[...]

It is then and then only that it can become a Subject of Consideration by what means I can cooperate in extricating him from the Embarrassment to which his own Imprudence has subjected Him."[52]

---

51. *London Chronicle*. 27 May 1788 – 29 May 1788; issue 4928.
52. Georgian Papers Online (http://gpp.rct.uk, July 2020). RA GEO/MAIN/16535 Copy of a letter from George III to the Prince of Wales, 3 July 1786.

Though the scaffolding at Carlton House and the festivities presided over by Maria Fitzherbert made it clear what was swallowing the more than generous allowance, the king wanted his son to personally account for himself. The Prince of Wales, unsurprisingly, wanted to do no such thing. Instead he wailed that he simply could not hope to meet his living expenses "out of so incompetent an Income as Mine". That incompetent income was £50,000. George did manage to force out an assurance that he had cut his expenses to the bone, but his austerity drive wouldn't last. Desperate, he swore that he would continue to let circumspection "be the Principle & Guide of my conduct till I have totally liberated my self from the Embarrassments which now oppress me, and the more so as I am persuaded that such a line when pursued with consistency will meet with the appropriation of every candid and dispassionate mind."[53]

To shore up his empty promises, George consulted Fox for advice. Fox suggested that he should offer to retire to Europe for a time, where he could live more cheaply until his debts were settled and his coffers back on track. The king rejected the offer, so in an effort to prove that he had changed, George called a halt to the building works at Carlton House, whilst his horses were sold and their stables shuttered. Yet with Carlton House echoing to the sound of lone footsteps rather than wild parties, London life rather soured for the heir to the throne. What he needed was some sea air.

A Seaside Romance

George III and Queen Charlotte adored Weymouth and when their children were young, it was there that they escaped the metropolis. The Prince of Wales preferred Brighton, which he fell for in 1783 whilst visiting his uncle, the Duke of Cumberland, and his scandalous wife. He became a regular visitor to the town and where the Prince of Wales went, fashionable society was sure to follow.

Whilst in Brighton, George stayed in a small farmhouse that charmed him so much that he bought it. Naturally a humble farmhouse was no place for the most fashionable gentleman in England, and though he had tightened his purse strings in London, in Brighton he opened that purse

---

53. Georgian Papers Online (http://gpp.rct.uk, July 2020). RA GEO/MAIN/16366-16389/29 Copy of a letter from the Prince of Wales to George III, 11 July 1786.

wide. He employed Henry Holland, the man behind the Carlton House renovations, to dream up a palace fit for a king and during 1785 and 1786, the Marine Pavilion began to take shape.[54] Just as Maria refused to live openly with her husband in London, in Brighton too she kept a separate residence a short distance away. It was far enough to maintain the respectable façade, but close enough for the happy couple.

The public and press were united in their liking of the widow who had seemingly tamed the worst of the prince's excesses and she was the darling of gossip columnists everywhere. The Georgian press was the most savage this country has ever known, but woe betide anyone who dared go against the current favourite of the day. When word got round that 29-year-old Maria was actually over 30, *The Times* dismissed those who repeated the rumour as "antiquated virgins and stale widows."[55] They fell over themselves to report on her trip to the Wax Work Cabinet exhibition at the Lyceum in the Strand, particularly when she visited the royal gallery there and "was observed to pass the greatest encomiums on the likenesses of all the Royal Family."[56] Maria could do no wrong.

In their seaside sanctuary, George and Maria passed the days in contented peace. Life was lived at a more bucolic pace, with little trace of the breathless round of entertainments and parties that had so occupied them in the city. Maria was sure that in time the rupture between father and son would be mended, and she saw this sedate new life as the key to that. Even the king and queen began to warm to Maria, who seemed to exert an entirely positive influence over their wayward son. Of course, the gossips of Georgian high society were soon trying to weed out an angle and in July 1786, they were sure that they had it.

"People talk much of the Prince of Wales' reform, particularly in this spot, which he had chosen as the place of his retreat," wrote the Earl of Mornington to the Duke of Rutland during that heady summer. "Mrs. Fitzherbert is here, and, they say, with child."[57] Those who hoped for scandal would be disappointed, for Maria was not with child

---

54. Later the Prince of Wales commissioned John Nash to overhaul the building again, creating the Royal Pavilion that stands today.

55. *The Times*. 4 April 1786; issue 398.

56. *The World*. 18 February 1788; issue 355.

57. Rutland, Charles Manners (1894). *The Manuscripts of His Grace the Duke of Rutland: Vol. III*. London: Her Majesty's Stationery Office, p.325.

and nor would she ever be, but her calm nature and restful influence had worked wonders on her mercurial man. Had their marriage been legal then perhaps it would have been the start of a new chapter for a reformed and freshly-matured Prince of Wales, but instead there was the constant worry that the day would come when a legal marriage would be necessary. When it did, all the bucolic pavilions in the world wouldn't be enough to stop it.

Marriage Denied

The Prince of Wales knew now that he would never get the unconditional bailout he had been so desperately hoping for. Maria's finances were stretched to breaking because of his spending, so there was nothing she could offer other than a shoulder to weep on. Though he tried to adjust to a quiet life in Brighton and forget about the glamorous London social whirl, his debts simply wouldn't evaporate. They were getting bigger all the time, as undeniable as the hulking scaffolding that blighted the elegant façade of Carlton House, where George's economy drive had left the renovations unfinished, the stables empty, and his domestic staff vastly reduced. Many of those who remained only did so after accepting substantial pay cuts.

Yet even with the building works halted and a skeleton staff, the prince couldn't service his debts. His father wasn't about to pay them off either, so he had no option but to go cap in hand to Parliament instead. The tearooms were filled with whispers of the secret marriage and everybody at Westminster had heard them. Should it be proven that the prince had married in contravention of the Royal Marriages Act and, horror of horrors, married a Catholic, then his embarrassment would be complete.

Of those who made it their business to make sure that the rumours were heard far and wide, the loudest was politician John Horne Tooke. He was an avowed enemy of Fox and that made him an enemy of the Prince of Wales too. In 1787, Horne Tooke penned a pamphlet entitled, *A Letter to a Friend on the Reported Marriage of His Royal Highness the Prince of Wales*. In it he argued that, though the rumoured marriage was contrary to the Royal Marriages Act, that did not mean it should be considered illegal in the eyes of the law. After a spirited rebuttal of the Act, Horne Tooke concluded that he had seen no definite proof that

Maria was still a Catholic, although there is absolutely no evidence to suggest that she had stopped going to Mass. And yet, he still argued that she should be considered a Protestant in the absence of any evidence to the contrary. And if Maria was a Protestant, he argued, then that made her the rightful wife of the Prince of Wales.

> "I think I am well justified in asserting, that since the period of her marriage, her royal highness [Maria] has not performed any one act of any kind whatever, which can justify such a denomination [as Catholic]. And not only my own opinion of her understanding and good sense assures me of it, but such authority as leaves no doubt in my mind confirms the assurance that that she is both ready and willing at any time to give proof of her conformity to the established religion of the land.
>
> I conclude therefore (and trust that others will conclude with me) that his royal highness's marriage is neither *unusual*, nor *improper*, nor *impossible*, nor *illegal*, nor affected by the act of *exclusion* or the act of *settlement*; but such as does honour to his sentiments and is highly beneficial to his country."[58]

If Horne Tooke's aim was to get people talking, he certainly succeeded. The press lit up with debates on Maria's faith and *The Times* was quick to warn him that his claim that Maria had not observed any Catholic rites for many months was bold indeed. It was well known that the prince's only hope of financial assistance rested with Parliament and the rumoured marriage stood in the way of financial help becoming a reality. As gossip gripped the nation, public opinion turned against the already less-than-popular young royal, whose apparent attachment to a Roman Catholic at the expense of the crown was seen as his greatest betrayal to date. Far from revelling in the romance of it, George's subjects wanted him to follow his father's lifelong example and put duty first. If the truth of his marriage was made public, any hope of financial aid would go up in a puff of smoke.

---

58. Horne Tooke, John (1787). *A Letter to a Friend on the Reported Marriage of His Royal Highness the Prince of Wales*. Dublin: P. Byrne, pp.24-25.

The Prince of Wales put all his trust in Fox, hoping that he might work some sort of magic in the Commons. But Fox refused to help, mindful of the damage that might be done should he argue the prince's case only to be embarrassed if the rumours later proved to be true. Denied the backing of the Whigs, George pressed an independent Member of Parliament, Alderman Nathaniel Newnham, to take up his cause. In reply to Newnham's requests for pecuniary assistance for the prince, Pitt tactfully replied that such assistance could only be considered if and when some exceptionally delicate matters had been addressed. These matters were so personal in nature, he continued, that the Prince of Wales should think very hard indeed before bringing them before the House.

It was an admirable attempt to head off any awkward discussion about Maria, but by this time George was desperate. Newnham pressed on and Pitt pressed back, warning again that the prince may not want his personal business to become a matter of public record. George's friend, Richard Brinsley Sheridan, believed that the Prime Minister was only making things worse. Should the Prince of Wales withdraw now, Sheridan warned that it would suggest he had crumbled in the face of thinly-veiled threats. It was as good as giving in to blackmail.

When Sheridan told the prince later that evening about the events that had taken place in the febrile House of Commons that day, George was troubled. Pitt had made his threats subtly but firmly enough and he understood that any effort to press for financial aid without acknowledging and denying the rumours of a secret marriage would see the gossip revived by one of his many enemies in Parliament. At that point it would be too late for a swift denial and the resultant enquiry could be long and ruinous. Yet if he authorised his supporters to acknowledge and deny the rumours without naming the lady concerned, the day might yet be saved, albeit at the cost of Maria's broken heart and stained reputation. The question was whether her husband loved money more.

On 30 April 1787, Fox delivered a statement to the House of Commons that he was sure would secure the gratitude and loyalty of the heir to the throne for the rest of his days. That it would also shatter Maria was immaterial. Fox cared for himself and his career; the trials and tribulations of the prince's latest fling meant nothing to him.

"[Fox assured the House that the rumour of a secret marriage] proved at once the uncommon pains taken by the enemies of his royal highness to propagate the grossest and most malignant falsehoods, with a view to depreciate [George's] character and injure him in the opinion of his country. [...] The whole of the debt the prince was ready to submit to the investigation of the House; and he was equally ready to submit the other circumstance to which he had alluded, to their consideration, provided the consideration of a House of Parliament could, consistently with propriety and decency, be applied to such a subject. Nay, his royal highness had authorised him to declare, that, as a peer of parliament, he was ready in the other House to submit to any the most pointed questions which could be put to him respecting it, or to afford his majesty, or his majesty's ministers, the fullest assurances of the utter falsehood of the fact in question, which never had, and which common sense must see, never could have happened."[59]

The prince's supporters believed that his denial would be an end to it, but his critics continued to press for more information. Had the prince himself authorised the statement, they asked, and if not then where had it come from? Fox replied that he "had direct authority" and the matter was now closed. The question was a germane one though, for just who *had* authorised Charles James Fox to disavow the unnamed Maria Fitzherbert?

The obvious answer was the Prince of Wales himself, who had once sent Fox a letter written in his own hand assuring him that the rumours of a forthcoming marriage were false. Or at least, he rather carefully danced around anything concrete at all, weaving a web of denial without being clear about exactly what he was denying. Fox had that letter as proof should he ever require it, but in so wholeheartedly coming to the aid of the Prince of Wales, he had won a valuable friend indeed. Maria was an enemy for the rest of his days.

---

59. Fox, Charles James (1815). *Speeches of the Right Honourable Charles James Fox in the House of Commons, Vol III*. London: Longman, Hurst, Orme, and Brown, pp.325–6.

Like everyone else in London society, Abigail Adams followed the twists and turns of the gossip during her extended stay in the capital. She reported the situation to her friend, Mercy Otis Warren, in letters that offer a glimpse of just how much of a talking point the private lives of the prince and Mrs Fitzherbert had become. The spelling is Abigail's own.

"Luxery dissapation and vice, have a natural tendency to extirpate every generous principle, and leave the Heart susceptable of the most malignant vices. To the total absence of principle must be asscribed the conduct of the Heir apparant to the British Throne, which is the subject of much speculation at this moment. The World have Supposed that a marriage had taken place between the prince, and a Lady known by the Name of Fitzherbert, whom for 3 years he persued driving her for more than half that time out of her country to avoid him. as she was in independant circumstances, of an ancient & respectable family; of a Fair Character and honorable connections every person presumed her married to him, [...] every step for more than a year has confirmed this Idea, as the Lady has attended him; not only to the Watering places, but into all publick, and private parties, and at the princs request has been countananced by the first persons in the Kingdom, and the publick papers have announced the report & given credit to it uncontradicted throughout all Europe, but now at a Time when he wishes to be relieved from the load of debt he has contracted, and finds that this affair is like to become a subject of parliamentary discussion, he authorizes Charles Fox (A Man as unprincipald as the prince) to declare the whole story a malicious falsehood, and in the most explicit terms to deny even the shadow of a marriage. yet not a person whom I have heard mention the subject since believes; a syllable of Mr. Fox's assertion thus does this young man set both Law & Decency at defience; his Friends are even so barefaced as to pretend that no connextion but of the platonick kind has ever subsisted between them, he a mere Scipio, & she a vestal."[60]

If Abigail Adams sounded disgusted at the conduct of Fox and George, then she was joined in her dismay by Maria Fitzherbert herself. When George called to see his wife the day after Fox's grandstanding performance at Westminster he found her in a state of agitation. The Earl of Minto was perfectly right to muse that events in the House "leave Mrs. Fitzherbert in an awkward way," and she knew it. Though Fox had not named her, Maria was in no doubt that everyone knew that the rumours concerned her, and her name was as good as mud thanks to his denial. Faced with her humiliation and fury George fell back on a familiar tactic. He lied. He swore that Fox had spoken without authorisation and demanded that Charles Grey make a mollifying statement in the House, but Grey flatly refused to be drawn into the whirlpool. With that avenue closed to him, George then summoned Sheridan, who promised that he could put right the damage done by Fox's speech. He wisely decided that would not do so until the matter of George's finances had been resolved in the prince's favour. Just like Fox, Sheridan's first priority was his own career. At an audience with Maria, he smoothly assured her that he was on her side and would do all he could to protect her interests. She believed him, because she had little other choice.

With the rumours of marriage officially denied, the Prince of Wales pocketed a sum in excess of £150,000. On 4 May 1787, Sheridan did his best to ignore the sniggers that ran around the chamber when he assured the Commons that the nameless woman who had been swept up in the rumours concerning the prince was a figure of unimpeachable honour. Nobody believed that there was anything in the least bit honourable about Maria Fitzherbert now. The press revelled in the seemingly mixed

---

60. "Abigail Adams to Mercy Otis Warren, 14 May 1787," *Founders Online,* National Archives, https://founders.archives.gov/documents/Adams/04-08-02-0019. [Original source: *The Adams Papers*, Adams Family Correspondence, vol. 8, March 1787–December 1789, ed. C. James Taylor, Margaret A. Hogan, Jessie May Rodrique, Gregg L. Lint, Hobson Woodward, and Mary T. Claffey. Cambridge, MA: Harvard University Press, 2007, pp. 45–49.]

messages being preached by the two senior Whigs, both of whom supposedly enjoyed the confidence of the prince.

> "Mr. SHERIDAN owes the respect paid to him at present, both by the Prince, and Mrs. Fitzherbert, to the ingenuity with which he destroyed the effect of Mr. Fox's declaration in the House of Commons- "That the Prince and Mrs. F. were not married." Mr. Sheridan at that time paid a very handsome compliment to Mr. [sic] *Fitzherbert's virtue*! and what other inference could the public draw from such a compliment, than that she was actually the Princess of Wales? This matter will soon be ascertained."[61]

The Prince of Wales had made a fortune from Fox's denial, but it had cost Maria her precious reputation. Fox had denied the marriage, tacitly branding Maria a mistress, but Sheridan would have it believed that she was virtuous. It was the worst possible outcome for Maria and she felt humiliated. Years later, when Fox tried to win back her favour with the promise of the rank of duchess, Maria held firm. She told a friend in her dotage that "she did not wish to be another Duchess of Kendal."[62]

Reconciliation

Despite George's denials, Maria couldn't come to terms with this fresh humiliation. Yet the prince was a habitual liar who left a trail of selfish chaos in his wake, so it's difficult to imagine exactly what other outcome she might have been anticipating. The Prince of Wales was enormously egotistical and economical with the truth, but he was also in a black hole of debt. He might well have crowed to Lady Dartmouth later about his plans to divorce Caroline and marry Maria once the king died, but there was never a grain of truth in the idea.

---

61. *The Times*. 24 January 1789; issue 1230.
62. The Duchess of Kendal was better known as Melusine von der Schulenberg, the lifelong mistress of George I. When Melusine was awarded the rank of duchess in an effort to elevate her reputation, the promotion was met with outrage in some quarters and humour in others.

As Lord Glenbervie wryly mused, "What seeds of domestic confusion, and too probably of civil war!"[63]

The romantic approach might well have been to admit to the marriage and face the consequences, and in truth, the sham wedding becoming public knowledge would have been constitutionally underwhelming. The marriage was invalid under the terms of the Royal Marriages Act, so the question of George's place in the line of succession according to the Act of Settlement was entirely moot. It would have certainly caused a constitutional kerfuffle, but not a catastrophe. What crisis there was ended up being purely domestic.

For a few weeks over the spring and summer of 1787, the Prince and his 'wife' went their separate ways. Maria no doubt confided in her friend and companion, Isabella 'Bel' Pigot, whenever George sent one of his breast-beating letters, but she didn't surrender. Miss Pigot, an admiral's daughter, knew the prince well; to him, she was affectionately known as 'Piggy.' When George's threats of suicide fell on deaf ears, he turned his ire on Fox instead. Surprisingly though, Maria's fears of humiliation were to prove ill-founded. She had expected to see her reputation destroyed, but instead public opinion turned in her favour. It didn't take much for people to dislike the spoiled and petulant George and Maria was considered very much the injured party. Despite this, she was her own worst enemy and loved the prince so much that it suited her to believe that Fox had exceeded his powers without permission. The more George pleaded, the more she weakened until the tide turned and she took him back. The couple departed for Brighton, where Maria presided over a round of glittering parties, queen of all she surveyed.

Maria's life with the prince was apparently settled at last, marred only by the death of her father in early 1788 and the occasional mishap that brought her back to the headlines. That summer she and George were travelling in his phaeton (a fashionable open carriage) in Hyde Park when they nearly collided with a stagecoach. As the prince tried to avoid a catastrophe the reins snapped and the phaeton overturned, pitching its two passengers out. The Prince of Wales was uninjured but

---

63. Bickley, Francis (ed.) (1928). *The Diaries of Sylvester Douglas (Lord Glenbervie), Vol I*. London: Constable & Co, p.351.

"Mrs. FITZHERBERT has sprained her ankle," reported *The World*, "by falling upon His HIGHNESS."[64] Make of that what you will.

As Maria's ankle healed, a fresh bout of trouble appeared on the horizon in the shape of the Marquis de Bellois, newly arrived from France. What happened next is a rather odd cocktail of rumour and scandal, but it appears that Bellois started a rumour that during her trip to France, Maria had conspired with influential Catholics to seduce and marry the Prince of Wales. With him in her clutches, the conspirators would launch a Catholic coup and seize the throne. These claims came just as the health of George III had taken a serious turn for the worst, leading to debates over who should rule should a Regency be necessary. The obvious choice was the Prince of Wales, so claims that he was the puppet of a Catholic conspiracy were serious indeed.

The status of Mrs Fitzherbert was again a matter of public debate, especially when it was confirmed by a mischievous journalist that "Mrs. FITZHERBERT will appear at the drawing rooms of the Regent – as Mrs. FITZHERBERT."[65] Once again, the marriage was denied in the House of Commons and once again, Maria cringed. Those who approved of the prince as Regent did so only "under the assurance of [Fox] that his Highness was not married to Mrs. Fitzherbert, as had been affirmed in a pamphlet," [66] and requested that this matter be discussed "whenever the Regency bill was regularly brought before the House."[67] Maria's private life was public business all over again.

Fox and the Whigs would do whatever it took to ensure that the Prince of Wales became Regent and carried them into government. The Whig press confidently asserted that there was no need to fear any breach of the Act of Settlement, for no marriage had taken place.

> "It will certainly be a satisfaction to the country to be assured, that the various stories circulated relative to the PRINCE OF WALES'S MARRIAGE WITH MRS. FITZHERBERT, are entirely void of foundation. The friends of his PARTY have pledged themselves to this; and declared in the HOUSE on

---

64. *The World*. 19 June 1788; issue 460.
65. *The Times*. 2 February 1789; issue 1236.
66. *Whitehall Evening Post*. 17 January 1789 – 20 January 2789; issue 6496.
67. Ibid.

Saturday, that had Mr. Fox ever had any reason to alter his former declaration, or any circumstance occurred which could have given him ground for it, they would have held him unpardonable, had he not come down to the House and declared what was his real opinion."[68]

Thanks to Fox, Maria was still distrustful of the Whigs who had denied her marriage, but she offered her services and her home to the supporters of the prince's case. She embarked on a PR offensive on her husband's behalf, singing his praises to those who had yet to make up their minds and doing all she could to ensure that her man won. On the other side of the argument stood Pitt and the Tories, with Queen Charlotte backing them. She had no desire to see her profligate and irresponsible son take control of the kingdom, fearing he would be as poor a manager of a nation as he had been of his own finances. Maria usually kept out of politics but this time there was no doubting on which side of the divide she stood. Claims of Catholic conspiracies had to be crushed.

Such claims were completely false, but that didn't stop Reverend Philip Withers, the author of an anonymous pamphlet entitled *Nemesis, or a Letter to Alfred*, from fanning the flames. In the pamphlet he claimed that Maria had been intimate with Bellois and had fled for Paris because "Plombiers [sic] was unable to furnish a midwife and other accommodations necessary for a lady obedient to the divine command – increase and multiply."[69] Following the supposed pregnancy, Withers posited that Maria had come home to England not out of love, but to marry the prince before he could find out what she had been getting up to in France.

Yet even this wasn't scandalous enough for Nemesis, who went on to write that Maria had borrowed £2,000 from Bellois, who demanded its return upon his arrival in London. When Maria refused to pay up, Bellois threatened to make public letters in Maria's own hand that he claimed would implicate her in the imaginary Catholic plot. Eventually the matter was settled for the far less hefty sum of £200, leading the author to conclude that, "the Lady rated her favours at eighteen hundred

---

68. *The World*. 9 February 1789; issue 660.
69. Anonymous (1789). *Nemesis, or a Letter to Alfred*. London: Privately published, p.9.

pounds. – I mean the favours of friendship and familiarity – and cheap enough, considering how dearly England has been obliged to purchase them."[70] Vast sums were supposedly handed over by a secret Catholic cabal to buy the silence of Maria's family, so they never admitted to the secret marriage, and even more money went to secure the support of the media and senior politicians for the rumoured wife of the heir to the throne. "There is danger," Nemesis concluded, "Of seeing Popery greatly encreased [sic] [and] of a secret cabal forming which will counteract the purposes of every wholesome administration."[71] It was heady stuff, but there was no truth in any of it.

In fact, the Marquis de Bellois made little impression on Maria during his trip to England, but the rumours of a Catholic conspiracy simply wouldn't die. They came back to haunt her when Lord George Gordon, who had played a small role in the death of Maria's second husband, resurfaced once more. He was being prosecuted for defaming Marie Antoinette, and was keen for Maria to appear in court to support his claims that he and Mrs Fitzherbert had spoken in Paris about intrigues between the French and British courts. Whether those intrigues involved her supposed role in a Papist conspiracy was not made clear, but the inference was obvious. When he called at Maria's London home in an attempt to subpoena her, Lord George Gordon was chased away by Maria's brothers and warned never to show his face again, unless he wanted to settle the matter once and for all with a duel.

> "Lord George Gordon asserts, that the laws of this country are contrary to the laws of God;- and Mr. Horne Tooke is of opinion, that an Act of Parliament may be contrary to law. If the arrangement and re-modelling of our laws were left to the former divine and the would-be reformer, what a glorious, wise, and happy people we would be!"[72]

Lord George Gordon and Philip Withers, the man behind *Nemesis*, did not meet with judicial sympathy. The former was found guilty of defaming Marie Antoinette and fled to the Netherlands. When French

---

70. Ibid., p.12.

71. Ibid., p.15.

72. *The Times*. 12 June 1787; issue 771.

pressure led him to be banished, he was forced to return to England and the five year sentence in Newgate that was waiting. Withers, meanwhile, got into a war of words in the press with Horne Tooke, after which he faced the formidable barrister Sir William Garrow at his libel trial. The court heard that "The Defendant, though a clergyman; was a professed libeller. He had not only attacked the character of the Honourable lady, the present prosecutrix, but he had directed his calumny against the House of Commons, whom in this pamphlet he had accused of having acted in a dastardly manner."[73]

Withers' defence was to claim that every word he had written was true and could not, therefore, be libellous. He added that he had rejected a massive bribe from nameless but powerful figures eager to buy his silence, selflessly preferring to make the planned Catholic coup public instead. The judge sentenced Withers to a large fine and a year in Newgate for his "gross and scandalous"[74] claims. He died behind bars. It didn't pay to cross the prince's wife.

The Split

After much handwringing and hairpulling over the question of who would head the Regency, George III unexpectedly turned the corner. For now at least, the danger of a slide into total mental collapse had been averted and he was once again fit to govern. It's tempting to speculate on what would have become of Maria had things gone the other way and the Prince of Wales been made Regent two decades earlier than he eventually was. Whether he would have kept his promise to abolish the Royal Marriages Act is doubtful, but even if he had done so, he still had to be willing to give up the crown if he wanted the marriage to stick. I think it's unlikely that he would have taken such a drastic step, especially after so many vociferous denials of the marriage in the House of Commons.

As the king recovered, Maria and George's happy homelife continued. Both spent more than they could afford, but they did so quietly by Georgian standards, and soon stories of the prince's womanising ways were replaced by approving reports of he and Maria paying court to a rather different sort

---

73. *Public Advertiser.* 16 July 1789; issue 17160.
74. *Bath Chronicle*. 26 November 1789; issue 1469.

of lady. At Maria's behest, in 1792 they visited a group of nuns who had been driven out of a French convent and had all their assets and money "seized on by the regenerate French."[75] George gallantly established a fund for their aid, "which in a short time amounted to upwards of one hundred pounds." Maria was still the subject of the occasional barb, thanks to her friendship with a certain *Great Personage*, but when the press wondered "in what character she is to be considered, whether as wife or widow"[76], it little troubled her. In her heart, she was a wife.

Though things at home were going well for the prince, tensions in the royal family were worse than ever. The king's health was fragile and the queen's temper was poor. She believed that George had secretly campaigned against his father to seize power and refused to let the two men meet without her present. When a fete was held to celebrate George III's return to health, both George and his brother, Frederick, were refused permission by their mother to attend. The more heated the feud at home became, the more the prince sought refuge in his old rip-roaring lifestyle, until tensions inevitably began to surface. The prince still loved to party whilst Maria was inclined to prefer the quiet seclusion that the couple had enjoyed during his austerity drive. Brighton was peaceful no longer though, and it had become the most fashionable resort in the land thanks to the wild parties George threw there. It wasn't Maria's idea of a good time.

Seeking a place to retire to away from the bustle of London and the noise of Brighton, Maria took a lease on Marble Hill House, the former home of Henrietta Howard, mistress of George II. For Maria, as for Henrietta before her, Marble Hill was a sanctuary and she settled easily into life in fashionable, bucolic Twickenham. She had plenty of friends nearby, including George's brothers, Frederick and William, and she still saw her husband regularly. What she hadn't realised was that George had started spending time with other women too. Add to that the ever-increasing pile of new debts that he was accumulating, and what they had was a recipe for disaster.

When George asked his father for a financial help, the king told him that he would not receive another penny until he was married. As far as the royal family was concerned, their eldest son was still on

---

75. *London Chronicle*. 30 October 1792 – 1 November 1792; issue 5648.
76. *York Herald*. 30 June 1792; issue 131.

the market and now more than ever there was no chance of having the secret marriage retrospectively recognised. Not only had it been twice denied in Parliament, but in 1793 a worrying precedent was set when George's younger brother, Augustus, married Lady Augusta Murray without permission from his father. When the king found out he invoked the terms of the Act and had the marriage annulled against Augustus' wishes. The possibility of Maria Fitzherbert's claim to the Prince of Wales being legally recognised was dead in the water.

With Maria spending more time at Marble Hill, George was free to acquire a new fancy in the shape of Frances Villiers, Countess of Jersey. Nine years the prince's senior, Lady Jersey was a capricious social climber and she and her husband were favourites of the king and queen. She knew full well that George's parents wanted him to marry a German princess and she knew too that George's attachment to Maria made him reluctant to do so. Should Lady Jersey be able to drive a wedge between the couple and push the prince into accepting his parents' plans, it would do her own prospects of advancement no harm at all. As the Duke of Wellington later noted, Lady Jersey had been determined to encourage an official marriage "simply because she wished to put Mrs Fitzherbert on the same footing as herself, and deprive her of the claim to the title of lawful wife."[77]

With that in mind, the manipulative Lady Jersey set to work. She took advantage of Maria's absences at Marble Hill to work on the Prince of Wales, becoming an understanding shoulder for him to cry on, seemingly sympathetic to his every trial. If seducing the prince was easy, convincing him that all his woes were caused by the troublesome Catholic influence of Maria Fitzherbert was surprisingly little challenge at all.

One June evening in 1794, Maria and George were to dine with his brother, Prince William, Duke of Clarence. After dinner the couple planned to travel to Brighton together for the summer, but George didn't appear. Instead he sent a note in which he told Maria that he had gone to Brighton without her and asked her not to follow. Maria correctly suspected that Lady Jersey was behind the change of plan. For six long years, she would not see the Prince of Wales again. She had been unceremoniously dumped a month shy of her thirty-eighth birthday.

---

77. Hibbert, Christopher (1974). *George IV: Prince of Wales.* New York: Harper & Row, p.135.

The Single Life

If George had expected Maria to race to Brighton and beg him to change his mind, he was to be disappointed. Instead she accepted his cruel dismissal with dignity and took a sojourn to Switzerland, where she nursed her broken heart. The prince interpreted her silence as a lack of affection and with Lady Jersey now firmly entrenched as his mistress, told his father that he would marry a German princess. It seemed like a small price to pay for what would be a large handout.

> "Much has been said respecting the jointure settled on Mrs. Fitzherbert, in consequence of a late separation; but the precise fact has never been hitherto stated. The truth is this:- When the incumberances [sic] of a certain Great Personage were put in a state of settlement, two or three years since, 3000l. a year was allotted out of his revenues for Mrs. Fitzherbert; which has been punctually paid by Mr. Coutts, the Banker. – This sum has been lately settled on the lady for life, which, with her own private fortune of 1800l. annually, will make her present income 4,800l. a year."[78]

When the news of the prince's engagement to Caroline of Brunswick was announced, Maria was as devastated as she was powerless. She had no legal rights over her husband and even though he promised to continue to pay the £3,000 that she had received since their marriage, it was little substitute for the happy days she had known in Brighton. Rumours in some sections of the press that she was voraciously seeking a payment of £4,000 and a title to buy her silence had no place in fact. The last thing on Maria's mind was money; instead, it was like being widowed for a third time. She made no statement on the announced nuptials and instead returned to England to resume her secluded life, unaware that the prince, on his way to his own wedding ceremony, had whispered to his chamberlain, "I shall never love any woman but Fitzherbert." Likewise, she didn't know that in the will that he made shortly after his marriage, George had poured out his heart and soul.

---

78. *London Packet or New Evening Post*. 6 August 1794 – 8 August 1794; issue 3897.

"By this, my last Will and Testament, I now bequeath, give, and settle at my death all my worldly property of every description, denomination and sort, personal and other, to my Maria Fitzherbert, my Wife, the Wife of my heart and soul. Although by the laws of this country she could not avail herself publicly of that name, still such she is in the eyes of Heaven, was, is, and ever will be such in mine.

[...]

I assure her as I now do, that I shall die blessing her, my only true and real Wife, with my parting breath, and praying the Almighty and Most Merciful Being [...] bless, protect, and guard her through this life, looking forward to the moment when our Souls in a better world may again be united, never more to part."

The Prince of Wales had made his choice. Immediately after the wedding ceremony, Orlando Bridgeman, who had attended the secret nuptials on Park Street, travelled to Maria's home to tell her that the prince had taken a wife. She fainted on the spot. Yet Maria wasn't necessarily blameless in her romantic travails. A tantalising clue remains in an exchange of letters between the Prince of Wales and the Duke of York.

"In short [Maria and George] are *finally parted*," George wrote to his brother on 29 August 1794. "From what you know of my temper, disposition, & the unvaried attention & affection I have ever treated her with, *you* will not lay the *fault*, *whatever it may be*, at my door." [79]

The Duke of York held Maria in high regard, yet his reply to George is sympathetic and suggests that Maria was far from a wounded innocent. Ill-used and given the run around as she was, don't forget Lady Anne Lindsay's assertion that *Fitz* treated men like dogs. If the Duke of York was to be believed, she'd kicked George once too often.

"[Let me] lose no time in expressing to you how sincerely I applaud your resolution of marrying our cousin Princess Caroline of Brunswick.

79. Aspinall, Arthur (ed.) (1965). *The Correspondence of George, Prince of Wales, Vol II*. London: Cassell, p.453.

> I have long been grieved to see how very miserably Mrs. Fitzherbert's unfortunate temper made you, and once, if you remember, some years ago, advised you not to bear with it any longer. I am rejoiced to hear that you are now out of her shackles."[80]

Hot temper or not, for months after the royal wedding in 1795, Maria succumbed to depression and ill health, but she could hardly speak of her situation for fear of reawakening the invasive curiosity that surrounded her. Instead, as the Prince and Princess of Wales struggled through their first year as man and wife and became parents for the first and only time, Maria made a gentle return to society from her new home on Tilney Street. She surrounded herself with trusted companions including Bel Pigot, her loyal live-in confidante.

As the decade wore on Maria faded from the newspaper columns, her name mentioned only when she took an occasional outing or made one of her characteristically generous charitable donations. Though back on the social scene, she went out of her way not to encounter George, avoiding Brighton and giving up the lease on Marble Hill. Instead she took a new home at Castle Hill in Ealing, where no memories of happier times would haunt her. But Maria had reckoned without the Prince of Wales' famously gadabout nature. Despite Lady Jersey and a royal wedding that ended in separation, her days on the arm of the heir to the throne weren't done yet.

Husband and Wife

When the Prince and Princess of Wales separated in the spring of 1796, there was only one person on George's mind. Lady Jersey had been cast off and he wanted to be with Maria again, but Maria had other ideas. She ignored his entreaties and rejected those that he tried to press on her via mutual friends, but George wasn't used to being told no. Soon his letters were nothing short of hysterical.

> "If you BREAK YOUR SACRED PROMISE, RECOLLECT I AM FREED FROM ALL TIES OF ATTACHMENT TO

---

80. Ibid., p.454.

THIS WORLD, *as there is no reliance, no more faith existing,* THEN I HAVE NO FEARS LEFT, NOTHING BUT HONOR IN A WORLD IN WHICH I HAVE EXPERIENCED NOTHING BUT MISERY & DECEIT, *in return for* THE FINEST FEELINGS OF THE HONESTEST OF HEARTS, NOTWITHSTANDING ALL APPEARANCE MINE HAS EVER BEEN TO ME; REITERATE YOUR PROMISE OR RECOLLECT YOU SIGN YOURSELF MY DOOM. OH, GOD! OH, GOD! WHO HAS SEEN THE AGONY OF MY SOUL & KNOWEST THE PURITY OF MY INTENTIONS, HAVE MERCY, HAVE MERCY ON ME: TURN ONCE MORE I CONJURE THEE, THE HEART OF MY MARIA, TO ME, FOR WHOM I HAVE LIVED & FOR WHOM I WILL DIE. You know not what you will drive me to FROM DISPAIR [SIC], YOU KNOW YOU ARE MY WIFE, THE WIFE OF MY HEART & SOUL, MY WIFE IN THE PRESENCE OF MY GOD."[81]

It was all too much for Maria. Remarkably, Queen Charlotte even wrote a letter begging her to take George back, but still she refused. She didn't change her mind until 1799, when the prince penned a desperate note in which he swore that he would publicly admit the secret marriage and implicate everyone who had been present at it if she continued to reject him.

Maria was terrified for the consequences such a revelation might have on her family and the prince alike. Despite herself, she still cared about him. A bout of ill health in 1799 had left her at such a low ebb that some outlets wrongly reported that "Mrs. Fitzherbert, who for so many years enjoyed the tender affections of a certain illustrious Personage, died at Bath [after] a lingering illness,"[82] but happily that wasn't the case. Maria's health had certainly been poor, but now she was on the road to recovery. The last thing she needed was even more upset.

Maria didn't know which way to turn. After much agonising she decided that this was a decision that only the Lord could make and she

---

81. Aspinall, Arthur (ed.) (1965). *The Correspondence of George, Prince of Wales, Vol IV*. London: Cassell, p.48.
82. *London Packet or New Evening Post*. 20 February 1799 – 22 February 1799; issue 4564.

asked her priest, William Nassau, to take her case to Rome. Maria told George that she would abide by whatever the church decided. If the Vatican agreed that they were married, then she would return to him. If the decision came back that the marriage was invalid, then she would not.

To George's delight, Rome gave the marriage the nod on the condition that he show true penitence for his sins. Naturally he swore that he was sorry and Maria returned to her errant prince. For months their reconciliation was private but in the summer of 1800 the couple threw a party in Tilney Street to celebrate their reunion. Maria admitted that "she hardly knew she could summon up resolution to pass that severe ordeal, but she thanked God she had the courage to do so."[83] The showy public breakfast had George's fingerprints all over it and once it was done they embarked on their social calls once more. In many ways it's unbelievable that Maria reconciled with George, but the Holy See had given her the thumbs up and George certainly *seemed* repentant. Yet some of Maria's support fell away as the public transferred their sympathies to the Princess of Wales, whose husband had abandoned her in favour of Mrs Fitzherbert. The secret marriage had remained a refuted rumour but there was no denying the very real marriage to Caroline of Brunswick. Maria Fitzherbert had become the thing she had always striven to avoid. She was the prince's *other woman*.

> "A Gentleman of high rank and Mrs. Fitzherbert are said to be once more *Inseperables*. Where one is invited, a card to the other is a matter of course."[84]

The Vatican's confirmation of the marriage was in many ways disastrous, not that Maria realised it at the time. She would consider herself to be the rightful wife of the Prince of Wales from that day forward. In more malicious hands this might have caused all sorts of trouble, but Maria was the only person who ended up with a broken heart. As long as the prince lived – and despite his self-abuse and parlous health, he lived a long time – Maria was a married woman. George would never be a

---

83. Langdale, Charles (1856). *Memoirs of Mrs Fitzherbert*. London: Richard Bentley, p.129.

84. *St James's Chronicle or the British Evening Post*. 3 July 1800 – 5 July 1800; issue 6637.

long-term prospect as a husband, yet Maria could take no other spouse. She had condemned herself to a lonely life yoked to a man who found fidelity an alien concept.

Yet perhaps Maria still believed that something permanent might come of it and for the early years of the nineteenth century, the couple were happy. The king and queen, though never exactly her greatest champions, appreciated both Maria's steadying influence on their eldest son and her quiet, reserved demeanour. She alone was able to quell George's wilder ways and for once things were relatively smooth in the royal household, despite the animosity that bubbled between the Prince and Princess of Wales. To her credit, even when things were at their absolute worst, the princess never so much as raised an eyebrow at Maria spending time with Charlotte, the estranged couple's only child.

Once again Maria returned to Brighton, where unsubstantiated rumours claimed that the prince had constructed a secret passage that linked the Royal Pavilion to Steine House, the fashionable home that was built to her specifications. No such passage has ever been discovered and constructing one would have been a wasted effort anyway, for George and Maria were open in their affections. George certainly had no need to sneak away to see Maria via underground tunnels.

Mary Seymour

> "A suit has been instituted in Chancery, to compel this lady to give up the infant daughter of the late Lord Hugh and Lady Horatia Seymour. [If successful] the consequences might be fatal, as [Mary] was very affectionate, and of a tender constitution, and that Mrs. F. had taken the place in her heart of her deceased mother."[85]

Though Maria never sought to cause drama and actively avoided the spotlight, sometimes it unavoidably found her. So it was in the matter of the case of Mary Seymour, a little girl to whom Maria Fitzherbert became a second mother. Mary was the daughter of Lord Hugh Seymour and his wife, Lady Horatia. The couple were close friends with both

---

85. *Bury and Norwich Post*. 3 April 1805; issue 1188.

George and Maria but when the prince married Caroline of Brunswick, a disapproving Lord Hugh cut George off.

When Mary was born in November 1798, Lady Horatia was already suffering with consumption and the difficult labour struck a serious blow to her health. She faced death unless she could escape the British cold, but the newborn's health was fragile and there was no way the little girl could travel. Maria offered to care for Mary until such time as Lady Horatia was sufficiently recovered to return to England and be reunited with her daughter. It was an ideal and selfless solution.

Mary, who was known as *Minney*, came to live on Tilney Street with Maria, who soon loved her as though she was her own. Lord Hugh and Lady Horatia went to Madeira, and then sailed on to Jamaica, but Horatia's health was already in terminal decline. The Seymours both died in 1801 within a few days of each other, Hugh of yellow fever and Horatia of consumption, orphaning their little girl and her five siblings. Though Lord Hugh's will expressly named his brother, Lord Henry Seymour, as the guardian to the five eldest children, the will was written before Minney's birth and she was not included in the list. Lord Henry believed that the best thing was to entrust the care of the little girl to her aunt Elizabeth, Countess Waldegrave, who was happy to accept the responsibility.

Maria was devastated. She and Lady Waldegrave had never been on the best of terms and she knew that if Minney went to live with the countess, she would likely never see her again. The Prince of Wales was fond of Minney too and it was she who gave him the notorious nickname *Prinny*, which echoed her own diminutive of Minney. George made representations to the Seymours on Maria's behalf, citing not only the mutual attachment between Mrs Fitzherbert and Minney, but also the upheaval the little girl had already faced in her short life. It was duly agreed after some wrangling that Maria could maintain custody of Mary until 1803, at which point she would have to surrender her. Even an offer of £10,000 from the Prince of Wales wouldn't change the family's mind.

Maria was determined to fight and retained the services of Samuel Romilly as her legal representative. The case became a cause célèbre in the Court of Chancery, where it dragged on for three long years. The arguments on both sides were simple enough: Maria loved Minney and Minney loved Maria, so the pair wanted to stay together. The executors of Lord Hugh Seymour's will, on the other hand, believed that Minney should be raised by family members. Although we might expect that their disapproval of Maria was occasioned by her relationship with the Prince of Wales, that wasn't the case. What actually set them against her was her religion, which made her "an unfit person to be entrusted with the guardianship"[86]. Should Minney be raised by Maria, they argued, then she would be raised a Catholic, a prospect at which "Every Protestant parent in the country would be justly alarmed"[87]. Maria's camp explained that she had no intention of raising Minney as a Catholic, but it was on this matter that the case hung.

Though he didn't appear in court, George submitted an affidavit in which he swore that Lady Horatia had begged him to care for Minney on her deathbed. The prince confirmed that he still considered himself the little girl's protector and stated that she could hope for no better care than that provided by Maria. In fact, far from trying to impose her faith on her ward, Maria had already placed Minney's religious education in the hands of a clergyman who had been personally recommended by the Bishop of Winchester. The bishop provided a sworn affidavit of his own to confirm that there was no question of Minney being raised a Catholic, regardless of what the Seymours might claim to the contrary.

It wasn't all going to go Maria's way though. Lady Euston, Minney's maternal aunt, had a very different opinion. She swore that the prince had fundamentally misunderstood the instructions of Lady Horatia, who had meant merely that he should look out for Minney's future wellbeing, rather than consider himself authorised to make decisions regarding her guardianship. Furthermore, she claimed that Lady Horatia had regretted allowing Maria to care for Minney at all, and that she would have removed her from Maria's care if she had realised her death was imminent.

In February 1805, the court made its decision. Minney was to be handed over to Lord Hugh's executors, Lord Henry Seymour and Lord Euston. Inconsolable, Maria lodged an appeal against the decision in the House of Lords but just as her health had gone into decline when George deserted her, once again her distress manifested as physical symptoms. She made a last desperate appeal for help to her friend, Isabella Ingram-Seymour-Conway, Marchioness of Hertford, whose husband was

---

86. *Morning Post.* 1 April 1805; issue 11384.
87. Ibid.

Minney's uncle, the Marquess of Hertford. Hertford was the head of the Seymour family, and Maria begged Lady Isabella to intervene in the case of Minney Seymour. George sweetened the request with personal visits to Lady Hertford as well as a trip to the Yorkshire home of her mother, where he delivered a gift of expensive Chinese lanterns. Fatefully, the closeness that grew between Lady Hertford and the Prince of Wales would result in her ousting Maria as George's favourite just two years later.

After so many years together Maria and Minney were like mother and daughter, and it's difficult to discern what benefit the court might have envisioned were they to change the arrangement. Once again, the affidavits were gathered and once again, the Bishop of Winchester said his piece, assuring the House of Lords that if the only obstacle to Maria's guardianship was her religion, then it need not be an obstacle at all. Minney was being raised in the Church of England, he declared, and that was all there was to it.

On the day that the case was to be heard in the Lords, a crowd gathered outside. They anticipated drama but instead they got a damp squib. Lady Hertford had worked her magic on her husband and as the packed gallery held its collective breath in anticipation of scandal, Lord Hertford rose to his feet. He explained that it pained him to see a private family matter aired in public and requested that custody of Minney be given to him, as the head of his family and the eldest brother of Minney's late father. The Lords voted unanimously in favour of the proposal and Minney, who was by then 7 years old, became the legal ward of Lord Hertford.

Lord Hertford immediately named Maria Fitzherbert as his official proxy and the person to whom he entrusted Minney's care. Maria wrote that "Words cannot do justice to the happiness I enjoy at the thought of my darling child restored to me, after the long series of misery and anxiety I have endured."[88] Though Lord Hertford's intervention had saved the day, Maria's idyll with the Prince of Wales was nearing an end. Lady Hertford would put the final nail in the coffin.

A Pecuniary Embarrassment

In the early years of the nineteenth century, drama came thick and fast for the Prince of Wales and Maria Fitzherbert. No sooner had the couple

---

88. Gore-Browne, Robert (1953). *Chancellor Thurlow*. London: Hamilton, p.35.

reunited than the Seymour case exploded into the headlines, followed all too swiftly by the Delicate Investigation of 1806, in which the Princess of Wales found herself accused of giving birth to an illegitimate child. That's a story for the second half of this book, but as Caroline's popularity grew, the prince's declined. The public disliked the showy, spendthrift heir to the throne intensely, and the more wronged his legitimate wife appeared, the more things they found to loathe about her husband. Nathaniel Jefferys, the prince's former jeweller and sometime Member of Parliament, reserved his animosity for Maria.

His dislike for Mrs Fitzherbert, which one can only assume was due to her being a Catholic *and* a mistress, began way back in 1790, when Maria had loaned George so much money that she had ended up in debt herself. George had asked Jefferys if he would lend her £1,600 and he had agreed without hesitation. The trouble started when Maria visited the jeweller to thank him and he took an instant dislike to her. Though his royal patron brought plenty of customers to Jefferys' door and he supported George throughout his parliamentary career, the prince was always tardy to settle his accounts. Eventually this cost Jefferys dear.

As the months passed, Maria made no effort to repay her debt. Even her custom was paltry, amounting to a total of £120 worth of goods, yet Jefferys did not dare broach the subject with her for fear of upsetting the prince and losing his patronage. Though it was George who had first requested the loan, it was Maria who Jefferys considered the sinner, never more so than once the Prince of Wales married Caroline of Brunswick. Jefferys received an order from the prince to provide jewels for the wedding and, with no spending limit imposed, duly selected pieces to the value of £64,000. When the time came to settle the account, no money was forthcoming and the case ended up in court alongside a further £24,000 bill that the prince hadn't paid. The judge found in Jefferys' favour and Lord Erskine, the Lord Chancellor, wrote to Jefferys to record his "extreme disgust at the evidence by which a JUST and HONORABLE CLAIM was attempted to be resisted."[89]

Yet still the prince didn't pay up, despite Jefferys writing multiple letters to him as his own circumstances deteriorated. Once a grand jeweller to the most flamboyant clients in Europe, by the turn of the century, Mr Jefferys had lost everything, and he was even being falsely

---

89. Ibid., p.23.

accused of anonymously smearing Maria in the press. He blamed the widow Fitzherbert for all of his misfortunes and those of the wronged Princess of Wales too. Indeed, he sniffily commented that the public "Will conceive an apology is due from me, for placing upon the same sheet of paper the names of the PRINCESS of Wales and that of *Mrs Fitzherbert*."[90]

Jefferys' resentment festered for years until, in 1806, he wrote a scurrilous pamphlet entitled *A Review of the Conduct of His Royal Highness the Prince of Wales*. In it Jefferys claimed that when Maria came to thank him for the money, she was aloof and ungrateful. After she left he considered, "if ever I should have the misfortune to lose the Prince's favour, I should have cause to lament the day when Mrs. Fitzherbert was under a necessity of thanking me for a service performed to her;- an observation I was induced to make, from the mortified pride visible in the countenance of that lady."[91]

Not only did Maria dodge her debts, spat Jefferys, but in her involvement with the heir to the throne, she had exposed the prince to "a charge, when proved, punishable by the laws of England with pillory, imprisonment, or transportation, as too frequently occurs at the sessions in the Old Bailey."[92]

Jefferys' words were those of a man in crisis, but the villain in this particular tale was George. The pamphlet caused an uproar and with the bit between his teeth, Jefferys went for the jugular, accusing the prince and Maria of whooping it up on the public purse whilst the Princess of Wales was treated like a pariah. Maria was devastated by the personal nature of the attack and the fact that once again, her dirty laundry was being aired in public. She retired to Brighton with Minney and remained there as the public digested Jefferys' pamphlet. This time there was little sympathy for Maria. The Princess of Wales was the new heroine of the hour.

Things seemed to go from bad to worse with the death of Maria's mother in the first weeks of 1807, and she withdrew further into the simple company of Minney Seymour. At the same time George's social

---

90. Ibid., p.64.
91. Jefferys, Nathaniel (1806). *A Review of the Conduct of His Royal Highness the Prince of Wales*. London: Privately published, p.15.
92. Ibid., p.67.

life was flourishing and central to it was Lady Hertford, the woman who had played such a significant role in securing Maria custody of her young ward. Things were changing again.

Isabella Ingram-Seymour-Conway, Marchioness of Hertford, had married the 2nd Marquess of Hertford, who was twice her age, when she was just 16. She swiftly joined the pantheon of celebrated society hostesses for whom the Prince of Wales developed a special fondness. His declarations of love failed to move her and his hysterical letters left her coldly unimpressed, but it just made him more determined. Maria had seen it all before with her husband's occasional follies, but she remained certain that she alone held the prince's heart. This time, she was wrong.

When Lady Hertford finally consented to become the prince's mistress, he couldn't leave Maria behind fast enough. To make matters worse, a condition of Lady Hertford's capitulation was that her reputation remain intact. That meant that whenever she had a liaison with the prince at his home, Maria also had to be present to lend an air of respectability. It was a humiliation that Maria endured for two years, perhaps fearing that Lady Hertford might have her husband snatch Minney away if she didn't. The stress began to play on Maria and as her health suffered, she summoned the courage to pick up her pen and write to George. She would play gooseberry no longer.

> "The constant state of anxiety I am perpetually kept in with respect to your proceedings, and the little satisfaction I experience when occasionally you make partial communications to me, have determined me to address you by letter.
>
> You must be well aware of the misery we have both suffered for the last three or four years on a subject most painful to me, and to all those who are attached and interested about you. It has quite destroyed the entire comfort and happiness of both our lives; it has so completely destroyed mine, that neither my health nor my spirits can bear it any longer. [...] You must decide, and that decision must be done immediately, that I may know what line to pursue. I beg your answer may be a written one, to avoid all unpleasant conversations upon a subject so heart-rending to one whose

whole life has been dedicated to you, and whose affection for you none can surpass."[93]

The letter leaves no doubt that relations between the couple were at their lowest ebb. The Dukes of York and Clarence attempted to stave off the inevitable heartbreak by assuring Maria that it was a passing fancy, but the die had been cast. As George III's health deteriorated and the possibility of a Regency or even George's succession became ever more likely, the politically shrewd Lady Hertford became something of a mentor. She warned her lover about the dangers of being so close to a Roman Catholic and with her guidance, George began to see the attraction of maintaining the Tory status quo, represented by her own husband, who had placed Minney in Maria's care. Perhaps George considered his relationship with Maria to be a relic of that old, flighty life when he had kicked against everything the king stood for. Now, with the crown tantalising close, he had no wish to rock the boat.

Prinny

As the first decade of the nineteenth century came to an end, George III's battles with mental illness grew ever more desperate. His physical health was failing too and it was all he could do to make his daily visits to the bedside of his youngest daughter, Princess Amelia, who was dying of consumption over the courtyard from his Windsor Castle rooms. When Amelia passed away in November 1810, the last threads of her father's tenuous sanity snapped. He would never recover.

> "The Regency bill has been printed. The following are the principal heads of it:-
>
> Prince of Wales to exercise the Royal authority, subject to restrictions.
>
> [...]
>
> Upon his Majesty's recovery, and declaration of his pleasure to resume his authority, this act to cease and no act done under it afterwards to be valid."[94]

---

93. Wilkins, William Henry (1905). *Mrs Fitzherbert and George IV*. London: Longmans, Green, and Co, p.314-315.
94. *Caledonian Mercury*. 19 January 1811; issue 13899

The Prince of Wales, once so devoted to his fashionable Whig friends and his Catholic wife, was to become the Regent and rule in his ailing father's place. He turned to Maria for advice, asking her whether he should grant the wishes of his hopeful Whig friends, who were expecting to be brought to power, or honour the decisions of his father and maintain the Tory status quo? Maria had no qualms about advising him to keep the political promises he had made to his friends. Perhaps some part of her hoped that he might yet rescind the Royal Marriages Act, but after twenty-five years as a secret wife, I would suspect that she had long since given up hope on this front. After all, rescinding the Royal Marriages Act wouldn't overturn the Act of Settlement and George had no intention of giving up the Regency now that it was finally in his hands. As he underwent the ceremony that confirmed him as Regent, no doubt he was considering the question of Maria Fitzherbert.

> "The magnificent suite of the state apartments had been previously prepared for the occasion. At the extremity of the largest apartment a canopy had been raised, under which the Prince Regent sate [sic]. The servants were all in state liveries, lining the hall and the passages. His Royal Highness was attended by the Princes; and by all the great Officers of the Household.[...] Pall-Mall and the adjoining streets and houses were crowded with spectators."[95]

Lady Hertford was as close to a suitable mistress as George would get and politically she was seen as a steady figure. Indeed, the *Courier* regarded her as "Britain's guardian angel". By the time of his first cabinet meeting the newly-minted Prince Regent had made his decision. He would follow the advice of Lady Hertford: the Tory administration would continue.

> "On Monday night, the Prince of Wales communicated to Mr. Perceval his determination respecting the continuance of the present ministry and the ground of that determination [...] although he cannot express to them his approbation of the principles upon which they have hitherto transacted the affairs of the kingdom – and although they must know that

---

95. *Leeds Mercury*. 9 February 1811; issue 2377.

it is only from a sentiment of filial respect for the choice of his Royal Father and Sovereign, that he can repose any degree of confidence in them."[96]

On the question of politics at least, Hertford had superseded Fitzherbert, and the two women could not be more different. One was Whig, one Tory, one was Catholic, whilst Lady Hertford was wholly opposed to the thorny issue of Catholic emancipation. Though Princess Caroline spoke highly of Maria, whose relationship with George had preceded her own ill-fated marriage to the prince, she dismissed Lady Hertford's affair with the prince as "a *liaison of vanity on her part* [...] but it will not last long, she is too formal for him."[97] By throwing his lot in with his new mistress, the Prince Regent had sent Maria a strong message. Prinny and Maria were reaching the end.

A Parting of Ways

Becoming Prince Regent didn't just mean that George now had more power and prestige than he had ever enjoyed before, it also gave him an excuse to throw one of his beloved parties. He decided that he would mark the occasion, as well as honour a visit by members of the exiled French royal court, by hosting a banquet at Carlton House. This would be a significant moment for Maria, for it was to be her first public airing on the arm of the Prince Regent. After the recent and unhappy experiences of playing second fiddle to Lady Hertford, she wanted to know precisely what her role would be. Caroline of Brunswick, naturally, was not invited. When a Carlton House insider informed Maria that she wouldn't be seated beside the prince, or even at his table - where the Hertfords would enjoy a choice position - she was in equal parts mortified and disbelieving. This had to be a mistake, Maria told herself, and she asked George to put it right.

When the Prince Regent told his wife of more than a quarter of a century that she had been correctly informed, Maria was devastated. She had no rank, George explained, and though he had been able to waive

---

96. Ibid.
97. Bury, Lady Charlotte Campbell (1838). *Diary Illustrative of the Times of George the Fourth: Vol I*. London: Henry Colburn, p.25.

such concerns of protocol when he was Prince of Wales, he could no longer do so now that he was the Prince Regent. "You know, Madam, you have no place," was his simple explanation. There were to be no sugarplums from *this* royal table.

For Maria, it was the last straw. She turned down the invitation, but when she attended a party thrown by the Duke and Duchess of Devonshire the following day and saw Prinny and Lady Hertford together, Maria knew that the end had come. She wrote to the prince to tell him that, "I can never submit to appear in any place or situation but in that where you yourself first placed me many years ago". He didn't reply. The tumultuous romance had finally come to an end.

The Prince Regent had other ideas. He had no desire to break with Maria completely, but neither did he relish the idea of consorting openly with a Catholic now that he was Regent. Knowing how capricious George could be, one wonders what he might have seen as a solution. Perhaps he would have offered Maria the opportunity to be his wife behind closed doors, a sort of domestic mistress, but certainly not in public. Maria would have had no interest in such an arrangement. There was no way forward.

Though their relationship was over, Maria wasn't exactly ruined. She had already secured her yearly pension when the couple split previously and now, with intervention from the Duke of the York and Queen Charlotte herself, that pension was raised to £6,000 per year. Though this might seem surprising, the queen had long since been able to see what a steadying influence Maria could be on her wayward eldest son. The two women might never have been friends, but they were certainly not enemies either.

Maria made no effort to see the prince again and nor did he seek out her company. Instead she went into genteel retirement and made the care of Minney her priority. Maria and Minney made their home at Sherwood Lodge in Battersea, but they were regular visitors to the city and Brighton too, and they even enjoyed a sojourn to Paris. Minney came out in 1817 and was welcomed at court, where it was roundly agreed that Maria had done a marvellous job of raising her. The Prince Regent remained as fond of Minney as he ever was and on her twenty-first birthday he sent her a banker's draft for a trust fund he had started in her name when she was an infant. The fund had matured to be worth £20,000.

Maria's name began to fade from the press and though she faced a mild resurgence of interest during the trial of Queen Caroline, all in all, she managed to keep her head down. She was in Paris during the trial but when she heard a rumour that the defence intended to call her as a witness, she hurried home to England. Upon her arrival in London, she cut the names of the witnesses to her wedding out of the marriage certificate, anxious that they might be open to prosecution. Maria's fears were unfounded though. With the Lords satisfied that the Royal Marriages Act nullified the marriage, she was not called to testify.

Queen Charlotte and King George III died within a few short years of one another, the first in 1818 and the second in 1820, but though she was now the wife of King George IV, Maria sought no advancement. She made no effort to communicate with George and certainly had no wish to attend his coronation. Even when Caroline of Brunswick died in 1821, Maria held her silence. Perhaps hoping to goad her into speaking her mind, when she and George accidentally found themselves at the same event, George told Maria that he was open to marrying again. She replied with a curt, "Very well, Sir", and immediately took her leave.

The King's Widow

The years of Maria's retirement passed without incident. She had given up any hope of reconciling with the king and as he cast Lady Hertford aside in favour of the ambitious Elizabeth, Lady Conyngham, Maria no doubt watched the development of this new affair with resignation. A relationship that she encouraged with rather more enthusiasm was that of Minney Seymour and Colonel George Dawson[98], the son of the Earl of Portarlington. Though Maria dreaded the day that Minney would marry and strike out on her own, she did everything she could to ensure that the marriage, which was certainly a love match, would be a roaring success. She also opened her house to her niece, Mary Anne Smythe, who was widely believed to have been the illegitimate daughter of Maria's brother, Jack. That said, there has been some speculation that the girl was Maria's child with the Prince of Wales. Speculation increased in 1833, when Lord Stourton asked Maria to sign a document vowing that she had never had a child with George, but she refused. Whatever her parentage was, Mary Anne Smythe would occupy the place that Minney

---

98. Later George Dawson-Damer.

had filled for so long. Minney and George Dawson were married in 1825. It was the end of another era for Maria Fitzherbert.

As Maria grew older she faced the deaths of those royal brothers who had been her friends. Now and then, usually when the king and his mistress were at odds, rumours resurfaced that there was to be a reconciliation between George and Maria, but there was never any substance to them, nor do we have any reason to suspect that Maria particularly wanted to reconcile. Though it's tempting to cast Maria Fitzherbert as some sort of dewy-eyed heroine, she was no such thing. She was by this point a woman in her seventies, and with Minney happily married off, her next project was securing the same happiness for her niece, Mary. She did so with an engagement to Captain Edward Stafford Jerningham, a member of a respected Catholic family. Mrs Fitzherbert was now the grand dame of Brighton, but she never forgot her husband.

For a long time the king's failing health had been a matter of public discussion. The former bon viveur was now a morbidly obese recluse who treated his ailments with alcohol and laudanum. He disappeared behind the walls of Windsor Castle just as his father had before him, with Lady Conyngham dictating his every move to her own advantage. Perhaps the king occasionally thought of Mrs Fitzherbert as his body grew weaker, for she certainly thought of him. When reports of George's failing health grew more dire than ever, Maria finally took up her pen and wrote to Sir Henry Halford, the king's physician, to enquire after his patient. Sir Henry replied with a chilling summary, informing Maria that the king was barely able to breathe. His days were growing short.

Nearly two decades had passed since they went their separate ways, but the thought of George dying without ever hearing from Maria again was too much for her. She wrote care of Sir Henry Halford and though the note is short, there is no mistaking the sentiment that inspired her to write it.

> "SIR, — After many repeated struggles with myself, from the apprehension of appearing troublesome or intruding upon Your Majesty, after so many years of continued silence, my anxiety respecting Your Majesty has got the better of my scruples, and I trust Your Majesty will believe me most sincere, when I assure you how truly I have grieved

to hear of your sufferings. From the late account, I trust Your Majesty's health is daily improving, and no one will feel more rejoiced [than I] to learn Your Majesty is restored to complete convalescence, which I pray to God you may long enjoy, accompanied with every degree of happiness you could wish for, or desire.

I have enclosed this letter to Sir H[enry] H[alford], as Your Majesty must be aware that there is no person about you through whom I could make a communication of so private a nature, attended with a perfect conviction of its never being divulged.

I have the honour to be, &c."

As soon as Maria had sent the letter, she rushed to London. There she waited for a reply and, she hoped, an invitation to attend the king in his final days. The invitation never came and Maria later confided to Lord Stourton that nothing had so "cut me up" as the king's ongoing silence. Though Sir Henry Halford gave the letter to his patient, George's illness had partially claimed his wits too. He could barely stay awake and when he did, he was frequently insensible; there was no hope of his being able to write to Maria, let alone summon her to his bedside. King George IV died on 26 June 1830, without replying to Maria Fitzherbert's last letter. As the Duke of Cumberland sent word that Maria was permitted to go into mourning for his late brother, the king was laid to rest. He went to his grave at Windsor with Maria's miniature around his neck, just as he had requested in his will.

"[I request that] the picture of my beloved wife, my Maria Fitzherbert, may be interred with me, suspended round my neck with a ribbon, as I used to wear when I lived, and placed right upon my heart."

Despite the years that had passed since they were together, Maria grieved deeply for her lost love. George's successor, King William IV, regarded her as a friend and with the assistance of the Duke of Wellington, the matter of her continued upkeep was soon agreed. The new king visited Maria at Brighton in the months after his brother's death and there she showed him her marriage certificate as well as other papers that confirmed

Pen and Sword Books
c/o Casemate Publishers
1950 Lawrence Road
Havertown, PA 19083

✄ HISTORY BROUGHT BACK TO LIFE WITH PEN & SWORD BOOKS

Pen & Sword Books have over 6000 books currently available and we cover all periods of history on land, sea and air.

If you would like to hear more about our other titles sign up now and receive 30% off your next purchase. www.penandswordbooks.com/newsletter/

By signing up to our free
discounts, reviews on new releases, previews of forthcoming titles and upcoming competitions, so you will never miss out!

Not online? Return this card to us with your contact details and we will put you on our catalog mailing list.

Mr/Mrs/Ms ....

Address..

Zip Code........................... Email address...

We hope you enjoyed this book!

her claim on the heart of George IV. William was greatly affected by her dignity and asked whether she would accept the title of duchess by way of both recognition and apology. Maria was unequivocal in her response. She thanked him but gently declined, saying that Mrs Fitzherbert would serve her as well now as ever. William IV accepted her reply and instead requested that she use his royal livery on her carriages and dress her servants in the same. These small measures were a tacit recognition of her status, as was his belief that Maria had every right to wear widow's weeds for the late king. For the rest of her days, Maria was to be a regular visitor to the court of King William IV.

Letters from a Prince

Though Maria was growing older, her wits remained as sharp as ever. She was keenly interested in current affairs, especially the progress of the Reform Bill, which would dramatically overhaul the electoral system of England and Wales, and she was perfectly happy to be out of the spotlight. The one thing she wanted was the return of the letters that she had written to George IV, which she believed were in the hands of the Duke of Wellington. Wellington offered to exchange them for the papers in Maria's possession that related to her relationship with the late king. Maria refused, countering that those papers were all that she had to prove her honour as a married woman, not a mistress. She would accept a compromise, said she, whereby she would appoint Lord Albemarle and Lord Stourton – to whom she later entrusted her memoirs – to act as her trustees in return for the letters she had written to the king.

Eventually the two sides agreed to destroy the contentious papers, with the exception of a handful that included the marriage certificate, the late king's will, and a hysterical letter George had sent to Maria alluding to the marriage when trying to win her back in 1799. In its heated and handwritten contents, there can be no doubt that George considered Maria Fitzherbert to be his wife.

> "Think not that Payne or any advice whatever will make me change my purpose, or FORSWEAR MY OATH. THANK GOD *my witnesses are living*, your uncle & your brother, besides Harris, who I shall call upon us having BEEN INFORMED BY ME OF EVERY, EVEN THE MINUTEST

CIRCUMSTANCE OF OUR MARRIAGE. Oh! my heart, my heart, but I am composed & calm. Whatever your answer may be & whatever the consequence STILL MY BLESSINGS WITH MY LOVE WILL EVER ATTEND THEE MY MARIA."[99]

The agreement was made. On 24 August 1833, the Duke of Wellington and Lord Albemarle met in Maria's drawing room and burned the vast collection of papers. Those that were preserved were deposited in Coutts's Bank. Maria Fitzherbert's honour, which she had always strived to protect, remained beyond reproach, but the burning of such precious letters caused her profound distress. She escaped to France, putting some much needed distance between herself and the fireplace at Tilney Street.

The Late Mrs Fitzherbert

The last years of Maria's life passed in a gentle round of visits to the royal court and happy days spent in the company of her friends. She spent the majority of her time at Steine House in Brighton, where she counted King William and Queen Adelaide amongst her closest friends. What little mention of her there was in the press was marked with approval for her dignity in the face of adversity. Her closeness to the royal household had been noted.

> "This amiable lady, who is a constant guest at the Pavilion, is held in great esteem by the King and Queen. Mrs. Fitzherbert's conduct throughout life has been exemplary; and her charities, distributed amongst the poor at Brighton, are upon a scale of liberality quite unequalled."[100]

In March 1837, 79-year-old Maria came down with a chill after taking an airing on the seafront at Brighton. She retired to her bed, where Minney and her family gathered as she received the last rites and said her loving goodbyes. Maria passed away on the evening of 27 March 1837.

---

99. Aspinall, Arthur (ed.) (1965). *The Correspondence of George, Prince of Wales, Vol IV*. London: Cassell, pp.49-50.
100. *Lancaster Gazetter.* 7 January 1832; volume 31.

"This Lady, whose health has for some considerable time been declining, died on Monday night, at ten minutes past seven o'clock, at her mansion on the Old Steyne, Brighton, in the 93rd [sic] year of her age. For some years Mrs. Fitzherbert has not joined many parties, but has received visits from all our leading fashionables."[101]

Maria Fitzherbert was buried according to the rites of the Roman Catholic Church. She was laid to rest in the vault of the church of St John the Baptist in Brighton, where she had often worshipped and to which she had made a number of generous charitable donations. As her cortege passed through the town, a vast crowed gathered to pay their respects to the late lady of Brighton. Although the funeral was a private one for close friends and family only, once Maria's grave had been sealed, a long line of well-wishers filed through the church to say farewell to Mrs Fitzherbert.

In the years that followed Maria's death, Minney commissioned a statue of her to be placed in the church where she was laid to rest. When John Edward Carew's respectful memorial was installed, it depicted a veiled Maria kneeling in prayer. On her left hand she wears not two, but three gold wedding bands, in honour of her secret marriage to King George IV.

---

101. *Morning Post.* 29 March 1837; issue 20686.

Act Two

Caroline of Brunswick
(17 May 1768 – 7 August 1821)

"If anybody say to me at this moment will you pass your life over again, or be killed, I would choose death, for you know, a little sooner or later, we must all die; but to live a life of wretchedness twice over, - oh! mine God, no!"[1]

The Little Princess

For the daughter of a royal house in the eighteenth century, the path was more or less set, from the cradle to the altar and all the way to the grave. And this was certainly the case for Caroline Amelia Elizabeth of Brunswick-Wolfenbüttel, who was born to Charles William Ferdinand, later to reign as the Duke of Brunswick-Wolfenbüttel, and his wife, Princess Augusta of Great Britain. Princess Augusta was the sister of King George III and she knew all about the lot of a royal woman.

Augusta was born in 1737 and had been married to Charles, her second cousin, since 1764. They made their home at the Grauer Hof and at first, the princess was taken by her handsome new husband, proudly telling her brother that, "I never knew anybody with a more real good heart you know he is sensible & clever in short he is monsterously [sic] fond of me & I am a happy woman."[2] She adored him, and when the celebrated soldier went away on military business, she was miserable. Caroline

---

1. Bury, Lady Charlotte Campbell (1838). *Diary Illustrative of the Times of George the Fourth: Vol I*. London: Henry Colburn, p.37.
2. Georgian Papers Online (http://gpp.rct.uk, September 2020). RA GEO/MAIN/51973 Letter from Augusta, Hereditary Princess of Brunswick, to George III, 11 December 1764.

was the third of the couple's seven children, six of whom survived into adulthood. Princess Hedwig Elizabeth Charlotte of Sweden memorably described the sons of the house like this:

"The sons of the Ducal couple are somewhat peculiar. The Hereditary Prince, chubby and fat, almost blind, strange and odd — if not to say an imbecile — attempts to imitate his father but only makes himself artificial and unpleasant. He talks continually, does not know what he says and is in all aspects unbearable. [...] The other son, Prince Georg, is the most ridiculous person imaginable, and so silly that he can never be left alone but is always accompanied by a courtier. The third son is also described as an original. I never saw him, as he served with his regiment. The fourth one is the only normal one, but also torments his parents by his immoral behaviour."[3]

Caroline's nurse was English – Augusta wouldn't have it any other way – and the little girl's childhood was already mapped out for her. She would be tutored in the arts of polite feminine society and prepared to one day become a bride. At first Caroline had the very best of example from her mother and father, but soon things at the Grauer Hof began to turn sour. Charles was an incorrigible flirt and the more he flirted with other ladies, the less happy Augusta became in Brunswick. She began to resent having left England for a man who wasn't devoted to her, and she complained about the "odd figures and manners of these [German] people"[4]. Augusta became ever more determined to not to settle in, keeping to her English customs for the duration of her long marriage.

The court of Brunswick was a world away from the domestic piety of its English counterpart. It was infamous for its ribaldry, so it's hardly surprising that the straight-laced Augusta wasn't happy there. She certainly wasn't happy with the way her husband held tight to the purse

3. Klercker, Cecilia (ed.) (1927). *Hedvig Elisabeth Charlottas Dagbok*. Stockholm: PA Norstedt & Söners, pp.210-220.
4. Georgian Papers Online (http://gpp.rct.uk, September 2020). RA GEO/MAIN/51978-51979 Letter from Augusta, Hereditary Princess of Brunswick, to George III, 19 February 1764.

strings, counting every penny unless he was spending money on his mistresses or himself. The trouble was, a lot of the money he lavished on those mistresses came from the £80,000 dowry that Augusta had brought to their marriage. After Augusta returned to her homeland in 1771 to see her dying mother, she returned to Brunswick even more determined to preserve her English way of life. The more she dug in her heels, the more time Charles William devoted to his mistresses, until the once happy marriage was soured beyond rescue. When Charles installed Luise von Hertefeld as his official mistress, Augusta decided to quit her life at court and devote herself instead to raising her children and studying religion under the tutelage of the Bishop of Fürstenberg. She wrote to tell her husband that:

> "I cannot hide from myself that my children need great attention on my part, and that I am responsible for them to God. I know I make you angry by speaking, but in time you would be more angry if I had let my weakness keep me silent, when it is a question of my children's well-being. In short, we could avoid a scandal if I lived less in public. The children will see nothing, and you will not consort with people who could do them harm."

The Brunswick court might have been wild, but Augusta was determined that Caroline wasn't going to see a moment of it. Instead she decided that her daughter would be raised in the strictest seclusion possible, kept safe from a world in which seduction and scandal were the everyday currencies. Yet in her lonely schoolroom, it swiftly became apparent that the young princess was not as compliant as her mother might have hoped. She was quick-witted and fearless and proud to be so. When the little girl rode on a carousel, her nurse warned her not to go too fast in case she made herself ill. Caroline assured her with characteristic confidence that, "Fear is a word of which a Brunswicker is ignorant."[5]

This particular Brunswicker was also ignorant to the attractions of the structured education that was provided by her governess, Countess Eleonore von Münster, especially when her mother and father were

---

5. Wilks, John (1822). *Memoirs of her Majesty Queen Caroline Amelia Eliz, Vol. I.* London: Sherwood, Neely, and Jones, p.42.

both trying to force their own ill-matched systems on her. Caroline was by no means unintelligent, but she found little to enjoy in formal lessons and preferred to debate and take the time to form her own opinions, rather than simply learn by rote. Though her education was intended to create the very model of a marriageable girl, Caroline was more excited by woodwork than needlepoint, and she had an enviable talent for music. Indeed, she often performed private harpsichord recitals for her family, though no outsiders were permitted to attend. It might be said that in her carefree ways and less than starched attitude, she was more her father's daughter than her mother's. It might also be said that she was a poor match for the fastidious Prince of Wales and his rigid familial court. Caroline's parents' marriage was an unpleasant spectacle and she spent her childhood watching from the sidelines as the strained union crumbled. The duke and duchess each tried to play her off against the other, leaving Caroline torn between the two of them, and she dreamed of making a life of her own, away from the domestic rigours of Brunswick. Such an opportunity would not be easily won.

Caroline did not stay a little girl forever, and by the time she reached her teenage years she had grown tired of her seclusion and the staid companionship of much older women. When balls were held, she was forbidden to attend them, and could only watch from the window as the guests came and went. George III's eldest daughter, Charlotte, Princess Royal, wrote to her friend Lady Elgin years after the royal marriage to bemoan the start that Caroline had been given. She might have more than her share of quirks, Charlotte argued, but with an upbringing like Caroline's, what else was to be expected?

"She is to be pitied for her bad education; indeed her relations are unpardonable for allowing those about her to treat her with such cruel severity. Will you believe it, at thirteen years old she had a governess who would not allow her to go to the window; she was seldom or never permitted to dine at table, or even come downstairs when there was any company; if she did her eyes were always full of tears, and her mother, instead of either speaking kindly to her or leaving her alone, always bid her go on crying, for it was only her naughtiness that made her so passionate. Was that the way either to soften her manner or do her heart good? Poor thing; the moment she obtained her liberty, having not the strength of principles to govern her passions, she allowed all her little evil impulses to get the better."[6]

It was a lonely life and when Caroline later found herself isolated at Carlton House just as she had been isolated in Brunswick, she fought back in a way that she never could as a girl. Even in her youth, she found ways to make friends, often interrupting her rides out so she could talk to the children she met along the way. Unsurprisingly, she got to know their parents too, and was soon making generous donations to the poorest families of the district. When she was 10 years old, she asked for money rather than a Christmas gift, and on the big day, she showed her parents what she had spent it on.

> "Immediately the doors were opened, and twenty-two new-cloathed [sic] children of her own age, subsisting by her bounty, sons and daughters of Brunswick soldiers [...] prostrated themselves before her parents. [...] In her early youth she was often heard to say – "Whoever is unfortunate may consider me as a friend."[7]

It was a charitable interest that was to create a great deal of trouble later in life.

Though philanthropy was all well and good, Princess Augusta drew the line at her daughter mixing with the poor rather than simply throwing money at them. It just wasn't the done thing for a girl with royal blood to visit hovels and mingle with the unfortunate people who lived in them, but that wasn't the reason for Augusta's disapproval. In fact, she suspected an even more scandalous reason for Caroline's behaviour. The duchess feared that her teenage daughter was using her philanthropic outings as an excuse to visit an illicit lover.

Concerned at where her headstrong attitude might lead, Augusta called for physicians to examine Caroline and they decided that the

---

6. Weigall, Lady Rose (1874). *A Brief Memoir of the Princess Charlotte of Wales.* London: John Murray, pp.4-5.
7. *Morning Post.* 18 October 1806; issue 11130.

1. Mrs Fitzherbert. John Condé, after Richard Cosway, 1792.

2. Caroline of Brunswick. Pierre François Ducarme, after an anonymous artist, 1820-1829.

Left: 3. His Royal Highness George, Prince of Wales. John Condé, after Richard Cosway, 1794.

Below: 4. George III and the Royal Family. Richard Earlom, after Johann Zoffany, 1771.

5. George III. William Wynne Ryland, after Allan Ramsay, 1794.

6. Charlotte of Mecklenburg-Strelitz. Richard Houston, after Johann Zoffany, 1772.

7. Princess Charlotte of Wales.
Anonymous.

Bartolomo Bergami.

8. Bartolomo Bergami [sic].
Anonymous.

9. HRH Caroline, Princess of Wales, and the Princess Charlotte. Francesco Bartolozzi, after Richard Cosway, 1799.

10. Mrs Fitzherbert, *Journal des Luxus und der Moden 1786*. Anonymous, 1786.

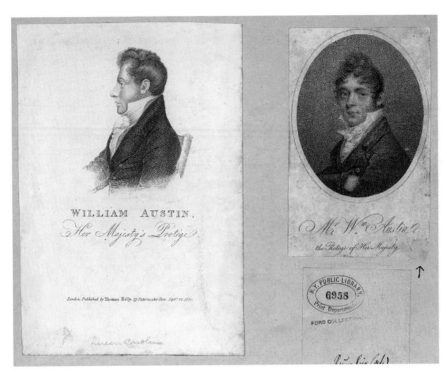

Above: 11. William Austin,
Her Majesty's Protege [sic].
Anonymous, 1820.

Left: 12. Their Royal Highnesses
the Prince & Princess of Wales.
Francesco Bartolozzi, after
H de Janvry, 1797.

13. Princess Charlotte Augusta holding her deceased child. Anonymous, 1818.

14. James Harris, Lord Malmesbury. Franciscus Sansom, after Sir Joshua Reynolds, 1784-1790.

PERGAMI.

Chez M. De Lion, libraire et Marchand de Musique Spuy Straat a la Haye

Left: 15. Baron Pergami. Anonymous, 1821.

Below: 16. *Ah! sure such a pair was never seen so justly form'd to meet by nature.* George Cruikshank, 1820.

THE ROYAL GEORGE AFLOAT;

OR,

TOM TOUGH IN HIGH GLEE.

A New Song—Tune—" My Name d'ye see's Tom Tough."

I.

My name is Royal G——ge, I have seen a little service,
Where pleasure like the Thames has its Tide of ebb
   and flow.
I've done duty for a Duke—now I do it for a Marquis ;
And in Matrimony's bed I've sung out, yo heave ho.
     And more would you be knowing
     I was Cock—swain to a blowing—
Who never turn'd her broadside from friend or from foe,
     I'm " at all in the Ring,
     Of Pleasure I'm the Spring"—
Except when I'm laid up with my damn'd Gouty Toe.

II.

But the worst on't was the time when *Old Snuffy* she
   got sickly,
And the people all rejoiced to find her on the go,
Death sent her Soul a-weigh, so sudden and so quickly,
I scarce could pack the Diamonds up for Oh, dear oh.
     But G——ge, though he drinks and smokes,
     Can love and feel like other folks—
His *interest* to forget, mus'nt come for to go—
     So I seiz'd on her Old Bags
     Stuff'd with Gold—and " rotten Rags,"
Stagg'ring off to Carleton House—singing *yo heave ho.*

III.

But now I am laid up in a devilish condition,
My wife has now attack'd me, which you very well do
   know,
Both C————gh and I, she will send unto perdition ;
Yes, she'll send us both to Hell with *a yo heave ho.*
     Ah, oh, my conscience pricks,
     On my rump I feel the kicks,
That are given devilish hard from *John Bull's* rusty toe,
     But the Devil take Reform,
     At Sea i'll face the storm
And my wife may go to hell—with a yo heave ho.

IV.

She's the people on her side, and that nobody can doubt,
Like a torrent in her cause they incessantly flow,
The dirty tricks of G——ge—oh ! at last they are found
   out,
What the *Devil* I'm to do—only God himself can know.
     In the boat with Mrs. N-sh
     To the Isle of Wight I'll dash,
In my cabin smoke and drink, and forget I have a foe ;
     There's C————e my Wife,
     She's the plague of my life,
And from her I'll make sail with a *yo heave ho.*

V.

Now the Yacht it is all ready, for the Isle of Wight i'll
   steer,
With the lovely Mrs. N-sh I am all upon the go,
I'll pack the husband off—for he has no business here,
With *his Wife* in pleasure's bark, I will jovially row.
     In the Place of Waterloo,
     He may fume, fret, and stew,
'Tis an *architect's* disgrace, and that the world does know,
     Here at Cowes I will revel,
     Kicking *Virtue* to the Devil,
With N-sh have a smash, singing *yo heave ho.*

VI.

Here, *Paget*, you I know are a cursed good fellow,
Thy hand shall guard me safe from every bitter foe ;
You'll stow me in the hold, when you find me rather
   mellow,
And let *lovely Mrs. N-sh* come to see her K—g below.
     But the Cottage is the thing,
     Where pastime wants the K——g ;
'Tis for the *Isle of Wight* I am all on the go,
     I'll forget the Q——n for ever,
     Cross o'er Southampton river,
And with lovely *Mrs. N-sh* sing out, yo heave ho.

Printed and Published by J. L. Marks, 37, Princes-street, Soho ; and 23, Fetter-lane, Fleet-street.—Price 1s. coloured.

17. *The Royal George Afloat; or, Tom Tough in High Glee.* J Lewis Marks, 1820.

18. *The Morning After Marriage, or, A Scene on the Continent*. James Gillray, 1788.

Above left: 19. Henry Brougham, 1st Baron Brougham and Vaux. Henry Hoppner Meyer, after James Ramsay.

Above right: 20. The Right Honourable Spencer Perceval. William Skelton, after Sir William Beechey, 1813.

Above: 21. *The Modern Paradise, or, Adam and Eve Regenerated*. Anonymous, 1786.

Right: 22. Sir William Sidney Smith. Edward Bell, after John Westbrooke Chandler, 1799.

23. *Installation of a Knight Companion of the Bath.* Theodore Lane, 1821.

24. Theodore Majocchi. Abraham Wivell, 1821.

Right: 25. Henry Brougham,
1st Baron Brougham
and Vaux. Friedrich
Rossmässler, 1833.

Below: 26. *Miss
Endeavouring to Excite a
Glow with her Dutch Play
Thing.* George Cruikshank,
1814.

27. *A Late Arrival at Mother Wood's.* Workshop of Robert Isaac Cruikshank, 1820.

28. Carlton House. John Pye, after an anonymous artist.

29. Coronation of King George IV in Westminster Abbey. Charles Turner, after Frederick Nash.

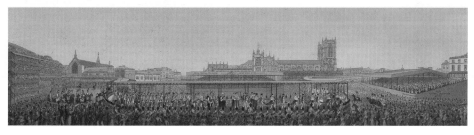

30. View of the Coronation Procession of George IV. Anonymous, 1821.

Left: 31. The Right Honourable Sylvester Douglas, 1st Baron Glenbervie of Kincardine. Edward Harding, after Sir Thomas Lawrence, 1794.

Below: 32. *View of the Funeral Procession of Her Late Majesty, Taken on the Spot*. Anonymous, 1821.

cause of her behaviour was essentially too much excitement - she was becoming too giddy. As a result, her already small world shrank even further, but Caroline wouldn't go down without a fight.

Teenage Maladies

In the early days of his illness, King George III's attacks always began with agonising physical pains that were followed by mental anguish. Over in Brunswick, his niece was beginning to show worryingly similar symptoms as a mysterious illness spiralled into hysteria. Fearful of her marriage prospects if word got out, Augusta had the already secluded young lady confined even more strictly to her rooms, where she was to remain until she recovered. "These are ills which I have feared all my life without knowing them," Augusta wrote to her brother, George III, to whom such illnesses were all too familiar. "These are hysterics, cramps, nerves, which make me despair, and believe she will be unhappy for all her life, by the care one must take. All that excites her arouses the disorder. So for a time she cannot appear, which gives her pain, and that can do her no harm."

Rumours soon spread that the young princess was incurably insane and when her cousin, Prince Frederick, Duke of York and Albany, arrived in Brunswick, Caroline was too ill to receive him for more than brief interludes. Despite her illness, Frederick was taken with what little he saw of the princess. He wrote to his mother to tell her that, "I never saw a more beautiful face or figure than Princess Caroline: she is not above thirteen years old, so that she is not allowed to appear in public but of a Sunday evening, and that for only half an hour, so that I could make the least acquaintance with her, but by what I have heard, she is very lively and sensible."[8]

Caroline's mother was bitterly disappointed by the fact that she couldn't encourage a friendship between York and her daughter. She was desperate to marry Caroline off to one of the British princes, and Frederick had seemed like the perfect candidate, but the young princess was hardly at her best. Though Augusta would continue to drop heavy hints about her

---

8. Aspinall, Arthur (ed.) (1963). *The Correspondence of George, Prince of Wales, Vol II*. London: Cassell, p.xvi.

ambitions, George III had never been fond of marriages between cousins, let alone when one of the parties was rumoured to be mad.

To everyone's relief, Caroline recovered from her mysterious illness, but the future looked no brighter as a result. She was still kept safely behind closed doors by her mother, who had helpfully told friends that she believed Caroline to be insane. Augusta was worried about letting Caroline mingle with wider society in case she fell ill again or, God forbid, developed a taste for the same licentious pastimes as her father. Yet there is little that fosters a yearning for freedom more than being denied it and the longer Caroline was forbidden to dance at those glittering balls and attend those glamorous fetes, the more desperate she became to do so. By the age of 16 she had had enough. If heartfelt pleas and polite requests brought her no joy, then she would resort to more desperate measures.

On the night of a particularly illustrious court ball, Caroline's chambers were rocked by howls of agony that brought her attendants running. They found the princess writhing on the floor, her belly swollen and her face tinged with a deathly grey pallor. Amid her convulsions and shrieks of pain she managed to gasp a confession that she was in the early stages of pregnancy and had gone into premature labour. Her attendants were thrown into a panic and summoned a midwife, as well as Caroline's parents. The duke and duchess arrived to find a scene of surprising calm and Caroline, who had been in agony mere moments before, perched before a mirror wiping away a thick layer of make-up. At her side was the pillow which had been stuffed up her dress. She greeted her parents with laughter, telling them that they should take this as a lesson. If they tried to stop her from being part of the fun again, then this was the least they could expect. The prank backfired badly and soon "it was the general opinion that in early youth the Princess had shown strong symptoms of insanity"[9]. That seems like quite a charge.

Caroline was a product of her peculiarly mismatched genetics and upbringing. She had inherited her soldier father's fearless, fun-loving streak, but she was raised according to her God-fearing mother's strict beliefs. What she really wanted was to go out and raise hell, but that

---

9. Hayward, A (ed.) (1864). *Diaries of a Lady of Quality from 1797 to 1844.* London: Longman, Green, Longman, Egberts & Green, p.186.

wasn't the done thing for a princess. A love of raising hell was one of the few things that Caroline and her future husband had in common.

The pregnancy prank sent a message to Caroline's parents that she wasn't to be trifled with, but it also sent a warning around neighbouring courts that this wasn't necessarily a young lady who would make the most ideal royal bride. Word spread very quickly across the continent whenever something was amiss with one of the aristocratic set, and this was no different. If Caroline's hands-on approach to helping the needy was unconventional, then painting her face grey and feigning labour was crossing the line. Further complicating matters were those troublesome rumours that she had developed attachments to the fathers of her charity children, and that some of those attachments went beyond unrequited crushes.

When it was suspected that Caroline was engaged in a clandestine romantic correspondence with one of her subjects, Augusta clamped down hard and Caroline's life became more suffocating than ever. In the years to come she would more than make up for her restrictive upbringing by living every moment as though it was her last. It is hardly surprising that a daughter of the House of Brunswick should struggle with married life. Quite apart from the strained marriage of her mother and father, Caroline could cite the disastrous examples of both her aunt's and her sister's marriages too. She didn't want to join those ranks.

Caroline's paternal aunt, Elisabeth Christine, had married her cousin, the hedonistic Crown Prince Frederick William of Prussia, when she was just 18. The marriage had turned sour almost immediately and Elisabeth Christine struck back against her husband's multiple affairs by taking a lover of her own. When the Crown Princess fell pregnant by a court musician named Pietro, the unfortunate minstrel was executed and Elisabeth Christine terminated her pregnancy with a herbal potion. The royal couple were divorced and Elisabeth Christine was placed under house arrest for the remaining seventy years of her life. Though it was a very pleasant version of house arrest that allowed her to have a full social life and plenty of fresh intrigues, it was hardly the sort of thing that the pious and God-fearing Augusta wanted to be associated with. Considering that Elisabeth Christine's former husband went on to marry three more times – twice bigamously – it might be considered that Elisabeth Christine had a fortunate escape.

A second scandal attached itself to Brunswick when the marriage of Caroline's eldest sister, Princess Augusta, spectacularly imploded after half a decade. Though her relationship with Prince Frederick of Württemberg produced four children in quick succession, things were not happy in Viipuri, where the couple settled after Frederick was appointed Governor General of Eastern Finland by Catherine the Great. Eventually Augusta fled her home and placed herself at the mercy of the empress, claiming that her husband had a violent temper and a veritable revolving door of male lovers. Catherine took Augusta under her protection and instructed Frederick to leave Russia. He was outraged and swore that his wife's allegations were false. Frederick told the empress that it was in fact his wife who had lovers hidden away everywhere, from stable lads to equerries.[10]

Whatever the truth behind the break up, the marriage was on the rocks. Augusta begged her parents in Brunswick to sanction a divorce but they refused, mortified by the scandal it would cause. Soon Augusta was beginning to get under Catherine's feet and Frederick's claims that she had a thing for grooms and stable lads seemed to be coming true. Embarrassed at her charge's behaviour, Catherine the Great rehomed Augusta at Lohde Castle, where she was to be attended by Wilhelm von Pohlmann. Pohlmann was nearly forty years Augusta's senior, but the couple soon became lovers and Augusta fell pregnant. When she began haemorrhaging in September 1788, Pohlmann delayed calling for medical help because he feared the consequences of their relationship being exposed. Augusta died as a result of blood loss, but the scandal still rang through the House of Brunswick. Not that the Hanoverian side fared any better when it came to avoiding disastrous marriages.

Augusta and George III's sister, Caroline Matilda, had been parcelled off to marry the troubled Christian VII of Denmark when she was just 15. Isolated, unhappy and increasingly unable to manage her new husband's spiralling moods and mental collapse, she began an affair with his doctor, Johann Friedrich Struensee. For a time, the queen and her lover ruled Denmark together as unofficial regents whilst the troubled king contented himself with the brothels of Copenhagen. Eventually the couple's opponents, led by the king's ambitious stepmother, mounted a coup to seize power. The upshot was a scandal that shook the court

---

10. Frederick later married George III's eldest daughter, Charlotte, Princess Royal. Their marriage was a peaceful one.

of Oldenburg to its roots. Struensee paid with his life whilst Caroline Matilda was placed in captivity. Her pleas to her brother, George III, to bring her home fell on deaf ears and she died under house arrest in Celle, aged just 23.

With three tumultuous, ultimately catastrophic unions already having plagued her family and that of her husband, Augusta would not suffer another failed marriage.

Caroline was smart, quick-witted and well-tutored in the necessary arts of making a royal wife. Naturally she had the looks for it too, but princesses always seem to, don't they? Sir John Stanley, who encountered Caroline when he was a young man undertaking his Grand Tour, rhapsodised over the "light-coloured hair hanging in curls on her neck, with rosebud lips from which it seemed that none but sweet words could flow, and [she was] always simply and modestly dressed," sighing that he knew he could never be good enough for her, though he dearly wished he was. Yet despite all these qualifications, romantic interest in Caroline from what her parents considered to be suitable gentlemen remained muted, perhaps because everyone seemed so sure that she was insane. As the years passed, the lack of suitors became more concerning than ever.

An Eligible Princess

> "One great recommendation of the PRINCESS of BRUNSWICK is, that the DUKE himself has, in a great measure, superintended the education of his children; and they are said to be, without exception, the best bred family in *Europe*. There is not any where a Court where *morals* are more regarded than in that of *Brunswick*, though in the neighbourhood of one where there is no great circumspection – on that point particularly."[11]

Caroline of Brunswick was accomplished, pretty, and intelligent, but she had a passionate temper and a sharp tongue. Her humour could be cutting and when the mood took her, she thought nothing of turning that humour on those around her to withering effect. It was one of the

---

11. *Oracle*. 27 September 1794; issue 18810.

few sports available to her. However, when soldiers and nobles loyal to the Bourbon cause started to use Brunswick as a base from which to observe the tumultuous beginnings of the French Revolution, Caroline's horizons – and targets – expanded with the court.

The Duke of Brunswick decided that he would lead a march on Paris that would scatter revolutionaries in its wake, and invited interested parties to join him. Among his followers was an unnamed German prince, who quickly fell for the unmarried princess. Dashing, perfumed and done up to the nines, he had the looks but none of the chat and Caroline was by far his intellectual superior. She mocked and teased him from dawn to dusk, but it did nothing to dent his interest.

Duke Charles, Caroline's father, was far from impressed by his daughter's bad behaviour. He couldn't afford for her reputation to get any worse than it already was, because when it came to court politics a good marriage could be valuable indeed. Marriage to a stupid prince was more useful than marriage to an intelligent pauper after all. Charles worked on the prince and his family until he received the proposal he had hoped for, but Caroline wouldn't even consider it. Not for her a wedding to serve the needs of her parents, she wanted to marry a man who she loved and would love her in return. As the years passed, she had to let go of that romantic ideal.

Though the German prince didn't take Caroline's fancy she was still only in her mid-teens, and at this time, there was another man who did. Later in life, Caroline tantalisingly claimed that the only man who had come close to winning her heart in those Brunswick days was a nameless yet devastatingly handsome Irish soldier, who had fought with distinction alongside the forces of Brunswick.

Like every woman at the Brunswick court, Caroline was utterly enchanted by the Irish Hussar as he posed atop his jet black stallion in a uniform topped with pristine white plumes. According to gossiping courtiers, Caroline somehow managed to sneak away from her attendants to enjoy romantic liaisons with the Hussar in the hope that she might be allowed to marry him. When her parents found out they spirited the princess away to a countryside retreat, where she was kept safely out of harm's way until the Irishman had left Brunswick for good. Of course, her sudden disappearance from court only stoked the fire of rumour harder until some were suggesting that she had fallen pregnant to the soldier. Worse still was yet to come, and soon there were even claims that at least one of the charity children who Caroline cared for was her own illegitimate child. There was no evidence for any of this, but Caroline never tired of telling those swooning tales of her lost Hussar. She was a born romantic though, so perhaps we should take it with a grain of salt.

Though Augusta was set on marrying her daughter to a son of George III, as the years passed, there was a distinct lack of marital overtures from England. Eventually she began to realise that the missed opportunity of the Duke of York's visit might have been her one and only chance of marrying off her wayward daughter to an English prince. With the golden goose seemingly having flown, Augusta began to cast about for an alternative until opportunity presented itself in the shape of the second son of the Margrave of Baden. The young man was rich and positively bristling with prospects, including the very real possibility that he would one day inherit the family title from his childless older brother. Augusta was certain that she had finally snared a bridegroom for her daughter and was desperate to see it through to the bitter end. "If this does not come off," she warned ominously, "I know of no more husbands for her."

Mysteriously, the longed-for match was abandoned at the eleventh hour, whilst expressions of interest from the illustrious houses of Orange and Hesse-Darmstadt came to nothing. Even as the Prince of Wales was marrying Maria Fitzherbert in London, in Brunswick, there was no change. Soon it seemed as though Caroline would never marry at all, and that would never do.

Paying Debts

As Caroline grew older and remained resolutely single, Augusta began to wonder what would become of her daughter. Today of course, staying single is really no big deal, but for a royal daughter of the eighteenth century, it was something close to disastrous. Things seemed to be going off kilter for all the surviving children of the ducal Brunswick family. The duke intended his sons to follow him into the military, but three of the four were found to be unsuitable for service due to physical and mental health concerns. Caroline's elder sister, Augusta, meanwhile, had made an excellent marriage to Frederick of Württemberg that ended in allegations of abuse, followed swiftly by a separation and her own premature death at the age of just 23. This time the marriage needed to stick, but who would be the groom?

Augusta had hoped to capture the hand of her nephew, Frederick, Duke of York, but she couldn't have dreamed of snaring the heir to the throne himself. Or rather, she couldn't have dreamed of it were it not for the prince's catastrophic finances. In England, relations between the king and queen and their eldest son were worse than they had ever been. Rumours of an illegal marriage to the Catholic Maria Fitzherbert plagued them and the Prince of Wales' debts had become a bottomless pit. The time had finally come to address the elephant in the room and to ensure that the heir to the throne was properly married off and ready to do his duty. The king made it clear to his eldest son that there would be no further handouts until he had taken a bride. Little known to George III, he had a supporter in George's mistress, Lady Jersey, who knew that she had nothing to fear from a wife who was taken for money, not love. An unwanted, legitimate bride would be far easier to deal with than Maria Fitzherbert.

With his parents, his mistress and even his political friends all singing from the same hymn sheet, the Prince of Wales eventually surrendered. He loved Maria, but he loved his lifestyle too and without money, that lifestyle would be impossible. With a resigned shrug and the observation that "one damned German frau is as good as another," George signalled that he would be willing to go ahead with a marriage to a Protestant German princess of his father's choosing. Across Europe the royal houses sat up and took notice. Their daughters had all been schooled in English in the hope that they might capture the heart of the Prince of Wales and now the moment of truth had come. All of them had their eyes on the prize, but "all, of course, but one, had a lucky escape"[12].

As the king considered the eligible princesses, his son, the Duke of Clarence, suggested that Caroline of Brunswick should be high on the list. She was the daughter of the king's own sister and despite her father's licentious ways, he was a celebrated soldier. Caroline had been raised in the bosom of respectability. No royal mother was more pious that Princess Augusta, who had devoted her life to her faith and her children, and few princesses could be expected to be more perfectly reared and educated in the ways of regal marriage than Caroline. Yet that didn't chime with the gossip that was doing the rounds of continental drawing rooms about the young princess. The rumours of attachments to soldiers

---

12. Littell, E (1845). *Littell's Living Age, Volume IV*. Boston: TH Carter and Company, p.631.

and other nameless men had taken root and Lord Holland spoke for everyone when he said that "even in that country, where they were not at that period very nice about female delicacy, the character of his bride was exceedingly loose."[13]

Such statements reflect gossip rather than proven fact, and it was all a gift to Lady Jersey. She didn't care that Princess Caroline would be nothing more than a pawn in her efforts to checkmate her rival, Maria Fitzherbert, because the less suited to one another the bride and groom were, the better it would be for her. Princess Caroline of Brunswick was the perfect candidate.

Queen Charlotte had more than a few doubts about the proposed match, not least because the other prime candidate was her niece, Princess Louise of Mecklenburg-Strelitz[14], and there was certainly no love lost between the queen and Caroline's mother. Charlotte rightly thought Augusta was a terrible gossip, and Augusta had never believed that Charlotte was good enough for George III. When the queen's brother, Charles, had considered Caroline as a possible bride after he was widowed, she was quick to disavow him of such an idea. She wrote to Mecklenburg to warn him, "That her passions are so strong that the Duke himself said that she was not to be allowed even to go from one room to another without her Governess, and that when she dances, this lady is obliged to follow her for the whole of the dance to prevent her from making an exhibition of herself." In concluding, Charlotte admitted that, "There, dear brother is a woman I do not recommend at all."[15]

Though Queen Charlotte had heard the gossip about Caroline and gave credence to it, the king had not, and Charlotte decided that it simply wasn't her place to smear his own sister's daughter. Given that Augusta, the bride's mother, later described Charlotte as "an envious and intriguing spirit"[16], it seems that the dislike between the two chatelaines was mutual, but still Charlotte wouldn't warn George III of what she had heard. Perhaps if she had, a twenty-five year disaster might have been

13. Anonymous (1854). *The Dublin Review Part 2*. London: Burns and Oates, p.6.
14. Later Queen of Prussia as a result of her marriage to Frederick William III.
15. Aspinall, Arthur (ed.) (1965). *The Correspondence of George, Prince of Wales, Volume III*. London: Cassell, p.9.
16. Malmesbury, 3rd Earl of (ed.) (1844). *Diaries and Correspondence of James Harris, First Earl of Malmesbury, Vol. III*. London: Richard Bentley, p.154.

averted. Lady Jersey was a cheerleader for Caroline too and was happy to remind her lover that marrying Princess Louise, who came from his mother's side of the family, might not be a wise move. All that would do was further extend Queen Charlotte's influence over him, and things were fractious enough between mother and son already. Lord Holland had the measure of Lady Jersey's motives when he mused that, "she may have decided his preference for a woman of indelicate manners, indifferent character, and not very inviting appearance, from the hope that disgust for the wife would secure constancy to the mistress."

Caroline herself wasn't exactly flush with romance when she was informed of her intended nuptials. She welcomed the marriage though, because it was a means to escape the stifling life of Brunswick at the very least. In a letter written in November 1794, she fondly dropped tantalising clues about the man she *really* loved. Whether this was her Irish Hussar remains a mystery.

> "I am about entering into a matrimonial alliance with my first cousin, George, Prince of Wales. His generosity I regard, and his letters bespeak a mind well cultivated and refined. My uncle is a good man, and I love him very much, but I feel that I shall never be inexpressibly happy. Estranged from my connexions, my associates, my friends - all that I hold dear and valuable, I am about entering on a permanent connexion. I fear for the consequences, yet I esteem and respect my future husband, and I hope for great kindness and attention. But, ah me! I say sometimes I cannot love him with ardour; I am indifferent to my marriage, but not averse to it. I think I shall be happy, but I fear my joy will not be enthusiastic. The man of my choice, I am debarred from possessing, and I resign myself to my destiny. I am attentively studying the English language; I am acquainted with it, but I wish to speak it with fluency. I shall strive to render my husband happy, and to interest him in my favour, since the fates will have it that I am to be Princess of Wales."[17]

17. Brougham, Henry (1839). *Opinions of Lord Brougham on Politics, Theology, Law, Science, Education, Literature, &c. &c. Vol* I. Philadelphia: Lea & Blanchard, p.13.

The king dispatched James Harris, later Lord Malmesbury, to Brunswick in late 1794. His mission was to finalise the wedding plans and to escort Caroline safely to England to begin her new life as the Prince of Wales. Malmesbury was the ideal candidate for the job, having enjoyed a long and successful diplomatic career first in Spain then in Berlin, where he won the respect of Frederick the Great. He understood the delicate balances of court life and could be trusted with carrying out the task assigned to him efficiently and without a shred of drama. Tellingly, Malmesbury already had suspicions that the match might not be made in heaven soon after he reached Brunswick. By the time he and the bride-to-be set foot on British soil, he was certain of it.

In Brunswick, however, hopes were high for the new princess, that "virtue meets with reward, and she whose study during life has been to confer happiness on others, will now deservedly be the most fortunate of her sex."[18] For her part, Caroline relished the chance to escape her stifling upbringing at last. She was by now in her mid-twenties and might have thought that hope was dwindling, but the king's decision had changed all that. Far from being left on a forgotten shelf, she was about to be married to the most eligible man in Europe. Perhaps thanks to her gossiping mother, Caroline had already heard of the prince's wayward love life and even his closeness to Lady Jersey, who was to be one of her Ladies of the Bedchamber, but she was willing to overlook all that for the chance of a new start. Lord Malmesbury summarised his first meeting with the bride-to-be in his diary.

> "The Princess Caroline (Princess of Wales) much embarrassed on my first being presented to her – pretty face – not expressive of softness – her figure not graceful – fine eyes – good hand – tolerable teeth, but going – fair hair and light eyebrows, good bust – short, with what the French call, "des epaules impertinentes." *Vastly happy with her future expectations.* The Duchess full of nothing else – talks incessantly."[19]

---

18. *Morning Post*. 18 October 1806; issue 11130.
19. Malmesbury, 3rd Earl of (ed.) (1844). *Diaries and Correspondence of James Harris, First Earl of Malmesbury, Vol. III*. London: Richard Bentley, p.153.

Knowing what we do now of the disastrous marriage, there is something rather sad in the thought of the *vastly happy* Caroline and her shy demeanour at the first meeting with Lord Malmesbury. Caroline's sheltered upbringing had left her hopelessly naïve and she had no idea that George was motivated by cash alone. The thought that a man might marry *only* for money, with not even a glimmer of affection, was unconscionable. The only cloud on the horizon as far as Caroline was concerned was the inescapable fact that she would have to leave behind the father she adored to travel to England, but if the Duke of Brunswick wished her to marry, she would do so. When that German prince had come calling Caroline still had the world at her feet, now she knew that her options were disappearing fast.

Augusta explained to Lord Malmesbury that though all the other eligible German princesses had learned English in the hope of marrying the Prince of Wales, Caroline was less than fluent in the language. She alone of the ambitious royal mothers had not imagined her daughter as worthy of such an honour. Besides, Augusta admitted, she had all but given up hope since her brother had left her in no doubt that he disapproved of weddings between cousins. Yet in order to finally curb the Prince of Wales' wayward spirit, George III was apparently now willing to overlook his doubts.

Malmesbury carried out his duties with aplomb, keeping the duke and duchess sweet as negotiations were brought to a satisfactory conclusion. He talked politics and tactics with the former and sat placidly as the latter merrily aired her many grievances against Queen Charlotte, safe in the knowledge that they had a shared aim. In the first week of December, the marriage treaty was drawn up in English and Latin. French was excluded, since Lord Malmesbury objected to it on account of poor Franco-British relations. Lavish gifts were exchanged at a ceremonial dinner to celebrate the signing of the treaty, but the duchess was more concerned with her daughter's future than with impressive presents. She took Malmesbury aside and quietly entreated him to be Caroline's advisor and friend on the long journey that awaited them. He assured her that he would take care of the young woman, little suspecting that taking care of Princess Caroline of Brunswick wasn't the easy job he was anticipating. The duke also took Malmesbury aside, but the conversation this time was a little less sentimental.

Duke Charles told Lord Malmesbury that he was perfectly aware of the flighty character and nature of the Prince of Wales and that he was concerned that George's character might be the cause of trouble between the newlyweds. Yet Charles knew that his daughter might bring challenges of her own and told Malmesbury that he should ensure that Caroline knew "not to *ask questions*, and, above all, not to be free in giving opinions of persons and things aloud"[20]. Malmesbury already knew that her mother had a tendency to do just that, having witnessed her bitter tirades against Queen Charlotte's jealous and venal nature. There was no love lost between them, so when Caroline admitted to Malmesbury that she was afraid of the British queen, he was left in no doubt that Duchess Augusta had been sharing her feelings with her daughter too.

The Prince of Wales was a hedonist. He loved to party and he adored pleasure, and Duke Charles had a feeling that Princess Caroline might yet share those qualities with her soon-to-be husband. "He dreaded the prince's habits,"[21] Malmesbury admitted, fearing that Caroline was already planning a life of luxury and amusement and hadn't considered the duties that came with the job. Malmesbury was as good as his word when he had the opportunity to advise Caroline on the best way to navigate the English court. He warned her against being too free with her opinions and told her not to upset Queen Charlotte at all costs. When Caroline wept, Malmesbury attributed her tears to her realisation that she would soon be leaving her home behind, but one can't help but wonder whether she had begun to suspect that the future might not be as glowing as she hoped.

> "[I told] her to avoid giving any opinion; to approve, but not to admire excessively; to be perfectly silent on politics and party; to be very attentive and respectful to the Queen; to endeavour, at all events, to be well with her. She takes all this well; she was at times in tears, but on account of having taken leave of some of her old acquaintance."[22]

Weary of the allegations of cronyism which were so quick to attach themselves to royal appointments, Malmesbury warned Caroline not to make promises regarding promotions or offices to anyone, no matter

---

20. Ibid., p.164.
21. Ibid., p.166.
22. Ibid.

how close or valued a friend. Instead, any candidates for office must be referred to Lord Malmesbury without exception. Caroline grew swiftly fond of her new mentor, but to his credit, he never made any effort to profit from her attachment. In fact, his dedication to the duty of preparing her for life at Carlton House is to be applauded, particularly given the doubts that had crept in during their acquaintance. Lord Malmesbury had not been sent to Brunswick to see whether the princess was suitable, that decision had already been taken. Instead, he had been sent to Brunswick to escort Caroline safely to England and she always trusted that he had her very best interests at heart. Though Caroline constantly told Malmesbury that she wanted him to remain close once they were in England, the old court hand wisely demurred. He knew too well that allying oneself too intimately to the incoming bride could end in tears. As he wryly noted in his diary, "I had the Duke of Suffolk and Queen Margaret in my thoughts."[23]

Malmesbury took the opportunity of the discussion on royal appointments to broach a few issues of court behaviour, advising Caroline that political opinions and affiliations were a no-no, just as favouritism ought to be. It was only now that Caroline revealed that she had somehow learned of Lady Jersey's intimacy with the Prince of Wales, but Malmesbury was sure that she believed they were just very good friends. Malmesbury assured his charge that Lady Jersey would behave in a manner befitting her role and station and that Caroline should remember that it was *she* who was Princess of Wales, not Lady Jersey. She must not be drawn into squabbles, he advised, and must never let the prince suspect even a flicker of jealousy. Instead, George should see only the sweetest side of his bride, whilst anyone who sought to stir up jealousy between them must be handled with the same studied politeness that he had recommended Caroline employ towards Lady Jersey. She need not be haughty, but she need not be humble either. Caroline's reply

---

23. William de la Pole, 1st Duke of Suffolk, negotiated the wedding of Henry VI and Margaret d'Anjou. He benefitted greatly from the match but his career went down in flames and as he fled into exile, he was beheaded by a mob. In his play, *Henry VI, Part 1*, William Shakespeare reimagined the story of Suffolk and Margaret as a secret love affair, with Suffolk engineering her marriage to Henry to keep her close by. In *Henry VI, Part 2*, the unfortunate Suffolk's severed head is a grieving Margaret's constant companion.

to this was simply to admit that she wished to be popular. In the years to come, she mastered that particular skill admirably.

What is apparent from Lord Malmesbury's Brunswick diary is his steady reiteration to Caroline that she must think before she spoke. Gregarious and social by nature, she had so long been secluded that the promise of a new start excited her beyond measure. She was filled with hopes of a world in which the people of Great Britain adored her, seeing for herself in this rose-coloured future the fun and extravagance she had been denied for nearly three decades. Malmesbury, of course, was careful to advise her not to get her hopes too high. When she admitted what she wanted most of all was to be loved, he corrected her again. On this occasion, as history would tell, Caroline of Brunswick chose not to listen to her mentor.

> "She says she wishes to be *loved* by the people; this, I assure her, can only be obtained by making herself respected and *rare* – that the sentiment can only be given to a few, to a narrow circle of those we see every day – that a nation at large can only respect and honour a great princess, and it is, in fact, these feelings that are falsely denominated *the love of a nation*; they are not to be procured as the good-will of individuals is, by pleasant openness and free communication, but by a strict attention to appearances – by never going below the high rank in which a Princess is placed, either in language or manners – by mixing dignity with affability, which, without it, becomes familiarity, and levels all distinction."[24]

Though he had his doubts that Caroline would make a suitable bride for the Prince of Wales, Malmesbury knew better than to say so. He was admired as a safe pair of hands precisely because of his talent for following orders to the letter, rather than interpreting them as he saw fit. In response to George's instructions that he should set off for home with the princess at once, Malmesbury crafted a smoothly placating response, assuring the heir to the throne that they would be there in good time.

---

24. Malmesbury, 3rd Earl of (ed.) (1844). *Diaries and Correspondence of James Harris, First Earl of Malmesbury, Vol. III.* London: Richard Bentley, pp.179-180.

More than anything else though, he was sure to get across the polite point that travel plans weren't his or the prince's to make. That privilege was the purview of the king alone.

> "I can only repeat, Sir, that on this side of the water no delay has arisen or will arise, and that not an hour shall be lost, whenever it shall please His Majesty's Ministers to inform me to what place I am to conduct the Princess, a point which was certainly not determined on [the] date of my last letters from England.
>
> The impatience of the Princess to get away is evidently her governing feeling; but it is tempered with so much good-humour and cheerfulness, that it is impossible not to consider her behaviour on this occasion as the most amiable possible.
>
> I am myself so very anxious that your Royal Highness should find every principle of happiness, that my judgment may be a little warped by my wishes; but I am sure I must have lost every power of discernment, if there does not exist in the mind of the princess the most fixed intention to make your happiness the study of her life, and in her heart, every affection to promote it."[25]

Malmesbury still nursed hopes that Caroline's enthusiasm would settle into something more befitting a Princess of Wales and queen-in-waiting. Long before rumours of illegitimate babies and dancing topless on Italian shores attached themselves to the bride from Brunswick, he saw in her the very future of the monarchy. She was likeable and keen, and if she listened to his good advice and learned a touch of diplomacy, it was in Caroline's power to "recover the dignity and respect due to our Princes and Royal Family, which had of late been so much and so dangerously let down by their mixing so indiscriminately with their inferiors"[26]. By the time the 1st Earl of Malmesbury died in 1820, the Princess of Wales had lived through enough scandal for two lifetimes. He could only give advice, after all, it was up to Caroline whether she chose to follow it.

---

25. Ibid., pp.227-228.
26. Ibid., p.174.

The Mentor

Lord Malmesbury was sent to Brunswick to serve as both a negotiator to the duke and duchess and a guide for their daughter. In both stations he succeeded admirably, yet we must ask ourselves whether he was exactly what Caroline needed. She was in her late twenties, sheltered, and the product of a tumultuous and isolated homelife. James Harris, future Earl of Malmesbury, was a man of the world who had enjoyed a long diplomatic career. He was in his late forties and a father of four, with nearly two decades of marriage under his belt. Though he could certainly speak with authority on how one conducted oneself at court, whether he could truly understand a sheltered woman who was about to leave everything behind to marry a stranger is debateable. He seemed to be fighting a tide of absurdity from England too, never more so than when the Prince of Wales threw protocol to the wind and dispatched an envoy with a letter to Caroline, telling her that he couldn't wait to embrace her. That amour certainly wouldn't last.

Even Caroline's strict upbringing hadn't been enough to crush her gregarious nature. She was the eternal optimist, and though she might nod sagely when Malmesbury advised her to behave in a manner befitting the Princess of Wales, in truth, she little understood the gravity of his words. Malmesbury, of course, was not the sort of man to indulge in idle gossip. His sage advice remained the same: Caroline need only behave properly and everything would fall into place. He must have known that it was wishful thinking, but Caroline truly believed that she might be able to make something of her marriage to the most eligible and fashionable man in Europe. She remained blissfully unaware of the existence of Maria Fitzherbert, let alone the prince's disinterest in her as anything but the means to settle his debts. The British press knew better.

> "A much more serious question has been mentioned in Parliament, and to which it is our duty to call the attention of our readers – we mean the proposition which has been made to grant an establishment to the PRINCE and PRINCESS of WALES, and *so free him from his present incumbrances* – With respect to the establishment, no man, who is a friend to the Constitution of the Country, will hesitate a moment in complying with it; and as to that part of the question

which relates to His Royal Highness's Debts, the same consideration, we mean the respect due to the Heir Apparent of the Crown, a respect which every friend to the Hereditary Monarchy of the Kingdom must feel, will operate forcibly in the determination."[27]

Whilst the matter of the prince's debts was well known, there was also the small problem of him already being married. Malmesbury certainly would have heard the rumours surrounding Maria Fitzherbert, but it would never have occurred to him to raise them with Caroline. Instead he did what he had been charged to do, and trusted the rest to fate.

And let us be clear, George's sense of urgency was not driven by sentiment or romance. As in so many things, he was motivated by money. He was keen to get the ring on Caroline's finger so he could see his allowance duly upped from that of a single man – a not so meagre £60,000 – to that due to a married heir to the throne, which amounted to a cool £100,000 a year.

Yet for all Caroline's excitement and enthusiasm, there were frequent hints that she had concerns of her own. From the mention of Lady Jersey to her constant reiteration of her need to be loved, it seemed as though she was seeking some kind of approval from the visiting diplomat that he was not able to give. He was right that wanting to be loved by a whole nation was a dangerous ambition, Caroline would learn that to her cost, but when it came to her fears regarding marriage itself, Malmesbury found his famed diplomatic skills tested to the limit. In a quiet moment, Caroline confessed that her paternal aunt, Augusta Dorothea, Abbess of Gandersheim, had told her that her marriage would be a miserable one and that men were not to be trusted. The Prince of Wales would break Caroline's heart, the abbess warned darkly, and she had seen enough of the world to be sure of it. Despite her religious role, Augusta Dorothea's spicy love life had driven a wedge between herself and Caroline's pious mother, just as Elisabeth Christine's illegitimate pregnancy and house arrest had soured relations between Duchess Augusta and her other sister-in-law. With nobody to confide in other than Malmesbury, Caroline had been dwelling on the words of her aunt, and now she looked to the British diplomat for some reassurance.

---

27. *True Briton*, 11 May 1795; issue 793.

When he heard what Augusta Dorothea had been whispering in her niece's pliant ear, Malmesbury furiously dismissed her warnings as "the nonsense of an envious and *desiring* old maid." Next time the Abbess of Gandersheim made such damning claims, he thundered, Caroline should hit back hard.

> "I desired the next time the Abbess held this language to [Caroline], to ask her whether, if she was to propose to exchange with her, and to take the Abbey of Gandersheim, and give her the Prince of Wales, whether she would think *men* to be such monsters, and whether she would not expose herself to all the dangers and misfortunes of such a marriage."[28]

On the one hand, Malmesbury dismissed Augusta Dorothea's warnings as the bitter pronouncements of a jealous woman. On the other, however, there remains the fact that the Abbess of Gandersheim was right. Whether she had heard gossip about the Prince of Wales is uncertain, but if she had, then her words might carry more weight had she expanded on exactly why she expected George to be a deadbeat husband. Perhaps Malmesbury was right to put it down to jealousy, but such a patronising dismissal of a woman simply because he perceived her as some sort of dried up old spinster shouldn't go unchallenged. Gossip about Maria and the prince had certainly followed the widow Fitzherbert to France and beyond, so it's not unthinkable that it got as far as the Abbess of Gandersheim.

The abbess had plenty to say about Malmesbury too, and she warned her niece to be on her guard against "*un homme dangereux.*" He took this news with a heavy sigh, especially when Caroline jokingly put it down to Augusta Dorothea being rather fond of him herself. Malmesbury was quick to stop any such silliness, perhaps thinking of Shakespeare's Suffolk and Margaret all over again. In the seething atmosphere of the royal court, careless talk could be dangerous.

By this point, Lord Malmesbury had very real fears for the royal couple. Caroline had no gift for reflection and precious little substance,

---

28. Malmesbury, 3rd Earl of (ed.) (1844). *Diaries and Correspondence of James Harris, First Earl of Malmesbury, Vol. III*. London: Richard Bentley, p.181.

he lamented, a characteristic that she shared with her husband-to-be. She needed a steady man, and the prince was anything but. As she prepared to travel to England, Caroline received another lecture on the importance of reserve and discretion with good humour, listening patiently as Malmesbury told her that "less talking" would serve her exceptionally well. But Caroline was a born talker. To be silent was not her way.

Leaving Home

As the time to sail for England approached, Malmesbury was busy making final preparations for the journey. Duchess Augusta wondered whether she should accompany her daughter all the way to London, but George and Charlotte wouldn't hear of it. She would go no further than the Dutch coast, after which two German ladies and the Honourable Mrs Harcourt, wife of the British general, would be Caroline's escorts. Augusta admitted to Malmesbury that she really wanted to come because Caroline's written English needed urgent attention, but the decision had been made. The duke was rather more heartfelt in his entreaties, making no mention of written English even as he beseeched Malmesbury to let Augusta travel with Caroline, who would benefit from her mother's direction. There was no way Queen Charlotte was going to let Augusta loose in England though.

Malmesbury had scarcely managed to settle the bride's parents when the unthinkable happened: an anonymous letter arrived from England. In it the author catalogued the many failings of the prince and, worst of all, directly warned Caroline that she must watch Lady Jersey at all costs. Although it had been sent to Augusta, the duchess thoughtlessly showed it to her daughter despite its sensitive contents and sent Caroline into a panic. Malmesbury was furious at the duchess' lapse of judgement and was sure that the letter was the work of a Mademoiselle Rosenzweit, who had been denied permission to travel to England with Caroline to act as her reader. The anonymous author warned Caroline that Lady Jersey was scheming to lead her into romantic indiscretions that would be used to blacken her name, but Malmesbury had been round the court block a few times. He resorted to scare tactics to shock Caroline into listening.

> "[Malmesbury explained that] it was *death* to presume to approach a Princess of Wales, and no man would be daring

enough to think of it. She asked me whether I was in earnest. I said such was our law; that anybody who presumed to *love* her was guilty of *high treason*, and punished with *death*, if she was weak enough to listen to him: so also would *she*. This startled her."[29]

As far as Malmesbury was concerned, that was an end to it. All that was left now was for the weather to clear and the party would be underway. As they waited for the moment to come, Malmesbury continued to observe Caroline and was even witness to her much-discussed philanthropic efforts. Even these gave him cause for concern, as he remained uncertain whether Caroline's charity stemmed from a desire to do good, or because she had shrewdly identified that it was one way to achieve her desire of being loved. If it was the latter, he feared that no good would come of it. Not for him any sympathy for the gadabout bride-to-be, all familiarity and *ma cherie* with her attendants, all scowls and tears when censured. He followed protocol to the letter. When Malmesbury refused to travel in the same coach as Caroline for fear of it being regarded as improper, she laughed off his concerns. Twenty years later, sharing a coach with another gentleman would lead her into all sorts of trouble, but Caroline never worried too much about propriety. There was only so much she was willing to learn.

> "BRITANNIA! – round thy sea-girt coast
> Awhile suspend the dreadful storm;
> Let Frenzy rouse the Gallic Host;
> Do you assume a milder form. –
> Lo! borne upon the azure main,
> A CAROLINE appears again,
> Thy Land of Freedom to explore;
> For thee she dauntless braves the deep,
> And views the curling surges sweep,
> Which lash thy whiten'd shore:
> While fav'ring breezes swell her snowy sail;
> And pour on Albion's cliffs the driving gail."[30]

---

29. Ibid., p.189.
30. *True Briton.* 9 April 1795; issue 712.

The party left Brunswick for England on 29 December 1794, in the middle of a harsh winter. Under instructions from the king and government they travelled by the quickest route that protocol would allow, stopping as infrequently as possible as they hastened for the Dutch coast and the British fleet that awaited them. By the time 1794 ticked over into 1795, the weather was dire and there still remained the question of whether they would actually be able to sail from Holland, or if the threat from the French might delay the departure still further. The last thing that Britain needed at this point was to lose the Princess of Wales in a naval bombardment.

In fact, it was this very prospect that finally gave Malmesbury something to admire in Princess Caroline. When the party learned that their journey would be delayed by a pitched sea battle between French and English ships, Caroline didn't so much as flinch. Instead she accepted the news with such good humoured stoicism that Malmesbury couldn't help but be impressed. It was his first hint of the fearless Brunswicker that dwelled beneath that flighty exterior.

Now things truly hung in the balance. French forces were beating the British into retreat and when they seized Holland, the way ahead was barred to the travellers. Should Malmesbury's party try to press on to the coast, they would have to pass through French lines. Caroline was all for it. She had no fear, she assured Malmesbury, for what Brunswicker did? Instead she urged him to press on and face the danger, but he favoured a more cautious approach. With French troops moving deeper into Holland, any attempt to cross to the coast now would have been reckless in the extreme.

The party retreated to the safety of Osnabrück, where Duchess Augusta, fearful that she might be seized by French troops, declared that she intended to leave Caroline in Malmesbury's hands and set off for home. He wouldn't hear of it, certain now that the duchess' attitude to propriety and protocol were as lax as those of her daughter, regardless of how long she had spent on her religious studies. He told Augusta that she would remain with the party until Caroline was safely handed over to her attendants and ready to set sail. There would be no exception.

With the duchess put firmly in her place, Malmesbury wrote to Lord Grenville to appraise him of the situation on the road. Were he travelling with his family, he informed the erstwhile Secretary of State for Foreign Affairs, he wouldn't risk a journey through Holland not only on account of the dreadful weather, but also due to the perilous political situation. Fearing that they may battle through danger only to discover that no British fleet was waiting to meet them, Malmesbury advised Lord Grenville that he, Princess Caroline and Duchess Augusta were all agreed that it was better to arrive safe rather than soon.

The royal party retreated further, eventually settling in Hanover. It seemed to Malmesbury to be the best choice, especially given his fears that taking Caroline back to Brunswick once all the formalities of leaving had been done was the best way to start gossip. There was already far too much of that about the new Princess of Wales. Brunswick was also, he told the Duke of Portland, the place in which Caroline was apt to be offered the sort of guidance that would do her no good whatsoever. Better for everyone that their next stop be somewhere that the Hanoverians called their own. There, he assured Portland, "the two months or more which will elapse from the time of our leaving Brunswick till that of our landing in England, will form and shape the Princess's mind and manners to her situation, and give her a more exact sense of it, than if the journey from the Palace at Brunswick to Carlton House had been performed with all the expedition we originally asked for."[31] Malmesbury already knew that the future was unlikely to be pretty.

One cannot help but feel for the long suffering, urbane Malmesbury, caught between the complaining mother and the tactless daughter as they bickered and carped. The former was fond of sharing indelicate stories about George III's childhood habit of wetting the bed, whilst the latter openly mocked her mother, with no trace of the diplomacy and good conduct that had been urged so many times.

In George's ancestral lands of Hanover, the party waited for word that their safe passage could be guaranteed. The British squadron that had been waiting for the princess had no choice but to retreat and for six weeks, Malmesbury devoted himself to moulding Caroline into a model British princess. By now having known her for a number of weeks, he made a note of his most recent character assessment in his diary. It hadn't really changed all that much from his first impression and when Caroline died 26 years later, the words written by Malmesbury in 1795 were still as germane as ever.

---

31. Malmesbury, 3rd Earl of (ed.) (1844). *Diaries and Correspondence of James Harris, First Earl of Malmesbury, Vol. III*. London: Richard Bentley, pp.236-237.

"On summing up Princess Caroline's character to-day, it came out to my mind to be, that she has quick parts, without a sound or distinguishing understanding; that she has a ready conception, but no judgment; caught by the first impression, led by the first impulse; turned away by appearances or *enjouement*; loving to talk, and prone to confide and make missish friendships that last twenty-four hours. Some natural, but no acquired morality, and no strong innate notions of its value and necessity; warm feelings and nothing to counterbalance them; great good humour and much good nature - no appearance of caprice - rather quick and *vive*, but not a grain of rancour. From her habits, from the life she was allowed and even compelled to live, forced to dissemble; fond of gossiping, and this strengthened greatly by the example of her good mother, who is all curiosity and inquisitiveness, and who has no notion of not gratifying this desire at any price. In short, the Princess in the hands of a steady and sensible man would probably turn out well, but where it is likely she will find faults perfectly analogous to her own, she will fail. She has no governing powers, although her mind is *physically* strong. She has her father's courage, but it is to her (as to him) of no avail. *He* wants mental decision; *she* character and *tact*."[32]

As Caroline waited in Hanover, she was all nervous excitement. Even as Malmesbury preached his mantra of reserve and circumspection and Caroline nodded along, very little of it was sinking in. It wasn't necessarily innocence and naïve anticipation that fuelled her either, but genuine anxiety about what awaited her in England. She had heard so many stories about the Prince of Wales by this point that George had metamorphosed in her imagination into something almost ogrish, and she feared their first meeting and what would become of her if the stories were true. Although Malmesbury assured her she would be made welcome by the king and queen so long as she behaved appropriately, he stopped short of telling Caroline that the tales she had heard of the prince were false. Instead, he did his best to coach her on how to approach her new husband should she wish to domesticate him. There was a hint of

---

32. Ibid., pp.202-203.

respect for his charge in his diary at this point, when he noted that he was certain that Caroline was more than up to the task. She had a robustness that he knew was the equal of the Prince of Wales' flightiness, it seemed, but he also knew that her lack of discretion was likely to cause trouble all on its own. It was one thing for the prince to assure Malmesbury that "there is no sort of respect, state and attention, that shall not be shown the Princess, the moment she sets foot on our dear little island,"[33] but it was quite another for him to put his grand sentiments into action once the party had finally reached Carlton House.

Gossip and indiscretion were something that Malmesbury could discuss with Caroline, but the one area that was most in need of attention was rather more intimate. Princess Caroline, he observed, had far too lax an attitude to her personal hygiene, and he took it upon himself to advise her on these matters in so far as a gentleman was able. Not only was he horrified by her bizarre decision to make a gift to him of a tooth she had had extracted, but he was also particularly concerned about her coarse and stained undergarments, which he had seen drying on the ship's deck, and he suspected were rarely changed and even less frequently washed. She took little care of her personal hygiene, as the occasional odour would attest, and for a fashion maven like the Prince of Wales, that would never do. Malmesbury engaged Mrs Harcourt to speak to the princess on these more intimate matters, but the Prince of Wales would later reflect that the situation hadn't changed for the better by the time he and his wife endured their first night alone as newlyweds.

The Last Leg

During the last week of March 1795, the party made for Cuxhaven. There the frigate HMS *Jupiter* and its captain, Jack Payne, awaited them in waters bristling with British warships. They left Hanover amid a sea of pageantry with an accompanying phalanx of Hanoverian guards as the garrison guns sounded a salute overhead, marking the departure of Her Serene Highness Princess Caroline.

The party paused at Muhlendorf and it was here that the Duke and Duchess of Brunswick said an emotional goodbye to their daughter. Caroline's father took Malmesbury aside and tearfully begged him to look out for the princess. Above all, he asked him to ensure that she wasn't hung

---

33. Ibid., p.249.

out to dry by more experienced and ambitious courtiers. They must have had their suspicions that their sheltered daughter was woefully unprepared for the fate that awaited her, but there was no question of the marriage not going ahead. What Caroline didn't already know, she would have to learn fast.

Princess Caroline embarked on the last stage of her journey to England on 28 March. For a time thick fog forced the ship to drop anchor and an anxious, excited princess could be glimpsed taking daily walks on the deck as she waited for the skies to clear and the voyage to resume. Yet the longer they waited, the more green Princess Caroline became until seasickness forced her back to her cabin. There she remained until Good Friday, when the fog lifted and the ship set sail again. It arrived at Gravesend on 4 April to be greeted by crowds desperate to catch a glimpse of the new princess. Lord Malmesbury was delighted at having achieved the better part of his mission so successfully and so unflappably, against sometimes stacked odds. So far, so good, but so far Lady Jersey had not been able to stick her troublesome oar in. Now Caroline was safely delivered to England, that was about to change.

The ship spent that night at anchor and the following morning, Princess Caroline's party left *Jupiter*. They transferred to the royal yacht *Augusta*, which carried Caroline to the Greenwich shore and a group of dignitaries who had gathered to welcome her.

> "The Princess of Wales has ever been known to entertain a strong partiality for England, and frequently to express that she considered herself more of an English woman than a German, her mother being of this country. When she landed at Greenwich, she pleasantly observed, 'I am now perfectly happy, for I have reached my country at last.'"[34]

It was at Greenwich that Caroline met Lady Jersey for the first time. She had managed to convince the Prince of Wales and the queen, with whom she was great friends, to engage her as Caroline's Lady of the Bedchamber. In this role, which afforded her an intimacy with the princess that few would share, Lady Jersey was perfectly placed to watch the newcomer's every move and report back to the Prince of Wales. It also gave her the

---

34. *London Packet or New Lloyd's Evening Post*, 6 April 1795 – 8 April 1795; issue 4001.

freedom to pick at Caroline and to undermine her, and to gather gossip that might come in useful one day. For now though, as far as Caroline was aware, every eye in England was turned towards her, and every heart was open. She was a romantic symbol of fresh beginnings on which the hopes of the nation were pinned.

Lady Jersey arrived at the appointed meeting place more than an hour late and brought with her a feather-trimmed dress of white satin. Caroline dutifully exchanged her simple muslin gown and blue petticoat for the showy but ill-fitting garment, but Lady Jersey wasn't done yet. Having succeeded in trussing her rival up like a Christmas turkey, Lady Jersey then declared that she couldn't possibly travel backwards in the lead carriage and must instead sit facing forwards. Lord Malmesbury had been around the block enough times to recognise this as a ploy to sit beside the princess and therefore grab as much limelight as possible, and he wasn't going to stand for it. After wryly remarking that perhaps Lady Jersey's temperament was not suited to the role of Lady of the Bedchamber, he offered her a place in his own coach instead, telling her that she could sit anywhere she liked in that case. This time Lady Jersey was outplayed. She accepted her fate and took the backwards-facing seat in the lead coach.

As Caroline peered excitedly from the window of a royal coach pulled by six horses, the procession made its way towards the city. All along the road spectators had gathered to greet the new princess and for the first time, Caroline was able to bask in that love she had so longed for. The public were tired of the profligate prince and his selfish ways and the rumours of marriage to Maria Fitzherbert had done his reputation no good whatsoever, yet here was a chance for a fresh start and a fairy-tale ending. They shared Caroline's hopes that the marriage might mark a new beginning for the prince and set him on the path of respectability that had stood his parents in such good stead.

> "Westminster Bridge, and all the avenues leading to the Park and Palace were crowded with spectators and carriages; but the greatest order was preserved. The people cheared [sic] the lovely stranger with loud expressions of love and loyalty; and she in return, very graciously, and with the utmost good nature, bowed and smiled at them as she passed along."[35]

---

35. Ibid.

Caroline had never known anything like it. Not so long ago she had watched enviously as guests gathered for balls she was forbidden to attend, but now the biggest crowds in England were turning out just to catch of glimpse of her. She arrived at St James's Palace to the sound of welcoming cheers and once inside, lingered before the window as she awaited her prince. This time she wasn't pulled back by unsmiling attendants, nor did she go unnoticed by the excited throng below. Instead, "the PRINCESS appeared at the windows, which were thrown up, that the people might have a sight of her charming person. [The] people huzzaed her, and she curtsied; and this continued some minutes."[36] There at the window the princess tarried, soaking up the adoration as the Prince of Wales hastened from Carlton House to meet his bride.

Meeting the Family

So the moment of truth had arrived. After thousands of miles, seasickness, war, and Lady Jersey's mischief-making, Princess Caroline was finally due to meet the man who would be her husband. There was nothing further that Lord Malmesbury could do to ensure that love blossomed, and he prepared to carry out the final duty of what had been a long and arduous diplomatic mission. Before the watchful eye of King George III, he would introduce the princess to her betrothed.

At the sight of the primped and powdered Prince of Wales, then 32, resplendent in the uniform of a hussar, Caroline dropped into a low curtsey. That was a good start, but that was where good impressions ended. We are indebted to Lord Malmesbury's diaries for a record of the very first moments of what was to be a disastrous relationship.

> "[Caroline] very properly, in consequence of my saying to her it was the right mode of proceeding, attempted to kneel to [the Prince of Wales]. He raised her (gracefully enough), and embraced her, said barely one word, turned round, retired to a distant part of the apartment, and calling me to him, said, "Harris, I am not well; pray get me a glass of brandy." I said, "Sir, had you not better have a glass of

---

36. *Sun*, 6 April 1795; issue 787.

water?" - upon which he, much out of humour, said, with an oath, "No; I will go directly to the Queen," and away he went."[37]

Malmesbury was mortified and Caroline was outraged. She rounded on the diplomat and asked what exactly had happened to turn the pretty young prince from the portraits into the plump fellow who had just been so very rude to her. Luckily for Malmesbury, he was summoned to an audience with the king whilst Caroline was hurried away to her apartments to prepare for dinner with her groom. In a matter of hours she would meet Queen Charlotte, about whom she had heard so much, as well as the Duke and Duchess of York, the Duke of Gloucester, Prince William and the unmarried daughters of George III.

The royal couple shared their first dinner as an engaged couple with the party of dignitaries who had received Caroline at Greenwich. When she witnessed the closeness between George and Lady Jersey, Caroline recalled the anonymous letter her mother had received and recognised immediately that the pair were intimately acquainted.

> "[The] first moment I saw my *future* [sic] and Lady J[erse]y together, I knew how it all was, and I said to myself, "Oh, very well!" I took my partie - and so it would have been, if – but, Oh, *mine* God!" she added, throwing up her head, "I could be the slave of a man I love; but to one whom I loved not, and who did not love me, - impossible."[38]

Throughout dinner, the room rang to the celebratory cheers of the crowd gathered outside. They roared Caroline's name, trying to draw her back to the window, but as she revelled in the popularity she had always longed for, the Prince of Wales bristled. When crowds called his name in those days it was usually with anything but adoration, yet the incomer at St James's had seemingly won the love of the people by doing nothing at all. Eventually George could stand it no longer and stalked to the window,

37. Malmesbury, 3rd Earl of (ed.) (1844). *Diaries and Correspondence of James Harris, First Earl of Malmesbury, Vol. III*. London: Richard Bentley, p.218.
38. Bury, Lady Charlotte Campbell (1838). *Diary Illustrative of the Times of George the Fourth: Vol I*. London: Henry Colburn, p.23.

where he "thanked them for this mark of their loyalty and attention to the PRINCESS; but he hoped they would excuse her appearance then, as it might give her cold. This completely satisfied the crowd, who gave the PRINCE three cheers."[39] With that, he slammed the window shut.

Caroline, however, had no fears of catching a cold: she feared nothing. As Lord Malmesbury looked on in horror, she threw aside all his advice about being circumspect and delicate and went for broke. Malmesbury wrote with thin-lipped disapproval that she was "flippant, rattling, affecting raillery and wit, and throwing out coarse vulgar hints about Lady [Jersey]. Who was present, and though mute, *le diable n'en perdait rien*[40]."[41] Malmesbury knew the Prince of Wales well enough to see that Caroline's performance was cementing George's dislike for her, but there was nothing he could do other than watch and cringe. That first meeting predisposed the prudish queen and sheltered princesses to dislike her too, though the king soon adored Caroline as though she was his own daughter. Perhaps he enjoyed seeing someone so unselfconsciously gregarious; he might also have rather liked the fact that Caroline could so easily annoy his wayward son.

Like a child on Christmas morning, Caroline was carried away on her own excitement. What horrified the prince and left Malmesbury dumbstruck was precisely what endeared her to the public, who celebrated this new arrival to the stiflingly proper court, finding her "good-humour is almost unequalled, and often takes the form of playful simplicity."[42] Yet hints about the prince's intrigues were everywhere, and the *Oracle* wrote that, "We sincerely hope that no *obtrusive improprieties* will offend her feelings in the mixed societies, which she condescends to decorate"[43]. They little knew how right they were.

Caroline, of course, simply didn't see it. She was drunk on the moment and the future, immature despite what was a reasonably advanced age for a royal bride, and entirely unprepared for the sort of marriage that awaited her. Only with the benefit of hindsight did she reflect ruefully that, "the

---

39. *Star*, 6 April 1795; issue 2068.

40. *The devil misses nothing.*

41. Malmesbury, 3rd Earl of (ed.) (1844). *Diaries and Correspondence of James Harris, First Earl of Malmesbury, Vol. III*. London: Richard Bentley, p.219.

42. *Oracle*, 11 April 1795; issue 18977.

43. Ibid.

moment one is obliged to marry any person, it is enough to render them hateful. Had I come over here as a Princess with my father on a visit, […] things might have been very different: but what is done cannot be undone."[44] Had she met the Prince of Wales as a visiting princess rather than a bride, perhaps things *would* have been different, but we shall never know. They certainly couldn't have turned out any worse.

Two days before the marriage took place, Princess Caroline told her bridegroom about the anonymous letter she had read in Brunswick. She knew all about Lady Jersey, she informed him, but he dismissed the contents of the letter as lies. George assured his fiancée that he and Lady Jersey were just good friends. Rather than disapprove of Lady Jersey, he went on, Caroline should thank her, since "the confidence resulting from so long a friendship had enabled her to offer advice which contributed not a little to decide me to marriage."[45] Good old Lady Jersey.

Inexperienced and naïve, Princess Caroline expected her husband's friendship at the very least, but she was one half of a business deal. George didn't have to like his bride, he just had to marry her.

The Royal Wedding

The wedding date was fixed for 8 April 1795, enough time for the bride to get over her journey, but not so long that the Prince of Wales could flee the country. Not that he would have done, of course, because he needed to have those debts cleared above anything else, and the king and queen needed an heir. After all, as *True Briton* sniffed with more than a hint of a raised eyebrow, "We should regret, indeed, were any pecuniary considerations to break in upon that domestic happiness which we hope will be without alloy."[46]

Though Caroline lacked the emotional maturity to recognise her fiancé's distaste at her garrulous behaviour, her thick skin stood her in excellent stead to withstand the many challenges she endured during her battles

---

44. Bury, Lady Charlotte Campbell (1838). *Diary Illustrative of the Times of George the Fourth: Vol I*. London: Henry Colburn, p.24.
45. Georgian Papers Online (http://gpp.rct.uk, August 2020). RA GEO/ MAIN/39169-39174 Letter from George, Prince of Wales, to Caroline, Princess of Wales, 21 April 1796.
46. *True Briton*, 10 April 1795; issue 713.

with the capricious Prince of Wales. With her every move watched by Lady Jersey she prepared for her forthcoming nuptials with barely contained excitement, keen to get started on the future that was waiting. Ever the optimist, Caroline was sure that she and George could make something of their marriage. It was a hope shared by her adoring public too.

> "The blooming Loves, on sportive wing,
> Appear and grace her beauteous train;
> Hov'ring aloft, their Praises sing,
> And joyful chaunt [sic] the nuptial strain.
> Mildness, Simplicity and Truth,
> Attendants from an early youth,
> Around her features play.
> Britons! behold the destin'd Fair;
> Your future treasure guard with care,
> And hail the happy day. –
> The Heir of Albion claims her as his own,
> To raise her virtues to an English Throne."[47]

Though the ceremony at St James's Palace was scheduled for the evening, from early that morning crowds were gathering. They were especially deep at the Queen's House, St James's Palace and Carlton House, where Queen Charlotte had commanded that a grand toilette be prepared in the chamber that had been appointed as Caroline's dressing room. She personally presented Caroline with the keys to the room, as a gesture of welcome into the royal family, but other wedding gifts such as a collection of plate valued at £12,000 carried a weight more pecuniary than symbolic. Caroline's simple shifts and threadbare petticoats were gone and in their place she wore a heavy gown of silver tissue, taffeta and lace, adorned with a jewelled miniature of the Prince of Wales. Her mantle of crimson velvet was trimmed with regal ermine and upon her head Caroline wore a diamond coronet, whilst around her neck glittered a necklace valued at 6,000 guineas. In her wedding attire, she shimmered.

Caroline looked every inch the Princess of Wales when she arrived at the Chapel Royal at St James's Palace, where John Moore, the

---

47. *Ode Written on the Nuptials of the Prince and Wales and the Princess Caroline of Brunswick. True Briton.* 9 April; issue 712.

Archbishop of Canterbury, was to officiate the wedding. Though what followed has become the stuff of grimly amusing legend, the ceremony must have been ghastly to endure for one so determined to make the best of everything as Caroline was, and if she glided into the chapel, the Prince of Wales virtually rolled. George was so drunk that he couldn't even walk, having drowned himself in brandy simply so he could face the sham ceremony that awaited him. The paralytic royal had to be propped up by the supportive arms of his groomsmen, the Dukes of Roxburghe and Bedford, just to get to the altar. If the wedding was a joke, then the punchline was Princess Caroline's optimistic dreams of a happy ending.

As George staggered to his position before the Archbishop, the most illustrious names in England watched in mute horror. Though his eyes were filled with tears, the prince barely looked at his bride but instead concentrated all his efforts on staying upright and conscious. No marriage, no money. The wedding rolled unstoppably on, as formal as the ceremony in that Park Street drawing room had been intimate, and Lady Jersey watched it all with a conniving gaze. She had succeeded in finding someone to supplant Maria Fitzherbert. In Caroline of Brunswick, there was no danger that the Prince of Wales might fall in love.

On her way to the chapel, Caroline had chatted with enthusiasm to the Duke of Clarence and now, at the moment of her greatest triumph, she was self-possessed and entirely regal. Whatever she might have thought of her groom's behaviour at the time, she certainly wasn't about to let it spoil her big day. Perhaps it helped that Caroline didn't love the prince any more than he loved her, though she was certainly a lot more polite about showing it. Her groom was considerably less circumspect, and his behaviour rang alarm bells for some.

When Dr Moore asked if anyone present knew of a lawful impediment to the marriage, the whole chapel held its breath. As though waiting for an actor to notice his cue, Dr Moore paused and looked meaningfully from the king to the prince, but the silence in the chapel lengthened. After a few seconds he resumed the service and, to the sound of the royal bridegroom's sobs, read not once but twice the passage in which the couple were reminded that they were now expected to live in nuptial fidelity. Fat chance.

The Prince of Wales wasn't so drunk that he didn't recognise the significance of the moment and certainly not so drunk that he hadn't been able to tell Lord Moira on his way to the ceremony that, "I shall never love any woman but Fitzherbert", but his agitation increased with every moment in the chapel. "H.R.H. was perpetually looking at his favourite Lady Jersey,"[48] noted the Duke of Leeds, and things came to a head when he rose to his feet during prayers and attempted to shamble from the scene. The king quickly rose from where he was kneeling and whispered something in George's ear. With those magic, secret words, the Prince of Wales returned to his position and the marriage was made official.

Across London church bells sounded and wine flowed, but as Maria Fitzherbert fell into a dead faint at Marble Hill, at St James's Palace the signs were no better. "I walked immediately before the Prince, who handed the Princess from the Chapel," wrote the Duke of Leeds, "And I could not help remarking how little conversation passed between them during the Procession, and the coolness and indifference apparent in the manner of the Prince towards his amiable Bride."[49]

Things didn't improve by the time the newlyweds arrived at the Queen's House, but whilst George was ashen and silent, Caroline was glowing and garrulous. "What an odd wedding," Lady Louisa Stuart mused, echoing the opinion of all those present.

"It is impossible to conceive or foresee any comfort from this connection," Malmesbury wrote ruefully after what should have been a happy event, "In which I lament very much having taken any share, purely passive as it was."[50] Such was the life of the diplomat.

At the end of the evening, the Prince and Princess of Wales returned to their marital bed at Carlton House. It was hoped that work on producing the heir and the spare would begin right away, but George's enthusiasm for brandy had already dashed that prospect. Instead, the paralytic prince collapsed in a heap on the floor of the bedchamber. "Judge what it was to have a drunken husband on one's wedding-day," said Caroline later, "and one who passed the greater part of his bridal night under the grate, where he fell, and where I left him!"[51].

---

48. Browning, Oscar (1884). *The Political Memoranda of Francis Fifth Duke of Leeds*. London: The Camden Society, p.220.

49. Ibid.

50. Malmesbury, 3rd Earl of (ed.) (1844). *Diaries and Correspondence of James Harris, First Earl of Malmesbury, Vol. III*. London: Richard Bentley, p.220.

51. Bury, Lady Charlotte Campbell (1838). *Diary Illustrative of the Times of George the Fourth: Vol I*. London: Henry Colburn, p.17.

The Honeymoon Days

Given the horrendous scenes at the wedding and the vitriolic split that came afterwards, it's tempting to imagine that the marriage of the Prince and Princess of Wales was like a battlefield from the off. In fact, that wasn't the case. Once George had sobered up, he managed to stagger to bed and despite his aching head, he and his new bride consummated their marriage. The arrival of their only child nine months almost to the day from the wedding can leave no doubt about that.

The newlyweds spent their honeymoon at Windsor, where Princess Caroline continued to woo George III. Given the emphasis he placed on piety and protocol, it might seem strange that the king was so fond of the new member of his family, but the very lack of sophistication that galled the Prince of Wales was a tonic to his father. Caroline was like the proverbial breath of fresh air, and she was vastly pleased with her new husband. Her new husband, on the contrary, was far from vastly pleased with his new wife.

A few weeks after the wedding ceremony, Lord Malmesbury attended a dinner at Carlton House and witnessed first-hand that the Princess of Wales had not taken any of his good advice on board. In front of the guest of honour, the Prince of Orange, Caroline was her usual light-hearted self and, horror of horrors, was so flighty and loud as to be virtually *indecent*, in Malmesbury's opinion. At the end of the dinner the prince took Malmesbury into a private room and asked him how on earth he had thought Caroline might make a suitable wife. Malmesbury was his usual urbane self and told George that the princess had been exceptionally well brought up and would, with a little direction, soon make an ideal partner. He advised the prince that Caroline's own father had said as much, and had been well aware of his daughter's exuberant ways.

George wasn't to be deterred and asked Lord Malmesbury why he hadn't sent word of *exactly* what Caroline was really like when she was still in Brunswick. He would have appreciated an advance warning, he whined, yet still the diplomat was unapologetic. Malmesbury had not been asked to make a decision on whether or not she was a suitable royal wife, he reminded the prince, but had been charged with arranging the marriage. This he had done with aplomb. Should he have presumed to make any comment whatsoever on Caroline's character or suitability, this would have been a direct contravention of the orders given to him by King George III, and he took such orders seriously indeed. What happened beyond that was nothing to do with him.

As rumours of trouble at Carlton House began to seep out, the press smelled blood. Little by little, reports appeared expressing concern that the prince had been seen at the theatre alone, or that Caroline's seat was empty in the opera box. Whenever such reports speculated on the marriage itself, they cast Caroline as the wounded innocent, yoked to an undeserving brat. Her dream was coming true: she was the epitome of the People's Princess.

> "This Lady seems to have a mind composed of *solid stuff*; let then her own mind govern her, at least in matters where only etiquette is concerned, and let her *graciousness* be unfettered. This will be POLITICALLY as well as MORALLY right.
>
> [...]
>
> The ENGLISH PEOPLE are great and noble, and brave and generous! and they *confer* as much honour as they *receive*. The crowds which attend the PRINCESS wherever she appears, reflect honour on *her*; and her excellent understanding and heart appear to feel it."[52]

Not quite twelve months later, Malmesbury learned from the prince that the princess' hygiene had not improved by her wedding night. He told Malmesbury that her neck and thighs bore odd scars and that her manner on their first night together spoke of extensive sexual experience, including lewd and admiring comments on the size of his manhood. Spying no blood from his supposedly virginal bride, George challenged Caroline as to how it was that there was no evidence whatsoever of her virginity. The following evening, if he was to be believed, Caroline mixed up a concoction of tooth powder and water and daubed it on her linens in an effort to convince her husband that she was indeed a virgin. When she showed George the proof, he was disgusted to see "such marks of filth both in the fore and *hind* part of her Linnen that she turn'd my stomach and from that moment I made a vow *never to touch her again*."

---

52. *Oracle*. 28 April 1795; issue 18991.

Yet Caroline had committed a wrong far worse than poor hygiene or bad manners. Her most grievous offence was simply being his wife, when Maria Fitzherbert was lost to him once more. That she was lost to him because of his own actions never quite dawned on the Prince of Wales. Lord Minto had his own opinions on what had caused the animosity between the pair. Quite apart from it being Caroline's hygiene, he suggested that it was a result of George's embarrassment at his lack of prowess in the bedroom. "The ground of his antipathy was his own *incapacity*," he wrote, "and the distaste which a man feels for a woman who *knows* his defects and humiliations."[53] Whatever the cause, the outcome was the same: the union was doomed.

Despite his revulsion, the Prince and Princess of Wales were intimate on three occasions in the first days of their marriage. George prayed that he had done enough to ensure that Caroline was pregnant and vowed never to lower himself to such activities with his wife again. It's all too easy now to see some gallows humour in this disaster, but for Caroline the situation was far from funny. Her character had been questioned and her husband was busy telling his friends about her personal hygiene, as well as her supposed lack of moral fibre. There remains, of course, the possibility that Caroline was indeed sexually experienced and that the rumours of her conduct in Brunswick were true, but I personally think it unlikely. The one thing Caroline seemed utterly unable to do was to lie and she had little control over her tongue. If she had taken a lover, she wouldn't have been able to resist telling someone about it. One can only feel pity for her as she faced up to the reality of her situation. She was the Princess of Wales and though the people certainly loved her, her husband categorically did not. To add to the catalogue of her perceived wrongdoings, Caroline's marriage to George didn't improve his finances as much as he had been expecting. Instead, much to his chagrin, Parliament decided that his income would remain at £60,000, £5,000 of which was ringfenced for his wife, who would also be in line for £50,000 should she be widowed. The increase in his allowance, which totalled more than £75,000, was put towards paying off George's monumental debts before he ever got his hands on it.

---

53. Aspinall, Arthur (ed.) (1965). *The Correspondence of George, Prince of Wales, Vol III*. London: Cassell, p.123.

The one thing that Caroline did right was falling pregnant. George was overjoyed when she announced that she was with child and celebrated not by lavishing his bride with care and attention, but by going back to his old gallivanting ways. The king's hopes that his son might settle down and learn the joys of a simple life were dashed when George took comfort once more in the arms of his mistress. Nobody was closer to him than Lady Jersey, who occupied an all-powerful position in the household of the princess, watching and undermining her every move. Though Caroline might under different circumstances have received some guidance and reassurance from her mother-in-law, that was not forthcoming. Neither Queen Charlotte nor her many daughters took it upon themselves to befriend the new arrival.

Duchess Augusta wrote to George III from Brunswick to complain of her son-in-law's behaviour, and it's not hard to see why Caroline felt so lonely. "HRH left her in the Country," she wrote, outraged, "Without even taking leave of her, or saying that he was going."[54] Eventually Caroline couldn't stand it any longer. She wrote to her mother from Brighton to tell her that she was utterly miserable and that Lady Jersey was the cause. She felt trapped.

By the time of their first wedding anniversary, the marriage was already on its last legs and Lady Jersey's power was increasing. "She twists every word the poor Princess sais [sic],"[55] opined Augusta to the king, but things would only get worse. Despite his mother-in-law's objections, George was about to place Lady Jersey at the centre of a new regime designed to ensure that his wife knew her station.

Princess Charlotte

> "The PRINCESS of WALES, like a widowed Dove, is still cooped up in her gilded Cage, at *Carlton House!* "Shame on't, oh shame!"[56]

---

54. Georgian Papers Online (http://gpp.rct.uk, August 2020). RA GEO/ MAIN/52171-52172 Letter from Augusta, Duchess of Brunswick, to George III, 7 October 1795.
55. Ibid.
56. *True Briton.* 9 September 1796; issue 1157.

The so-called *Carlton House System* was supposedly a result of the prince's need to economise following Parliament's shattering decision regarding his debts. Under this new regime the once glamourous palace was shuttered and the ballrooms fell dark and silent. By now heavily pregnant, Caroline was isolated in her marital home and she confided in a letter to a friend that, "I do not know how I shall bear the loneliness". The few visitors who were allowed to see her were shocked to see the decline in the spirits of the once gregarious princess, whose only regular companion was Lady Jersey.

Under the Carlton House System, Caroline's life was as restricted as it had ever been in Brunswick. She had no real friends, but instead a "list of Persons that were fixed upon to compose Her Royal Highness' Parties,"[57] which had been approved by her husband, the queen and Lady Jersey. These were not people Caroline would have chosen. Forced to spend long hours alone with Lady Jersey during the day, when evening fell, Caroline was sent to her rooms whilst the prince and his mistress headed out on the town together. If the prince and princess dined at Carlton House, Lady Jersey joined them and conversations were conducted in English, simply so Caroline would struggle to keep up. She had been the only eligible German princess who hadn't made learning English the focus of her education, and George knew it. Yet Caroline's pregnancy offered a glimmer of hope, and she prayed that the birth of her child might be enough to put right what had gone wrong.

Princess Charlotte Augusta of Wales was born on 7 January 1796, after a long and agonising labour. The royal family was delighted and hoped that her birth would be the start of a more settled life for the Prince of Wales. The fact that he wrote a will that left everything to Maria Fitzherbert just a few days after his daughter's birth is proof that such hopes were ill-founded. Princess Caroline had given the royal family their heir and as far as her husband was concerned, he had done his duty. As the press railed against the restrictions placed on her, Caroline contented herself with the company of her little girl. Charlotte was in the care of a handpicked nursery team headed by Lady Dashwood, whilst

---

57. Georgian Papers Online (http://gpp.rct.uk, August 2020). RA GEO/ MAIN/39281 Letter from Lord Cholmondeley to George, Prince of Wales, 24 August 1796.

her subgoverness was Frances Garth[58], who would become an invaluable friend to both the Princess of Wales and her daughter.

To her husband's distaste, Caroline flung herself into motherhood with the same enthusiasm that she approached everything else, but she felt smothered in London. She wanted to really experience the country that was now her home and was tired of being kept a prisoner in Carlton House, where she and the prince were fighting a war of attrition. The royal couple exchanged furious letters written from opposite ends of the building – either the Blue Room or the Yellow Room, depending on which party had written them – and they simmered with resentment. Eventually, when she correctly intuited that things were never going to change, Caroline appealed directly to the king to intervene and to remove Lady Jersey. The Prince of Wales ground his heels in hard, claiming that "[Lady Jersey's] removal would confirm every slander which has been so industriously propagated relative to her conduct [...] as well as to the nature of her intimacy with me."[59] But this time, Caroline wouldn't take no for an answer.

Rumours of discord in the royal household were by now regularly alluded to in the press, which was concerned by the "alarming symptoms of decline observable in the habit of the PRINCESS of WALES,"[60] which they put down to "acts of *indifference*" on the part of her loathed husband. There was no doubt who the villain of the piece was either and it made Lady Jersey uneasy. She might have been ambitious, but the last thing she wanted to be was infamous.

> "Lady JERSEY, though she still maintains the nominal office of *Lady of the Bedchamber* to the PRINCESS of WALES, has certainly received her dismission from the *Public*, who, as well as her Royal Mistress, have dispensed with her attendance at *Carlton House*."[61]

---

58. Miss Garth was the niece of General Garth, who enjoyed a long and secret romance with Princess Sophia, the sister of the Prince of Wales. You can read the full story in my own book, *Daughters of George III: Sisters & Princesses* (Pen & Sword Books, 2020).

59. Georgian Papers Online (http://gpp.rct.uk, August 2020). RA GEO/ MAIN/39190-39191 Letter from George, Prince of Wales, to Caroline, Princess of Wales, 27 May 1796.

60. *Oracle*. 21 June 1796; issue 19352.

61. *Sun*. 25 June 1796; issue 1170.

Despite Lady Jersey's vilification in the press, she retained the Prince of Wales' loyalty. Wherever he went, he found himself heckled by members of the public who loathed him for his extravagance and selfishness and found a rallying point in Caroline. Despite their dislike of George, however, the public and press alike longed for a reconciliation between the royal couple and the general opinion was that the ousting of Lady Jersey would be the thing that brought it about. Far from trying to reconcile though, the thoughts of the Prince of Wales turned more and more to the prospect of a separation. The Duke of Clarence, who had recommended Caroline to his father, told friends, "My brother has behaved very foolishly. To be sure, he has married a very disagreeable person, but he should not have treated her as he has done, but have made the best of a bad bargain, as my father has done. He married a disagreeable woman but has not behaved ill to her."[62]

What should have remained a private family quarrel exploded into the public arena when Lady Jersey took delivery of a packet of letters Caroline had written to her mother. Lady Jersey had come into possession of the letters when a Dr Randolph, who was charged with delivering them, was delayed by ill health. He preferred to return the papers to Caroline until he was able to set out on his journey and was told to do so via Lady Jersey, who promptly opened them. Finding the letters highly critical of the Prince of Wales, his mother and her household, Lady Jersey showed them to Queen Charlotte, who read that Caroline "had spoken in a very disparaging manner of the Queen, and had said, in particular, that she had found her to be as disagreeable as the Duchess had taught her to expect."[63] Worried for his own reputation, when Dr Randolph found himself accused by Princess Caroline's supporters of leaking the contents of the letters, he pointed the finger at Lady Jersey instead.

If Lady Jersey expected the press to round on Caroline for criticising her husband and mother-in-law, she was in for a surprise. Instead they heaped the blame onto his mistress' shoulders instead, bemoaning the lot of the poor, beleaguered princess who was forced to keep such a cuckoo in her nest. The criticisms of Lady Jersey became so furious that her husband, "feeling the character of his EXCELLENT LADY

---

62. Bickley, Francis (ed.) (1928). *The Diaries of Sylvester Douglas (Lord Glenbervie), Vol I*. London: Constable & Co, p.71.
63. Bickley, Francis (ed.) (1928). *The Diaries of Sylvester Douglas (Lord Glenbervie), Vol II*. London: Constable & Co, p.13.

assailed by the *malicious* and *scandalous* paragraphs of the Newspapers, has thought it his duty to vindicate her from such aspersions, by a publication, assuredly the most extraordinary that ever honoured the BRITISH PRESS."[64]

The case of the letters shone a spotlight on the Carlton House System and the mistress who commanded the Princess of Wales. This time, there would be no saving Lady Jersey. Yet when the prince's mistress handed in her resignation, it was with the same high-handedness that had become her trademark. One can only imagine what sort of conversations might have passed between her and her friend, Queen Charlotte, on the subject of Princess Caroline.

> "Lady JERSEY has written a letter to the Princess of WALES, on her resignation, which is one of the more disrespectful we ever recollect to have read. Her Ladyship begins by stating that her wish was to have resigned long since, but that his Royal Highness would not suffer it, on the ground that it would only tend to justify the calumnies reported of her. She then intimates who the person is who has propagated all the scandal against her, and concludes by assuring the Princess she shall to the last moment of her life *be proud to serve the Prince of Wales*. Throughout the letter, there is not one word of respect towards her Royal Highness."[65]

The king wrote to his son to impress upon him the importance of treating Caroline with courtesy and to inform him that Lady Jersey must not be admitted to "any other House [other than Carlton House] where the Princess resides." In doing so, he hoped that her absence "[would] speedily enable Me to restore harmony into Your House, for I find [Caroline] begins to think the Public suppose Her adverse to a reconciliation."[66] Even now, the king and Caroline still hoped for a happy ending.

---

64. *Oracle*. 20 July 1796; issue 19378.

65. *The Times*. 25 July 1796; issue 3644.

66. Georgian Papers Online (http://gpp.rct.uk, August 2020). RA GEO/ MAIN/39252 Letter from George III to George, Prince of Wales, 23 June 1796.

Caroline naively believed that if she could be rid of Lady Jersey, then her marriage would still be able to recover. She was badly mistaken. Just as there was no saving Lady Jersey's public face, there was no way back for the royal marriage either. George felt bruised by Caroline's victory over his mistress and had no intention of a sham marriage, nor of keeping Lady Jersey around forever. After all, if he *were* to achieve a separation from his wife, why would he settle for his mistress when his first bride was still holding onto his heart?

A Domestic Estrangement

By the summer of 1796, the Prince and Princess of Wales could no longer endure their unhappy pantomime of a marriage. With his heart set once again on Mrs Fitzherbert, George turned to Lord Malmesbury and launched into a litany of complaints about Caroline, sparing none of the gory details when it came to her hygiene and manners. Though it was clear that he wanted to end his marriage, George assured Malmesbury that he wouldn't embarrass her unduly by seeking any formal separation just yet. Of course, the worldly diplomat would have seen right through such empty claims. Lord Malmesbury knew Caroline as well as anybody and though he certainly had his reservations when it came to her giddy manner and toilette, his sympathies rested with the wronged woman. As he had believed ever since his trip to Brunswick, with a decent man Caroline stood every chance of a happy marriage. With George, Prince of Wales, she had no chance at all.

Caroline herself was unsurprised and relatively unperturbed to learn of George's fresh attachment to Maria. She even pronounced, "that is the Prince's true wife; she is an excellent woman; it is a great pity for him he ever broke vid her. [When] the Prince had married me, she would not believe it, for she knew she was herself married to him."[67]

In Georgian England, divorce or separation wasn't unheard of, but nor was it easy or painless. For the heir to the throne and the woman who was destined to one day become his queen, any problems were magnified tenfold. Malmesbury was quick to remind him of that.

---

67. Bury, Lady Charlotte Campbell (1838). *Diary Illustrative of the Times of George the Fourth: Vol I*. London: Henry Colburn, p.28.

"Let me humbly remind your Royal Highness that in your exalted situation it is not your private feelings alone, whatever they be, that you have to consult upon a measure of such magnitude; your interests and happiness are so closely united with those of the country at large that it is impossible for you to take any material step on which the public will not claim a right to form a judgement and expect that a very considerable degree of deference should be paid to it. From a conviction of this truth it was that your Royal Highness did me the honour to say on Friday last you were first induc'd to think of marriage; the motive, Sir, was worthy of you, and the public saw in it a pledge of your regard for them. Let the same laudable & becoming motive still guide your Royal Highness in preserving a connection, the breach of which will far more deeply affect the public mind than your not having ever thought proper to form it could possibly have. A measure so unexpected could not at any time fail to excite a very strong sensation throughout the country."[68]

George replied immediately, stressing that he had "neither used an expression nor acted in a manner that can even in the most distant point of view savour of the smallest degree of harshness."[69] That was a lie, unless the prince believed that paralytic was the ideal condition for a groom on his wedding day, or that a loving husband would keep his wife confined with precious few friends and under constant watch from his own mistress. The Prince of Wales was shameless, but Caroline of Brunswick was more than his match. This was no wilting royal flower.

Scarcely two months after the prince informed Malmesbury that he had no intention of embarrassing Caroline by seeking a separation just yet, he went back on his word. All his efforts were by now fixed on Maria and he and Caroline resumed their communication through letters

---

68. Georgian Papers Online (http://gpp.rct.uk, August 2020). RA GEO/ MAIN/39156-39157 Letter from Lord Malmesbury to George, Prince of Wales, 24 March 1796.

69. Georgian Papers Online (http://gpp.rct.uk, August 2020). RA GEO/ MAIN/39158-39160 Letter from George, Prince of Wales to Lord Malmesbury, 26 March 1796.

seasoned liberally with tit-for-tat. Still Caroline claimed that she didn't blame her husband for her situation, but she was forced to face up to the fact that her unhappiness had not been entirely Lady Jersey's doing. Lady Jersey was out of the picture, but life was as miserable as ever.

Caroline never criticised Maria. To the contrary, she spoke of her admiringly, no doubt impressed by just how patient and understanding she must have been to have put up with the vagaries of the selfish and unpopular Prince of Wales. The two women never met but there doesn't seem to have been any animosity between them. Yet George received concrete proof of his plummeting approval ratings when Caroline visited the opera a matter of days before he wrote to his father and told him that their situation was untenable. The Duke of Leeds, who was present on the evening concerned, wrote of the outpouring of love for the princess in his diary.

> "I was in my box at the opera when the Princess of Wales arrived. The Pitt [sic] and some of the Boxes began to applaud, and the whole House almost instantly rose and joined the Applause. [...] The applause and Huzzas [sic] continued several minutes. She appeared much struck [...] After repeated curtseying to the audience she sat down; the audience called for God save the King, which the orchestra immediately played; the Princess rose instantly, as did the whole House, and the acclamations were universal of God save the King; one Person with great emphasis calling out, God save the *Princess* too, say I."[70]

It was an indication of what the future held for the prince and princess and George was furious. When people began to notice that Caroline was no longer taking her place at the front of the box but instead preferred to retire to the back, they asked why. Was she being compelled to withdraw by her husband's family? More to the point, "How comes it that the Portrait of the PRINCESS of WALES is not to be seen at the *Queen's House*, among the other Portraits of the ROYAL FAMILY? The

---

70. Browning, Oscar (1884). *The Political Memoranda of Francis Fifth Duke of Leeds*. London: The Camden Society, p.220.

DUTCHESS [sic] of YORK's has been there some time; and, without the PRINCESS, the illustrious groupe [sic] is strangely incomplete."[71] Private quarrels had become public business again.

Although the royal couple had apparently reconciled following the drama of Lady Jersey's resignation, they were essentially living apart. George summered in Brighton and Caroline in London, where she incensed both her husband and his mother by inviting visitors who were not on the list of approved friends. She took her lead on this from a letter the prince wrote to her in 1796, which she interpreted to mean that her restraints had been loosened. That was definitely not the case.

> "We have unfortunately been oblig'd to acknowledge to each other that we cannot find happiness in our union. Circumstances of character & education, which it is needless to discuss now, render that impossible. It then only remains that we should make the situation as little uncomfortable to each other as its nature will allow.
>
> [...]
>
> Let me therefore beg of you to make the best of a situation unfortunate *for us both*, which is only to be done by not *wantonly* creating or magnifying uncomfortable circumstances."[72]

Caroline and George were equally well aware that her victory over Lady Jersey had been a significant one. In a letter to his father George whined that gossips had poisoned Caroline's mind against him, but her little rebellion played right into his hands too, giving him the moral excuse he needed to renew his relationship with Maria. As far as the prince was concerned, there was no loving wife waiting at home whose heart would be broken, there was only Caroline. George's sisters and mother were more than happy to rally round and join the chorus of disapproval, but the Prince of Wales knew that convincing the king to release him from his marriage was easier said than done.

---

71. *True Briton.* 9 September 1796; issue 1157.
72. Georgian Papers Online (http://gpp.rct.uk, August 2020). RA GEO/ MAIN/39169-39174 Letter from George, Prince of Wales, to Caroline, Princess of Wales, 21 April 1796.

George wanted out. He didn't care what Caroline wanted and he didn't for a moment consider the embarrassment he would cause her, not to mention the public loathing he was already subject to. As Caroline continued to break free of the Carlton House System, George wrote to his father and informed him that "it would now be absolutely ruinous to my character & interest, as well as destructive to my peace of mind, for the rest of my life, to have further communication or intercourse of any kind with so dangerous a person as the Princess."[73] There was no question of reconciliation. Instead, George declared that he had no other option but "to supplicate your Majesty to order measures for our final separation." George III had other ideas.

> "You seem to look on your disunion with the Princess as merely of a private nature, and totally put out of sight that as Heir Apparent of the Crown your marriage is a public act, wherein the Kingdom is concerned; that therefore a separation cannot be brought forward by the mere interference of relations. The public must be informed of the whole business and being already certainly not prejudiced in your favour, the auspices in the first outset would not be promising.
>
> [...]
>
> I once more call on you to look with temper at the evils that may accrue to you by persisting in an idea that may lead to evils without bounds, and if more cannot be effected, have the command on yourself that shall, by keeping up appearances, by degrees render your home more respectable and at the same time less unpleasant. If you bring yourself to wish to have this effected, I do not see that the prospect of success is desperate, but in a contrary line of conduct nothing but evils appear.
>
> I most devoutly call on the Divine Providence to direct your mind to receive this fatherly and friendly advice with that temper that may make me ever subscribe myself, my dear son, your most affectionate father."[74]

---

73. Georgian Papers Online (http://gpp.rct.uk, August 2020). RA GEO/MAIN/39192-39195 Letter from George, Prince of Wales, to George III, 31 May 1796.
74. Georgian Papers Online (http://gpp.rct.uk, August 2020). RA GEO/MAIN/39199-39200 Letter from George III to George, Prince of Wales, 2 June 1796.

The prince and princess had long since passed the point of harmony though, and the seemingly endless reports of her rapturous public appearances were the final nail in the coffin. George suspected that the acres of approving newsprint had been planted by Caroline or her supporters with an eye to embarrassing him. At the top of his list of suspects were his critics Lord Thurlow and the Duke of Leeds, but there was no end of candidates happy to stir the pot. For Queen Charlotte, who had disliked her daughter-in-law from the off and who had lived her life out of the limelight as far as any queen could, such gossip was mortifying. She was so embarrassed that she asked her husband for permission to abandon her remaining drawing rooms for the rest of the season, certain that Caroline's spies would be present and looking to sow the seeds of further discord.

> "There will be a legal question of great importance to settle,
> in case of the separation of the PRINCE and PRINCESS
> of WALES. Will her Royal Highness be entitled to her *full
> dower of* 50,000l. a year as a *separate maintenance?*"[75]

As the press dug the knife in and the thorny issue of the separation went undecided, Caroline's horizons began to shrink again. George imposed restrictions on her access to Charlotte, who had just turned one, and ordered a schedule for the little girl's care that was virtually militaristic in its precision. Frances Garth, who had become Caroline's ally and arranged secret meetings between mother and daughter, resigned her position in the nursery after her wages fell nearly a year into arrears and instead became a Woman of the Bedchamber to the Princess of Wales. Caroline finally had a friend in her household and she had another in the royal nursery too, in the adored shape of Ann Hayman, Charlotte's subgoverness. With Miss Hayman present, Caroline could be sure that she would be allowed to visit her daughter without fear of anyone reporting her movements back to her husband and his mother.

Caroline moved out to Charlton for the summer, but she was forced to leave Charlotte in the city when the Prince of Wales refused permission for his daughter to travel. Caroline was heartbroken at the forced separation and split her time between London and Charlton, taking care never to be

---

75. *The Times.* 22 June 1796; issue 3618.

present when George was also visiting the nursery. Once again she took her grievance to the king and it was decided that Princess Charlotte and her attendants would be placed in their own establishment at Montague House in Blackheath. It was the ideal compromise, for whilst her mother could visit whenever she wished, Charlotte couldn't be said to be living with one parent to the detriment of the other.

But George didn't like the fact that Miss Hayman and Caroline had grown close. When Caroline asked if Miss Hayman could help with her accounts, he used that as an excuse to fire her, claiming that she would not be able to care for Charlotte adequately if she was spending her time on Caroline's financial affairs. As Lord Minto noted, "Miss Hayman has just been dismissed by the Prince because, being uncommonly agreeable and sensible, the Princess liked her company."[76] Caroline railed that she had not been allowed to bring any of her German ladies with her and pointed out the strange coincidence that sooner or later, all the friends she made in England seemed to fall from grace too. She told George and the king that she would like Miss Hayman to join her household as Keeper of the Privy Purse and they acquiesced. By this point, Caroline was under no illusions about her situation.

The Princess of Wales struck the death blow at a meeting with George at the close of 1797. In the presence of Lord Cholmondeley, she delivered a prepared speech that marked an end to any hopes of a reconciliation. Though she addressed her husband in French, she spat the last word in English.

"I have been two and a half years in this house. You have treated me neither as your wife, nor as the mother of your child, nor as the Princess of Wales. I advise you that from this moment I have nothing more to say to you, and that I regard myself as being no longer subject to your orders, or your rules."

Blackheath

Though Caroline had made her decision, her advisors counselled caution. With George III on her side she had a powerful friend in the royal household and the last thing they wanted was for her to lose that

---

76. Aspinall, Arthur (ed.) (1965). *The Correspondence of George, Prince of Wales: Vol III*. London: Cassell, p.375.

invaluable champion. Caroline wasn't the sort of woman who liked to lie low, but Lord Thurlow advised her that that was precisely what she ought to be doing. Things had never been so precarious, and Caroline had to maintain her role as the innocent party, even if that meant being seen to submit to a husband who was making her life impossible. Yet still the king refused to grant a formal separation, urging his son and daughter-in-law to find some common ground on which they could move forward together. Lord Loughborough, as intermediary for the prince, and Lord Thurlow, as intermediary for the princess, tried to hash out some sort of compromise, but it seemed impossible.

When Caroline took the lease on Montague House in Blackheath, where her daughter had previously been billeted, the die was cast. She began to spend most of her time in what was being touted as a country retreat but was actually the place she went to escape her husband. The letters that the couple and their advisors now exchanged pertained more and more to the matter of a separation, even as George's political friends pushed for reconciliation. Their favourite was the heir to the throne, after all, and the heir to the throne had scarcely been as unpopular as he was now. There was to be no reconciliation though and instead the couple continued to unofficially live apart. George had been able to monitor and control his wife's social circle in London, but at Blackheath his powers were sorely limited.

Caroline constantly shone, regardless of the circumstances. When two coachmen, Isaac Rawlinson and Matthew Ingram, careened into the Princess of Wales' carriage on the Greenwich road and seriously injured her attendant, they were arrested for dangerous conduct. At first the papers were disgusted that coachmen could be arrested for simply doing their jobs and argued, "let our Cockney Horsemen avoid the Greenwich Road; for as it commonly happens that they cannot guide their horses, they may chance against a Royal Groom, and be condemned to the Gallies [sic] during life for their unskillfulness."[77]

It was a rare moment of backlash for the Princess of Wales, but it didn't last long. Soon it was being reported that Caroline was frequently subject to hooliganish behaviour on the road, when drivers refused to clear a way for her and insisted on thundering past at dangerous speeds. As the tide of public opinion began to turn, the stricken coachmen appealed to the Prince of Wales for clemency and it was duly granted.

---

77. *Morning Post.* 5 August 1797; issue 7925.

Although found guilty and sentenced to two years hard labour, the prisoners were released after paying a nominal fine. Guess who got the credit? Certainly not the Prince of Wales. Instead the judge told them:

> "[Had] it not been for the interference and recommendation of Her Royal Highness the PRINCESS of WALES, whose endearing qualities of mercy and clemency shine with redoubled lustre on this occasion, you would have met with a heavy and exemplary punishment."[78]

If Carlton House had been a prison to Caroline, Montague House was where she could kick up her heels. It became a place of pilgrimage for her husband's Tory opponents and Caroline loved it. In 1799, as the Prince of Wales and Maria Fitzherbert were anxiously awaiting word from the Vatican on the standing of their marriage, Caroline was the hostess of the hour to guests including the Prime Minister William Pitt, Lord Chancellor Lord Loughborough, and a veritable *who's who* of senior government figures. What's most surprising wasn't who was present, but what Caroline managed to convince them to do.

> "[At Montague House] we *did* play at musical magic. Mr. Dundas [Treasurer of the Navy] was made, by the power of harmony, to kiss Miss Emma's hand, on his knees. Lady Charlotte [North, daughter of the former Prime Minister] was to present the Queen of Prussia's bust to Mr. Pitt, and make him kiss it, which, after some difficulty, he performed. The Princess was to tie Mr. Long and Mr. Frere together, and make each nurse a bolster as a baby. Mrs. Crewe, with all her caution, was the most frisky in the company, which amazed some of us much; but the most charming part of all was that of Mr. Dundas."[79]

As the house rang to the sounds of laughter, Henry Dundas, future Viscount Melville, "though he could not be tipsy, for I sat by him

---

78. *Oracle.* 15 January 1798; issue 19831.
79. Minto, Countess of (ed.) (1874). *Life and Letters of Sir Gilbert Elliot, First Earl of Minto, Vol III.* London: Longmans, Green and Co., p.61.

at dinner and saw no excess, [squeezed] the Princess's hand in the tenderest manner possible, called her angel repeatedly, and said he hoped no one but himself would know how much he loved her."[80] Whilst it's unlikely that this was anything beyond a courtly flirtation, it wasn't only Caroline's fun-loving character that drew the Tories to her. She was the wife and mother of the heirs to the throne and the most obvious candidate to serve as regent should Charlotte succeed her father before she reached her majority. It made sense to keep her sweet, especially when the Prince of Wales was so committed to his Whig circle.

It wasn't to everyone's taste, of course. Lady Hester Stanhope's thin-lipped recollections of Caroline capture perfectly the sense of indecorous silliness that sat so badly with the sophisticated ladies of the royal inner circle.

> "Oh! what an impudent woman was that P[rince]ss of W[ales].! [...] How the seacaptains used to colour up when she danced about, exposing herself like an opera girl; and then she gartered below the knee:- she was so low, so vulgar!"[81]

What Minto referred to as Caroline's "frisks" were harmless on the face of it, but he counselled her to behave with more discretion, concerned about the sort of capital her husband could make of these flirtatious, silly gatherings. Jack Payne, a close friend of the prince's who had captained *Jupiter* and brought Caroline safely to England, had become George's trusted intermediary with Maria Fitzherbert and was now employed to serve the same function between Maria and Caroline. He enquired as to whether Caroline would be willing to meet Maria, one assumes to discuss the strange situation that existed between the two women. Caroline understandably declined the offer, along with one to join the prince for dinner in London. Instead, she replied that the prince would be welcome to attend her in Blackheath, which Lord Minto interpreted as an earnest desire to reach a reconciliation.

---

80. Ibid.
81. Stanhope, Lady Hester (1846). *Memoirs of the Lady Hester Stanhope, Vol I*. London: Henry Colburn, p.267.

More likely, I suspect, Caroline was merely being polite. If the prince wanted an invitation to her table, he would have to get in line.

> "The Princess of Wales is now giving a merry round of dinners, not to persons of her own sex, but to a vast circle of Gentlemen, political and military [...] but no ladies are invited to any of the parties."[82]

That wasn't actually strictly true. Memorably, when Caroline invited Lord and Lady Lavington to spent an evening at Blackheath, she ordered that a double bed be made up for the couple. There was much drama when the Lavington's servants exclaimed that they had not shared a bed in years, and would not want to do so now. Caroline dismissed the concerns with a wave of her hand and told her housekeeper that it was a double bed or nothing. The next morning, Lady Lavington confided in her hostess that it had been a long time since she had enjoyed a night so much.

Without her husband to clip her wings, Caroline could give full rein to her enthusiastic, indiscreet manner. She thundered around with Princess Charlotte, crawling across the rugs and rolling on the floor with her daughter just as George III once had with his own children, and she flirted up a storm with her Tory admirers, especially future Prime Minister George Canning, for whom Caroline retained a special affection. The status quo was now firmly established, with the princess in Blackheath and the prince and Maria in London. And so it went on for several years, until a very messy scandal came calling.

An Infamous Calumny

As a young lady in Brunswick Caroline had devoted herself to charity children, and in Blackheath she once again returned to her favourite philanthropic pursuit. In 1801, she took in an abandoned baby girl and named her Edwardine Kent, in honour of her brother-in-law, who became the infant's godfather. Caroline got on well with Edward and George's other brothers, although they tried to keep out of the crossfire between the prince and princess.

---

82. *The Ipswich Journal.* 24 April 1802; issue 3609.

Though Edwardine's arrival passed off with little comment, that wasn't the case with the little boy who followed her. He became the subject of a scandalous and shocking episode.

In 1802 a Deptford woman named Sophia Austin came to Montague House, having heard of the princess' charitable ways. She was poor, hungry and desperate to earn a few pennies to feed her baby, William. Her husband, Samuel, had been laid off from dockyard work and Sophia wondered if Caroline would be able to intervene and land him a job. Although she was unable to do that, Caroline offered to take baby William in and raise him in the comfort of Montague House. *Little Willikins*, as he became known, would still be able to see his parents as often as they wished, but he would enjoy a lifestyle that they couldn't hope to give him. Though her advisers thought the scheme odd to say the least, the Austins jumped at it.

Caroline had enjoyed a close friendship with Lord and Lady Douglas, her Blackheath neighbours, but her favourite was Sir Sidney Smith, a dashing naval hero. Caroline and Smith flirted outrageously and he regaled her with tales of his impressive naval victories, which she never tired of. He was everything that her husband wasn't: a man of action and a bona fide hero, who loved to spend time with the Princess of Wales. Their relationship almost certainly went beyond platonic and Caroline revelled in it. That she and Smith shared a bed seems entirely plausible.

In 1802, hot on the heels of little William Austin, another new arrival came to Montague House. This was Captain Thomas Manby, and Caroline wasted no time in adding this second dashing naval hero to her collection. The princess took an instant shine to the handsome Captain, who became a neighbour whilst his ship was being fitted out at Deptford dockyard. She flirted with him in front of Smith, who watched in mute fury as the couple played footsy before sharing a kiss at the end of a particularly ribald evening. Sir Sidney Smith's reign in Blackheath was over. From now on, it was Captain Thomas Manby who would share Caroline's bed.

Caroline was by now exhibiting every quality that Lord Malmesbury had warned her against. She had abandoned any pretence of discretion and openly consorted with Manby at Blackheath, where her life became ever more extravagant. It was as though she thought that word would never reach her husband or there would be no consequences if it did. Even better, in Lady Douglas, Caroline was sure she had found a confidante in whom she could entrust all her greatest secrets. She was wrong.

Caroline had reckoned without Lady Douglas' own attachment to Captain Manby. She had expected a fair division of the spoils, with Caroline pairing off with Smith and herself with Manby, so when the princess effectively pounced on Manby too, Lady Douglas was fuming. When Manby stayed with the Douglases, the lady of the house liked to take him breakfast in bed and sit with him as he enjoyed it. Once he and Caroline became friends though, it was the Princess of Wales who was invited to share his breakfast behind locked doors. Soon it was whispered that she had added Manby to her list of lovers, but Caroline had gossip of her own to share.

"The Princess of Wales does not seem to believe in attachment of any husband and wife to one another, nor in the chastity of any married woman," wrote Lord Glenbervie. "She has anecdotes of intrigues without end of all the women of her society or of her acquaintance,"[83] and it should come as little surprise that she had plenty of anecdotes about Lady Douglas in her collection. No sooner had the gossip about the princess started than Lord Douglas received a series of obscenely illustrated anonymous letters, accusing his wife of an affair with Smith. The Douglases were convinced that the letters were in Caroline's handwriting and their thoughts turned to revenge.

With his wife's reputation on the line, Sir John Douglas showed the letters to Sir Sidney Smith, who gallantly replied that he and Lady Douglas were nothing more than friends. Captain Manby, meanwhile, received some anonymous letters of his own in which the writer urged him to speak up about his adulterous relationship with the Princess of Wales. It was turning into a right royal mess.

As the king recovered from another bout of serious ill health in 1806, he once again signalled his support of Caroline by appointing her Ranger of Greenwich Park. He also took young Princess Charlotte under his wing, to prevent her from becoming a pawn of her warring parents. She was to live at Windsor, with both her mother and father allowed access to her whenever they wished. A house was set aside for Caroline's use whenever she needed it and, with the king as her champion, she

---

83. Bickley, Francis (ed.) (1928). *The Diaries of Sylvester Douglas (Lord Glenbervie), Vol II*. London: Constable & Co, p.80.

was freely consulted on Charlotte's upbringing. The Princess of Wales recognised this as proof of the sovereign's affection, and she revelled in "the pleasure of having my child as she is my greatest comfort in this world."[84] The Prince of Wales was altogether less pleased, since his expenses included £5,000 for the education of his daughter, which would be clawed back if the king took charge of Charlotte's schooling. Lord Essex wrote to Lord Lowther of the monarch's continuing affection for his daughter-in-law, noting, "whenever he is in town on a Thursday, instead of dining at the Queen's House or going back to there, he constantly dines with the Princess at Blackheath and returns *late* in the evening across the country to Kew."[85] George III's chatty dinners with his eldest son were considerably less common. It sent a strong message.

As Ranger of Greenwich Park, Caroline was empowered to make decisions regarding the crown properties on the estate. Since she was settled at Montague House, she leased the Ranger's House to the newly-established Royal Naval Asylum, and offered the use of a number of other houses to the Asylum for its teachers and staff. When Lord and Lady Douglas learned that their own residence was amongst those likely to be handed over, it was the final straw. Sir John Douglas informed his acquaintance, Prince Augustus, Duke of Sussex, of the anonymous letters the couple had received, liberally sprinkling the tale with stories about the Princess of Wales' bedfellows. The duke invited the Douglases to repeat their accusations to his brother, the Prince of Wales, and to sign a statement swearing to their veracity. They agreed, and Lady Douglas added an allegation that Caroline had said she would claim William Austin was the child of the Prince of Wales, sired during a two night stay at Carlton House. In fact, said Lady Douglas, he was really the result of a tryst with an unnamed lover.

In case that wasn't evidence enough, she added that Caroline had grown fat in 1802 and had confided to Lady Douglas – who was herself pregnant at the time – that she was with child. When the baby came along, Caroline was supposedly determined to suckle him herself and did so whilst carrying on monologues about the shortcomings of the royal family.

---

84. Aspinall, Arthur (ed.) (1965). *The Correspondence of George, Prince of Wales, Vol IV*. London: Cassell, p.145.

85. Aspinall, Arthur (ed.) (1965). *The Correspondence of George, Prince of Wales: Vol V*. London: Cassell, p.160.

This was dynamite because if Caroline and George had a son, he would move ahead of Princess Charlotte in the line of succession. If Lady Douglas' claims of a bastard child were to be believed, then Caroline was guilty of treason, plain and simple.

Lady Douglas never believed for a moment that William was Caroline's child. Caroline was saucy, silly and never knew when a joke had gone too far. Though she might have gone on a flight of comical fantasy and imagined the scenes if she *did* claim William was the heir to the throne, the chances of her actually doing it were virtually non-existent. Edwardine Kent and William Austin filled a yawning sadness in Caroline's life at a time when her access to her only child was tightly controlled, but William was never intended to be a changeling heir to the throne. Though he remained with Caroline until her death, William always knew where he came from.

George retained the services of Samuel Romilly, who had advised Maria in the case of Minney Seymour, to investigate whether there was a case to be made against Caroline. By the end of May 1806, he had concluded that there was. The Delicate Investigation was on.

It was with a heavy heart that the king agreed to call a commission of four senior politicians to ascertain whether the Princess of Wales had indeed conspired to pass off a bastard child as the heir to the throne. Fearful of the impact on the royal family should the scandal become public knowledge, George III impressed upon Prime Minister William Grenville, who was the head of the commission, that the investigation was to be kept completely secret. Perhaps surprisingly, one of the people who knew nothing of its existence was Caroline, the very woman who was being investigated. The charge against her was a simple one.

> "That her Royal Highness had been pregnant in the year 1802, in consequence of an illicit intercourse, and that she had in the same year been secretly delivered of a male child, which child had ever since that period been brought up by her Royal Highness, in her own house, and under her immediate inspection."[86]

---

86. *Hansard* HC Deb. Vol. 24 Cols.1106-23, 4 March 1813. [Accessed August 2020]. https://api.parliament.uk/historic-hansard/commons/1813/mar/04/the-princess-of-wales

Returning from a summer excursion to Devon with little Willikins, Caroline was informed by the Duke of Kent that she was to be approached by a solicitor named Thomas Lowten. Lowten was gathering evidence and statements on behalf of the prince, and wished to speak to members of the princess' household. Caroline's calm exterior when she heard the news belied her fury and she wrote to the king to protest her innocence in a letter that is as bewildered as it is heartfelt.

> "I approach you, with a heart undismayed, upon this occasion, so awful and momentous to my character, my honour, and my happiness. I should indeed, (under charges such as have now been brought against me,) prove myself undeserving of the continuance of that countenance and protection, and altogether unworthy of the high station, which I hold in your Majesty's illustrious family, if I sought for any partiality, for any indulgence, for any thing *more* than what is due to me in justice. My entire confidence in your Majesty's virtues assures me, that I cannot meet with *less*.
>
> The situation, which I have been so happy as to hold in your Majesty's good opinion and esteem; my station in your Majesty's august family; my life, my honour, and, through mine, the honour of your Majesty's family have been attacked. Sir John and Lady Douglas have attempted to support a direct and precise charge, by which they have dared to impute to me, the enormous guilt of High Treason, committed in the foul crime of Adultery."[87]

Caroline was determined not to lay herself open to any further allegations of wrongdoing. Upon learning that her servants were to be questioned, she asked the Duke of Kent to wait with her until Lowten had arrived, to provide an assurance that she hadn't attempted to coach her household. Though Caroline was understandably anxious, her old friend Lord Minto assured her that there was no need to be. It was obvious that the Douglases had acted in revenge for Caroline deciding to take possession of their residence, he said, and nobody would take their allegations as

---

87. Cobbett, William (ed.) (1813) *Cobbett's Political Register, Vol XXIII*. London: Richard Bagshaw, p.411.

anything more than bad blood. "Yet all one knows of her unreserved and indiscreet manners may make one understand how an unfavourable judgement may have been formed without any real foundation,"[88] admitted Minto, acknowledging that Caroline was occasionally the author of her own misfortunes.

The whole case against Caroline hinged on Lady Douglas' allegations that the princess had intended to pass William Austin off as the son of the Prince of Wales. Lady Douglas painted herself as an innocent woman, wide-eyed in the thrall of the showy and smothering princess, who had become her constant and cloying shadow. She had been raised to respect royalty, said Lady Douglas, and though at first she felt honoured to attend Caroline, she soon became "so extravagantly fond of me, that, however flattering it might be, it certainly was very troublesome."[89]

Lady Douglas didn't quite accuse Caroline of pursuing her as a lover might, but the implication was clear. Caroline, said Lady Douglas, "would push past my servant, and run up stairs into my bedchamber, kiss me, take me in her arms, and tell me I was beautiful, saying she had never loved any woman so much."[90] In case the point hadn't been driven home hard enough, she assured the commission that she asked Caroline to restrain herself only to be told, "believe me, you are quite beautiful, different from almost any English woman; your arms are fine beyond imagination, your bust is very good, and your eyes, Oh [sic], I never saw such eyes – all other women who have dark eyes look fierce, but yours (my dear Lady Douglas) are nothing but softness and sweetness, and yet quite dark."[91] Lady Douglas was overegging the pudding.

She spoke of Caroline's indiscretion and drunkenness, of her dismissal of Sir John Douglas as less of a man than her naval admirers and of her fury at being told that the royal family might disapprove of her relationship with Sir Sidney Smith. Upon learning that the Duke of Clarence was keeping an eye on her and Smith, Caroline supposedly warned Lady Douglas spitefully, "I will cheat him and throw the dust in

88. Minto, Countess of (ed.) (1874). *Life and Letters of Sir Gilbert Elliot, First Earl of Minto, Vol III.* London: Longmans, Green and Co., p.389.

89. Huish, Robert (1821). *Memoirs of Her Late Majesty Caroline, Queen of Great Britain: Vol I.* London: T Kelly, p.131.

90. Ibid., p.132.

91. Ibid.

his eyes, and make him believe Sir Sidney comes here to see you, and that you and he are the greatest possible friends. I delight of all things in cheating those clever people."[92] It was all a little too convenient. Lady Douglas had done all she could to dissuade the princess from an unwise course of action, she promised, warning her, "that it rested with herself to keep her acquaintance at a proper distance and, as Sir Sidney was a lively, thoughtless man, and had not been accustomed to the society of ladies of her rank, he might forget himself, and she would then have herself to blame."[93] What a friend.

Soon the testimony read like a penny dreadful and Lady Douglas' claims that she was afraid of the crass and vulgar princess when the two women were clearly good friends reeked of bad feeling. Though it's perfectly believable that Caroline mocked the royal family and confided that she hoped for a formal separation, the idea of Lady Douglas secretly clutching her pearls rather than lapping it up doesn't carry the slightest ring of truth. Likewise, if Caroline did make an ill-conceived comment about passing William Austin off as the heir to the throne, then she was guilty of nothing but telling a bad joke and Lady Douglas' claim that her friend might actually have given birth to the child herself was nothing but stirring the pot. She knew William wasn't Caroline's child, but she had been badly piqued by the anonymous letters alleging adultery and wanted to stick the knife in. She wanted to secure the favours of the Prince of Wales too, who was sure to become Regent sooner or later if his father's much-publicised struggles with his mental health were anything to go by. The best way to do that, Lady Douglas surmised, was to lay it on with a trowel.

> "Such was the person we found her Royal Highness the Princess of Wales, and as we continued to see her character and faults, Sir John and myself more and more, daily and hourly, regretted that the world could not see her as we did, and that his Royal Highness the Prince of Wales should have lost *any popularity*, when, from her own account (the only account we ever had) *she* was the aggressor from the beginning, herself *alone*, and I, as an humble individual, declare that from the most *heartfelt* and unfeigned

---

92. Ibid., p.137.
93. Ibid., p.136.

conviction that I believe, if any other married woman had acted as her royal highness has done, I never yet have known a man who could have endured it; and her temper is so tyrannical, capricious, and furious, that no man on earth will ever beat it; and, in private life, any woman who had thus played and sported with her husband's comfort, and her husband's popularity, would have been turned out of her house, or left by herself in it, and would deservedly have forfeited her place in society."[94]

Lady Douglas certainly told a good story, but in embroidering the truth, she crossed the line into melodrama. If it came down to one woman's word against the other, the commission was walking a potentially very delicate path. Unsurprisingly, when Caroline retained Spencer Perceval to act as her representative, he swiftly dismissed Lady Douglas' testimony as "a greater farrago of gossiping trash and malignant accusation [than] can hardly be conceived."

Despite Lady Douglas' lurid claims, the matter of treason proved surprisingly easy to resolve. Perceval swatted away the claims of an illegitimate child by producing a grateful Sophia and Samuel Austin, who testified that although Caroline had taken their child into her home and cared for him as though he was her own, from bottle-feeding him to changing his dirty nappies, they were not mother and son. Sophia Austin even supplied evidence from a lying-in hospital of the little boy's birth, but by this point the commission had seen enough.

> "We are happy to declare our perfect conviction, that there is no foundation whatever for believing that the child now with the Princess of Wales is the child of her Royal Highness, or that she was delivered of any child in the year 1802; nor has any thing appeared to us which would warrant the belief that she was pregnant in that year, or at any other period within the compass of our inquiries."[95]

---

94. Ibid., p.144.
95. Urban, Sylvanus (1813). *The Gentleman's Magazine: Volume LXXXIII*. London: Nichols, Son, and Bentley, p.260.

The question of adultery was not so easy to dismiss. The defence case wasn't exactly helped by Robert Bidgood, Caroline's page and a long-time retainer of the Prince of Wales. He claimed that Manby routinely spent the night at Blackheath and added that he had seen the reflection of the couple exchanging passionate kisses in a mirror. Caroline's former footman plainly stated that "the Princess is very fond of fucking," whilst Lord Moira, a friend of the Prince of Wales, told anyone who cared to listen that Captain Manby was in possession of an ornamental bag that contained a clipping of the princess' pubic hair. Lord Ellenborough dryly commented that they might have trouble proving its provenance unless they were able to compare it to another specimen of the same. Somewhat more troubling was a statement from Fanny Lloyd, Caroline's coffee-room attendant. She claimed that she had heard that Mary Wilson, a housemaid, "went into the Princess's bedroom to make up the fire [and] found the Princess and Sir Sidney [Smith] *in the act*; that [Wilson] immediately left the room, and fainted at the door." Imagine how traumatised she would have been if she'd been employed by the hedonistic Prince of Wales instead.

When the remaining servants were questioned, however, all of them denied that they had witnessed scenes of adultery. Even Mary Wilson, whose story Lloyd had recounted, denied that she had seen Caroline and Sir Sidney *in the act*. Little by little Lady Douglas' statement began to crumble. The commission didn't accuse her of lying under oath though, accepting that Lady Douglas had merely repeated what the princess – who she herself had dismissed as a liar – had told her.

"[Nor] did Lady Douglas *ever say in unqualified terms* that the Princess was in the family way," her husband wrote, ever ready to defend his wife's questionable honour. "*Such* an assertion being impossible for any human to have uttered. She said what she will *ever* repeat: that the princess told her so, and from her own observations and circumstances she had no reason to doubt her assertions."[96]

If Lady Douglas had been misled, Sir John reasoned, then she could hardly be held responsible. I doubt Lady Douglas was misled at all. She had lied, but had the good sense to provide herself with an escape route.

---

96. Aspinall, Arthur (ed.) (1965). *The Correspondence of George, Prince of Wales: Vol V*. London: Cassell, p.389.

Let's not naïvely assume that every word she said was untrue, because Caroline *did* consort with plenty of close male friends at Blackheath and it's perfectly believable that she was sexually active. It's believable too that her servants, loyal to a fault, rallied round to protect their mistress' reputation and when she eventually quit England for Brunswick, Caroline certainly rewarded them handsomely. The only witnesses who could be found to speak against Caroline were long-time retainers of the Prince of Wales, who she scarcely knew. It was hardly a smoking gun and the report of the commissioners, which was finalised on 14 July 1806, formally cleared her of being the mother of an illegitimate child once and for all.

> "The identity of the child now with the Princess, its parents, age, the place of its birth, the time and circumstance of its being taken under her Royal Highness's protection, are all established by such a concurrence both of positive and circumstantial evidence, as can, in our judgment, leave no doubt on this part of the subject. The child was, beyond all doubt, born in Brownlow-street Hospital, on the 11th day of July, 1802, of Sophia Austin."

The commission reached a less favourable conclusion on the matter of adultery. Although Caroline had not been given an opportunity to speak in her own defence, the commission of four cabinet members decided that, on the subject of her relationship with Thomas Manby, there remained sufficient doubt.

> "[Though] the facts of pregnancy and delivery are to our minds satisfactorily disproved, so, on the other hand, we think that the circumstances to which we now refer, particularly those stated to have passed between Her Royal Highness and Captain Manby, must be credited, until they shall receive some decisive contradiction; and, if true, are justly entitled to the most serious consideration."

Had the case been heard in a court of law, which would have been a very high-risk strategy for the prince, adultery would have been a matter of high treason, but the Delicate Investigation was a talking shop. It had not been conducted as a court case would and lacked any legal jurisdiction. When the commissioners decided that there was not sufficient evidence to clear the Princess of Wales of adultery, the resultant stain on Caroline's reputation was a moral, rather than a legal, one.

The Aftermath

Though the investigation was over, Caroline and Perceval weren't about to take its repercussions lying down. Caroline was not allowed to attend court or see her daughter whilst the commission was ongoing, and she was determined to resolve the matter as speedily as possible. Although the commission was supposedly conducted in the utmost secrecy, heavy hints about it were appearing in the press across the country. Every new report brought a fresh outpouring of support for the princess, who was regarded as an innocent punching bag for her husband's spite. As her mother correctly forecast in a letter to George III, "she now will be more in view, & cause much envy to her mortal enemy [the Prince of Wales]"[97]. The public loved her charitable ways and little Willikins was living the life of Riley in Blackheath, whilst his guardian was lapping up the adoration that poured in for her charitable acts. Yet Lady Hester Stanhope saw it differently and watched the scenes at Blackheath with horror.

> "[As] as for the P[rincess] of W[ales].'s adopting [William Austin], and making such a fuss about it, it was only pure spite to vex the Prince. He was a nasty boy. Oh! how Mr. Pitt used to frown, when he was brought in after dinner, and held by a footman over the table to take up anything out of the dessert that he liked.
> [...]
> It was unpardonable in the P[rince]ss to lavish her love upon such a little urchin of a boy, a little beggar, really no better. To see him brought in every day after dinner, bawling

---

97. Georgian Papers Online (http://gpp.rct.uk, September 2020). RA GEO/ MAIN/52224 Letter from Augusta, Duchess of Brunswick, to George III, October 1804.

and kicking down the wine, and hung up by his breeches over the table for people to laugh at; and so ugly!"[98]

Caroline had been forcibly separated from her own child and in a world where the likes of Lady Hester Stanhope sneered at her every wrong, it's impossible not to root for the princess just a little bit. At times she was her own worst enemy, but even if she wasn't, there were plenty of people willing to fill that role.

As Perceval got busy sowing sympathetic stories about Caroline in the press, he urged her to insist on being allowed to attend court again. Though it was the last thing she wanted to do, Caroline recognised that this would force the king to make a decision on the commission's report. Her mother wrote to the king and urged him to end Caroline's limbo, reminding him that she was his niece as well as his daughter-in-law, but George III still held back. Perceval forced the king's hand and sent the report to the Prince and Princess of Wales. It was the first time Caroline had actually seen the full extent of the charges and statements against her and it made for damning reading. Her husband had expected the commission to find in his favour, and instead it had done no such thing. He was wholly unprepared for it.

The Delicate Investigation had not proved the hammer blow that the Prince of Wales had anticipated, but it did damage Caroline's standing with the king, who took few things more seriously than his marriage vows. Perceval intended to exploit George III's fear of embarrassment by publishing the full report of the commission, but his real aim was to convince the Privy Council to pursue charges against Lady Douglas for lying under oath. As Caroline and Perceval sat down to write her defence in preparation for public consumption, the princess' team went in hard on Lady Douglas. They attacked her lies and her reputation, even conjuring up witnesses who swore she was intimate with Bidgood, who had spilled the beans on Caroline's affair with Manby. Perceval sent all the evidence to George III, accompanied by a lengthy and heartfelt statement by Caroline in which she protested against her treatment and the embarrassment it had caused her. Central to the defence was the repeated argument that Lady Douglas had been motivated by malice to lie.

---

98. Stanhope, Lady Hester (1846). *Memoirs of the Lady Hester Stanhope, Vol I.* London: Henry Colburn, p.268-269.

There was certainly more of Perceval than Caroline in the arguments against the legality of the secret commission, which had excluded not only Caroline but the voices of her supporters.

A similar package went to the prime minister, and the dam of secrecy broke beneath the tidal wave of Perceval's efforts. The press divided down party lines and the Delicate Investigation became the hottest topic in the land. Even Caroline was feeling the pressure, and before 1806 concluded with a run of catastrophe, she had confided in friends that she longed to go home to Brunswick.

The first disaster was the death of her eldest brother, Hereditary Prince Charles. He was born blind and suffered from conditions that affected both his physical and mental health. Despite this, he was married to Princess Louise of Orange-Nassau, who had once been befriended by Maria Fitzherbert. Louise served as her husband's nurse in a childless but surprisingly happy marriage. The prince was just 40 years old when he died.

Princess Caroline herself narrowly escaped serious injury in early October when the carriage she was travelling in collided with a tree and overturned. Miss Cholmondeley, Caroline's friend and attendant, died almost instantly from her injuries, and the princess took to her bed for weeks as she recovered. There was worse yet to come. Soon Caroline would need all the public adoration she could get.

> "Under these circumstances of distress, under these losses with whom she might claim kindred, and from whom she may hope for comfort, the generous people of England will feel that this illustrious and amiable PRINCESS has a stronger title than ever to their attached and affectionate support."[99]

Declaring that "I will die as I have lived – with honor [sic]!"[100], Caroline's father barely survived the wounds he sustained on the battlefield at Auerstädt, where the forces of Prussia were fighting Napoleon's armies. He was taken to Altona for treatment, where he was joined by his wife and two of their children. Over the weeks Duke Charles William's condition deteriorated and on 10 November 1806, he died. Caroline adored him

---

99. *Morning Post*. 11 October 1806.
100. *The Morning Chronicle*. 26 November 1806; issue 11709.

and his death shattered her already weakened spirits, especially now she had been robbed of the company of the king, who had become a surrogate father. Her only comfort was the erstwhile Lord Malmesbury, who had known her father well thanks to his diplomatic missions to Brunswick, and who visited Caroline to share his condolences and lend a shoulder to cry on.

Faced with this catalogue of misfortunes, it would hardly have been surprising if Caroline had folded under the pressure. The Prince of Wales no doubt prayed she would, even if the chances of her going back to Brunswick now Napoleon was on the scene were close to zero. Her spirits were broken though, and perhaps he hoped that this would rob Caroline of the will to fight. Instead, the opposite happened. Caroline became more determined than ever to clear her name and in December, she made her case to the king.

> "Your Majesty's own gracious and Royal Mind will easily conceive what must have been my state of anxiety and suspense whilst I have been fondly indulging in the hope that every day as it passed would bring me the happy Tidings that Your Majesty was satisfied of my innocence in every part of their charge.
>
> [...]
>
> The World in total ignorance of the real State of the Facts begins to infer my Guilt from it. I feel myself already sinking in the Estimation of Your Majesty's Subjects, as well as of what remains to me of my own Family into a State (intolerable to a Mind conscious of its Purity and Innocence,) a state in which my Honour appears at least equivocal and my Virtue is suspected, From this state I humbly entreat Your Majesty to perceive that I can have no hope of being restored, until either Your Majesty's favourable opinion shall be graciously notified to the World, by receiving me again into the Royal presence, or until the full disclosure of the Facts shall expose the Malice of my accusers, and do away every possible ground for unfavourable Inference and Conjecture.
>
> The various Calamities with which it has pleased God of late to afflict me, I have endeavoured to bear, and I trust I have borne with humble resignation to the Divine will.

But the effect of this Infamous charge, and the delay which has suspended its final termination by depriving me of the Consolation which I should have received from Your Majesty's presence and Kindness, have given a heavy addition to them all, and surely my bitterest Enemies could hardly wish that they should be increased.

But on this Topic, as possibly not much affecting the Justice, though it does the hardship of my Case I forbear to dwell.

Your Majesty will be graciously pleased to recollect, that an occasion of assembling the Royal Family and Your Subjects, in dutiful and happy Commemoration of Her Majesty's Birthday, is now near at hand – If the increased Occupations which the approach of Parliament may occasion or any other Cause should prevent the Commissioners from enabling Your Majesty to Communicate Your pleasure to me before that time, the World will infallibly conclude (in their present state of Ignorance) that my answer must have proved unsatisfactory and that the infamous Charges have been thought to be but too true.

These Considerations, Sire, will I trust in Your Majesty's Gracious Opinion, rescue this address from all imputation of impatience – For Your Majesty's Sense of honourable Feeling, will naturally suggest, how utterly impossible it is that I, conscious of my own Innocence, and believing that the Malice of my Enemies has been completely detected, can without abandoning all regard to my Interests, my Happiness, and my Honour, possibly be contented to perceive the approach of such utter ruin to my Character, and yet wait with patience and in silence till it overwhelms me.

I therefore take this liberty of throwing myself again at Your Majesty's feet, and entreating and imploring of Your Majesty's Goodness and Justice in pity for my Miseries which this delay so severely aggravates, and in justice to my Innocence and my Character to urge the Commissioners to an early Communication of their advice."[101]

---

101. Georgian Papers Online (http://gpp.rct.uk, August 2020). RA GEO/MAIN/40871-40874 Letter from Caroline, Princess of Wales, to George III, 8 December 1806.

George III had dragged his heels long enough. If he didn't welcome Caroline back into the bosom of the royal family, her camp would publish the entire proceedings of the commission – heavily annotated in their favour – and let the public decide. On advice from the Cabinet the king announced that he would cautiously welcome Caroline back into his presence, but only once she had been warned that she must exercise more discretion in future. Caroline was delighted to be back in George III's favour, but their relationship had been irreparably damaged. Never again would he be like a second father to the Princess of Wales, but she had yet to realise it.

Still the Prince of Wales refused to give up. He had come to the conclusion that the commission's belief that Caroline had committed adultery bore further investigation by his own representatives. Whilst this was ongoing, the king informed Caroline that he could not see her. To Spencer Perceval that meant only one thing: publish and be damned.

Behind the scenes a battle raged over the best way to resolve the situation with minimum embarrassment. Perceval's manuscript, known simply as *The Book*, was printed and ready to go and the prince's supporters dreaded what it might contain. What would it say about Maria Fitzherbert and the rumours of a secret marriage? Would Lady Jersey be a supporting character? What of George's other romantic entanglements? Soon the whole country would devour its scandalous contents, but at the eleventh hour fate intervened. The Grenville ministry collapsed and Caroline found her Tory supporters holding the reins of power, with none other than Spencer Perceval occupying the office of Chancellor of the Exchequer. Caroline was in the public gallery when her defender made his maiden speech as chancellor and the new administration brought with it sweeping change. They immediately advised the king that he should welcome the Princess of Wales back into the royal presence and he was quick to obey, even making apartments in Kensington Palace ready for her use should she require them. The public welcomed the news with open arms.

> "The PRINCESS of WALES was present yesterday at Her MAJESTY'S Drawing Room [...] the cause we have so strenuously advocated has at length triumphed, and the calumniated PRINCESS is acknowledged to rank among the purest and most exalted of British subjects. – What a

triumph to the Princess of WALES! What a humiliation to her enemies!"[102]

Having claimed the victory, Spencer Perceval held a bonfire of *The Book* at Lincoln's Inn Fields. Inevitably copies escaped and made their way onto the black market, despite Perceval offering a cash reward for their recovery. Needless to say, he didn't track them all down.

Caroline didn't have things all her own way and both the king and the Prince of Wales were agreed on the fact that Princess Charlotte must never spend time with William Austin. Caroline agreed to the condition and after recovering from a case of shingles, resumed her life at court, where she revelled in her triumph.

The appearance of the princess at a drawing room in honour of the king's birthday led to premature celebrations amongst those who had been hoping for a reconciliation between the Waleses. The *Morning Post* excitedly exclaimed, "may the interest thus evinced be rewarded as a perfect re-establishment of that domestic concord, the interruption of which has been so long lamented."[103] There was fat chance of that.

Family Life

In Brunswick, the world had changed. Immediately after the death of the duke in Altona, the French army had advanced deeper into his territory, leaving his widow and children with no home to return to. Instead they fled to the Duchy of Augustenborg, where Augusta's nephew-in-law, Frederick Christian II, reigned. They remained in Augustenborg until 1807, when George III granted Duchess Augusta permission to join her daughter in England. She arrived from the turbulent continent in July and went straight to Blackheath, where the Princess of Wales waited. At first Caroline accompanied her mother everywhere she went, including visits to the royal family. Indeed, Augusta refused to attend any court occasions unless her daughter was invited too and for a little while, it seemed as though the old friction from Brunswick had been forgotten. Caroline needed friends too, because her allies in the royal household

---

102. *Morning Post*. 15 May 1807; issue 11307.
103. *Morning Post*. 5 June 1807; issue 11325.

were disappearing at a rate of knots until only the Duke of Cumberland, never a fan of his eldest brother, remained.

The king was polite because he had to be, but *The Book* was the greatest betrayal he could have imagined. Nothing was more precious to him than his domestic privacy and the thought that his own daughter-in-law was willing to lay bare to public scrutiny one of the royal family's greatest quarrels was utterly abhorrent to him. Before the Delicate Investigation, the king and princess were as close as father and daughter. Once it had concluded, that intimate friendship was over. Though he might – at a pinch – have forgiven Caroline her own indiscretions, he would not forgive the threat of *The Book*. Nowhere was this more evident than in the fact that he ceased to consult her on issues regarding Princess Charlotte's care. The house that had been set aside for Caroline's use at Windsor was quietly given to his daughter, Princess Augusta, and when the king did meet his daughter-in-law, warm friendship had given way to cool civility.

Duchess Augusta had supported Caroline and protested her innocence throughout the Delicate Investigation. Whether the prudish and holier-than-thou duchess ever read the detailed report remains open to conjecture, but if she did, she never mentioned it to anyone. Perhaps she broached the subject with Caroline, or perhaps she preferred to brush it and the uncomfortable questions it invited under the rug. It had been a difficult twelve months, after all. The arrival of the Duchess of Brunswick in England did little to improve her daughter's lot. They had not been the best of friends in Germany and in Blackheath, that didn't change.

The two women were mother and daughter, but that's where the things they had in common began and ended. In fact, having Augusta close by curtailed the independence that Caroline so valued and seeing her once compliant daughter as a self-possessed adult didn't entirely please Augusta. Soon they began to argue, and it became clear that something had to change. Augusta moved out of Caroline's home and into the neighbouring Brunswick House, with her visits to Caroline now scheduled in advance. It was likely the only thing that prevented yet another all-out domestic war.

On a more positive note, now Augusta was in England, Princess Charlotte visited her every weekend. That Willikins was also a familiar figure around Montague House cannot be disputed, but what Augusta made of him we can only guess. In Brunswick her daughter's charity children stayed in their own homes and it was one more sign of Caroline's strong-willed personality that in Blackheath, they were as part of the family.

In her newly refurbished apartments at Kensington Palace, previously the rooms of Caroline of Ansbach, George II's queen, Caroline played the society hostess to the hilt. She was served by her attendants, siblings Lady Sheffield and Lady Glenbervie, and by Lady Charlotte Lindsay, a newcomer to the inner circle. One notable exception from the group was Lady Townshend, who had resigned from her role as Mistress of the Robes in 1808, after she and Caroline disagreed on the best way to deal with William Austin's future. Lady Townshend believed that the time had come to send him home and simply pay for his care, but Caroline wouldn't hear of it. Willy stayed, Lady Townshend went, and Caroline, Lord Glenbervie noted, "seldom misses an opportunity of abusing her, and imputing to her intrigues of both sorts."[104]

Even the Duke of Cumberland, an unlikely ally to his sister-in-law, withdrew from her company as a result of arguments over Willikins, but Caroline had other admirers waiting in the wings. Soon she was being squired about town by George Pitt, 2nd Baron Rivers of Stratfield Saye and Sudeley Castle, a dandy in his late fifties who had a wide and admiring social circle. Whether the two were lovers is a matter of debate, but it's possible. Rivers was a charming, engaging man and Caroline loved charming, engaging men.

At long last it looked as if the royal marriage had finally settled down and though the prince and princess wouldn't live together, nor would they agitate for any change to the current circumstances. The Prince of Wales continued with his circle and the Princess of Wales with hers, whilst Charlotte was perfectly happy with her governess, Lady de Clifford. The young princess was not flourishing as a student though, having lost so much time to the warring wishes of her parents, who would replace one tutor with another as a matter of routine, often leaving delays between appointees.

Caroline became a regular fixture at Kensington Palace, far away from her mother in Blackheath. It was one way to guarantee that their frequent clashes grew more intermittent. The Delicate Investigation had

---

104. Bickley, Francis (ed.) (1928). *The Diaries of Sylvester Douglas (Lord Glenbervie), Vol II*. London: Constable & Co, p.21.

changed nothing and she was as loud and proud as she always had been. Never was this more the case than when her brother, Frederick William, Duke of Brunswick-Wulfenbüttel, arrived triumphant in England from the continent. Like his father he was a soldier to his bones, and he was welcomed as a hero. In fact, Frederick William's successes had been scant and his lands had been absorbed into the Napoleonic Kingdom of Westphalia after the defeat of Prussia and the Fourth Coalition. The duke had fled for Baden and there mustered a new fighting force under the auspices of the Austrian Empire. This force seized control of the city of Braunschweig during the War of the Fifth Coalition, at which point he had headed for England. There he and his troops were welcomed into the British Army, with Frederick William being awarded the rank of Lieutenant General[105].

Frederick William summoned his sons from Europe and Caroline was quick to let her brother know that life with her mother was as difficult as ever. He kept his own counsel, perhaps already aware that Duchess Augusta was in the process of altering her will to leave her home not to Caroline, but to his own sons instead. It was a mark of her fractious relationship with Caroline that she had long since abandoned her promise never to visit the king and queen without her daughter present too, and now did so quite happily. Absence might make the heart grow fonder, but living next door to one another had reawakened all the old animosity between the mother and daughter from Brunswick.

Caroline hardly cared, because she barely went to Blackheath now anyway. Why would she, when she had those apartments in Kensington Palace at her disposal? She was as free with her company as ever and, like her husband, free with her purse too, until her debts climbed to over £50,000. Those debts were the responsibility of the Prince of Wales and they were soon under discussion in the House of Commons. Fearing that any resistance to making a contribution might not go in his favour should the Regency become a reality, the Prince of Wales agreed to pay up. He settled on a figure of £50,000, with the outstanding £2,000 to come from Caroline's own purse.

It was money that ended the friendship between Caroline and Spencer Perceval, who had defended her so passionately before the commissioners

---

105. Frederick William was killed at the Battle of Quatre Bras in 1815, the night after he had danced at the Duchess of Richmond's fabled ball.

of the Delicate Investigation. By failing to secure a complete settlement of her debts, Caroline decided that Perceval had failed her and by the time he became prime minister in 1809, she was his enemy. That signalled a change in her political allegiances as the once Tory Princess of Wales threw her weight behind the Whigs for the first time. She became a regular sight in the gallery of the House of Commons, where she watched debates and divisions with fascination. "The speaker would not allow the Tellers to declare the numbers until the doors were shut," said the *Morning Chronicle*. "He audibly pronounced – "Strangers must withdraw"- It was some time before the princess took the hint."[106] Wasn't it always?

Charlotte shared Caroline's support for the Whigs, her lackadaisical schooling not having dented her inherited love for politics. It was one of the few interests that the Waleses all shared. Their political colours, however, were decidedly different. Once an avowed Whig, under the influence of Lord and Lady Hertford the Prince of Wales was turning to the Tories, just as his father had for so many years. With the Regency now imminent, which side the Prince of Wales chose would shape the future of the country.

The Regency

Half a decade of strained family relations had passed since George III had withdrawn his once enthusiastic support from Caroline, and Queen Charlotte gritted her teeth and accepted Duchess Augusta as a regular fixture at court. The elder stateswomen of England and Brunswick were no fonder of one another than they had ever been, but their relationship was one of stiffly polite tolerance. It came with the job.

Though the relationship between the king and his daughter-in-law had cooled, Princess Caroline was still keen to remind people in her own unique way that she was a member of the royal family. Not for her a message of goodwill; instead, she told Lord and Lady Glenbervie that George III had been so desperate to see her that he had fled St James's on horseback with a pack of equerries, grooms and soldiers at his heels. He led the chase to Blackheath, where he demanded to see Princess Caroline alone and then, if the princess was to be believed, "he threw

---

106. *Morning Chronicle,* 25 January 1810; issue 12702.

her down on one of the sofas, and would certainly have ravished her, if happening to be without a back, she had not contrived to get over it on the other side." When she protested, the king answered that it was quite all right, because "on occasion when the Queen was laying in, the late Lady Harcourt had humbly offered to supply her Majesty's place till her recovery."[107] Such gossip did little to help Caroline's cause.

Though she was once close to the king, there is little evidence that his illness left Caroline sympathetic to the queen and her daughters. They had rallied firmly behind the prince when it came to his marital dispute and were virtual strangers to the Princess of Wales. There is equally little evidence that she recognised the impact that the king's precarious state of health might have on her own way of life. Caroline was as different to the ladies of the House of Hanover as it was possible to be. She was a party animal, given to indiscretion in her anecdotes and wildness in her manner. Her dress could be unconventional and all the caution that Lord Malmesbury had counselled fifteen years earlier had been shoved aside in the pursuit of liaisons with an ever-widening, often embarrassed social circle. What she had certainly reckoned without was the fact that her husband's loathing of her had not dimmed. He would act quickly to exert his authority when he was appointed Regent.

George had been Prince Regent for barely two months when he made his move and forbade 15-year-old Charlotte from attending any social engagement convened by her mother. Caroline wasn't so clueless that she thought she might be a part of the celebrations her husband was planning, but their opulence no doubt took even her by surprise. She would very likely also have been surprised to discover that invitations from the estranged wife of the Prince Regent were not half so attractive as invitations from the estranged wife of the Prince of Wales. With George's new role, Caroline's days of flirtatious gatherings and political dinners came to an end. There were precious few movers and shakers who would throw their lot in with her now it was her husband who ruled in his father's stead. All of her new, adoring Whig friends flounced back to the company of the prince in the hope of winning him over to their cause, and Caroline had long since burned her Tory bridges.

---

107. Bickley, Francis (ed.) (1928). *The Diaries of Sylvester Douglas (Lord Glenbervie), Vol II*. London: Constable & Co, p.87.

As the new regime took hold, Caroline's once-crowded Kensington Palace apartments became quiet and their occupant grew bored. Tired of hearing the echoes of parties and gatherings that she was not invited to, Caroline returned to Montague House. She had lived the life she had longed for, she had been loved by the public and lauded as the hostess of innumerable parties, so the silence that now engulfed her was deafening. Yet in the Palace of Westminster, things were anything but quiet.

> "Yesterday afternoon, at about a quarter past five, as Mr. Perceval was entering the Lobby of the House of Commons, he was shot by a person of the name of Bellingham, who had placed himself for that purpose at the side of the door leading from the stone staircase. [...] Immediately on receiving the ball, which entered the left breast, he staggered and fell. [...] The only words he uttered were, "Oh! I am murdered," and the latter was inarticulate, the sound dying between his lips."[108]

When Spencer Perceval was shot by John Bellingham on 11 May 1812, the moment was significant in more ways than one. To date he remains the only British prime minister to have died at the hands of an assassin and his death marked the passing of an era, as the old Georgian order, typified by Perceval's traditional powdered wig and breeches - by 1812 long out of style - gave way to the new. The old king was hidden away at Windsor and as the Prince Regent glittered, a new government would rise too. At the head of the incoming administration was Lord Liverpool, who had no sympathy for the Princess of Wales. Liverpool would become forever associated with hardline government, but his name was a long way down the Regent's list of replacements for Perceval. In the event, he would become the longest serving prime minister of the nineteenth century.

The Prince Regent was quick to capitalise on the change of regime and sought the support of Lord Liverpool for new measures aimed at governing Princess Charlotte and further restricting her relationship with her mother. Under the new rules, Caroline was informed by the Lord Chancellor that, "The Princess Charlotte of Wales should at present

---

108. *Morning Chronicle.* 12 May 1812; issue 13420.

reside at Windsor; and that The Princess Charlotte, for the purpose of waiting upon Your Royal Highness at Kensington, should come from London once a fortnight."[109] This uncompromising new system left Prinny satisfied that his teenage daughter would be brought up according to his wishes, with as little influence from her wayward mother as possible.

If George had expected Caroline to take it lying down, he was sorely mistaken. She was already bored, so these fresh restrictions gave her something to rail against. Though Spencer Perceval no longer stood at her back, Caroline gained a new ally in the fiercely ambitious Whig politician, Henry Brougham. He had no personal liking for Caroline, but the two shared a mutual friend in her attendant, Lady Charlotte Lindsay, and in the ongoing war of attrition between the prince and princess, Brougham recognised an opportunity for advancement. He would become Caroline's adviser, for better or worse, until the end of her life.

When the Prince Regent abandoned his Whig friends in favour of the Tories, he put himself in direct opposition to his daughter as well as his former friends. Charlotte had inherited her parents' shared sense of theatre and she demonstrated it at the opera, where she blew flamboyant kisses towards senior Whig, Earl Grey, sending a clear signal that she was a child no longer. As her daughter grew into a woman, Caroline's horizons began to widen too. With everything settled on the continent, it was time to travel.

The Regent's Valentine

Charlotte and Caroline's relationship had been put under lifelong pressure by the Prince Regent. When her daughter was young Caroline had relied on friends in the royal nursery to facilitate secret visits, but once she lost the favour of the king and George tightened his restrictions, the opportunities for stolen moments became few and far between. Up until this point, Charlotte had more or less toed the line, but when she stood up in her opera box and blew kisses in the direction of Earl Grey, she was done with being a good girl. She and her mother wanted more

---

109. Georgian Papers Online (http://gpp.rct.uk, July 2020). RA GEO/ MAIN/49678-49679 Letter from Lord Eldon, Lord Chancellor, to Caroline, Princess of Wales, 17 June 1812.

than their appointed fortnightly audiences, and Brougham was just the man to make that happen.

Yet whilst Caroline and her Whig friends were selling the public image of a conscientious and wronged mother, behind the scenes, the lady was almost as scandalous as her opponents claimed. Though her meetings with Charlotte were supposedly limited, she stole additional time wherever possible and during one of their meetings, Charlotte confessed that she had fallen for Captain Charles Hesse, rumoured by some to be the illegitimate son of her uncle, the Duke of York. There was no hope of Charlotte being allowed to marry Hesse, but Caroline gave the burgeoning romance her full support. She passed notes between the princess and the soldier, helped to arrange clandestine meetings and even locked the couple in her bedroom together, no doubt hoping to speed the courtship along. When the Regent discovered what had been going on, he went through the roof. Charlotte's attendants were fired and replaced by handpicked appointees headed by Charlotte's new governess, Lady Leeds. She was unquestionably loyal to the Prince Regent and under her watchful eye the chances of secret meetings with anybody were nil. This still wasn't enough for George, who was determined to put a stop to his daughter's flirtations once and for all. As her access to Charlotte tightened even further, Caroline turned to her advisors for help. She needed to make her complaints known, and she needed to do it as loudly as possible.

Brougham wrote a heartfelt letter from the princess to her husband that *somehow* found its way into the public arena, reigniting the smouldering debate about the discord that had engulfed the royal family. The infamous letter was even read out on the floor of the House of Commons and when it appeared in the press in February 1813, it became known as *The Regent's Valentine*. To the horror of the royal family, it was the only topic of conversation among the gossiping classes of England.

> "I presume, Sir, to represent to your Royal Highness, that the separation, which every succeeding month is making wider, of the mother and the daughter, is equally injurious to my character and to her education. I say nothing of the deep wounds which so cruel an arrangement inflicts upon my feelings, although I would fain hope that few persons will be found of a disposition to think lightly of these. To see myself

cut off from one of the very few domestic enjoyments left me - certainly the only one upon which I set any value, the society of my child - involves me in such misery, as I well know your Royal Highness could never inflict upon me if you were aware of its bitterness. Our intercourse has been gradually diminished. A single interview weekly seemed sufficiently hard allowance for a mother's affections - That, however, was reduced to our meeting once a fortnight; and I now learn that even this most rigorous interdiction is to be still more rigidly enforced.

But while I do not venture to intrude my feelings as a mother upon your Royal Highness's notice, I must be allowed to say, that in the eyes of an observing and jealous world, this separation of a daughter from her mother will only admit of one construction - a construction fatal to the mother's reputation. Your Royal Highness will also pardon me for adding, that there is no less inconsistency than injustice in this treatment. He who dares advise your Royal Highness to overlook the evidence of my innocence, and disregard the sentence of complete acquittal which it produced - or is wicked and false enough still to whisper suspicions in your ear, betrays his duty to you, Sir, to your daughter, and to your people, if he counsels you to permit a day to pass without a further investigation of my conduct. I know that no such calumniator will venture to recommend a measure which must speedily end in his utter confusion. Then let me implore you to reflect on the situation in which I am placed; without the shadow of a charge against me - without even an accuser - after an enquiry that led to my ample vindication - yet treated as if I were still more culpable than the perjuries of my suborned traducers represented me, and held up to the world as a mother who may not enjoy the society of her only child.

[...]

Is it possible, Sir, that any one can have attempted to persuade your Royal Highness, that her character will not be injured by the perpetual violence offered to her strongest affections - the studied care taken to estrange her from my society, and even to interrupt all communication between us? That her love to me, with whom, by his Majesty's wise and gracious arrangements, she passed the years of her infancy and childhood, never can be extinguished, I well know, and the knowledge of it forms the greatest blessing of my existence.

[…]

The plan of excluding my daughter from all intercourse with the world, appears to my humble judgment peculiarly unfortunate. She who is destined to be the sovereign of this great country, enjoys none of those advantages of society which are deemed necessary for imparting a knowledge of mankind to persons who have infinitely less occasion to learn that important lesson: and it may so happen, by a chance which I trust is very remote, that she should be called upon to exercise the powers of the crown, with an experience of the world more confined than that of the most private individual. To the extraordinary talents with which she is blessed, and which accompany a disposition so singularly amiable, frank, and decided, I willingly trust much; but beyond a certain point the greatest natural endowments cannot struggle against the disadvantages of circumstances and situation. It is my earnest prayer, for her own sake as well as her country's, that your Royal Highness may be induced to pause before this point be reached.

[…]

The pain with which I have at length formed the resolution of addressing myself to your Royal Highness is such as &c. should in vain attempt to express. If I could adequately describe it, you might be enabled, Sir, to estimate the strength of the motives which have made me submit to it. They are the most powerful feelings of affection, and the deepest impressions of duty towards your Royal Highness, my beloved child, and the country, which I devotedly hope she may be preserved to govern, and to shew by a new example the liberal affection of a free and generous people to a virtuous and constitutional monarch."

The letter hit the Prince Regent like a hand grenade. Even Jane Austen weighed in, telling her close friend Martha Lloyd, "I suppose all the World is sitting in Judgement upon the Princess of Wales's Letter. Poor woman, I shall support her as long as I can, because she *is* a Woman, & because I hate her Husband – but I can hardly forgive her for calling herself "attached & affectionate" to a Man whom she must detest – & the intimacy said to subsist between her & Lady Oxford is bad – I do not know what to do about it; but if I must give up the Princess, I am resolved at least always to think that she would have been respectable, if the Prince had behaved only tolerably by her at first." The Prince Regent was more Wickham than Darcy in Austen's eyes.

As soon as the letter was published in the *Morning Chronicle*, the prince decided that Charlotte would not be permitted to see her mother as previously agreed. At his urging, Parliament dredged up the Delicate Investigation all over again in the hope of using it against Caroline, but it proved to be a fateful move. The public was outraged at what they regarded as a second unfair trial for the princess and even worse, those copies of *The Book* that had escaped the bonfire begat new editions that were selling at a rate of knots. Caroline's supporters had never been louder and all she had to do was sit tight and let it unfold around her.

When the Duchess of Brunswick died on 23 March 1813, sympathy for the Princess of Wales reached an all-time high. In Brougham she had found her champion. Driven by his own disdain for the Prince Regent, he would steer her cause through the stormy waters yet to come.

A Royal Wedding

Caroline had the support of the majority of the public, but that did nothing to change her husband's mind when it came to their daughter and he certainly wasn't about to consult her on matters of marriage. Though his arranged union with Caroline had been disastrous, that didn't mean that he was about to let Charlotte choose her own husband. Instead, as his daughter approached her eighteenth birthday, Prinny turned his attention to the serious business of finding her a bridegroom.

With no input from his wife, George chose Prince William of Orange to fill the vacancy. He brushed aside his daughter's dissent and in 1814, signed the marriage contracts that guaranteed the match. Perhaps the Regent had expected Charlotte to take his decision lying down, but she did anything but. When he told her that she was to be moved to the secluded Cranbourne Lodge at Windsor, it was the final straw. Charlotte fled from her father and dashed into the London streets. She leapt into a cab and headed straight for her mother's home.

Though Caroline would have loved to have Charlotte with her, this impromptu change of address could only end in tears. On behalf of the Princess of Wales, Lord Brougham and the Duke of York explained to Charlotte that she couldn't simply choose to abandon her father in favour of her mother. If she did so, the consequences would be visited upon Caroline, not Charlotte, and could result in legal proceedings. Charlotte grudgingly agreed to go home, but not until Caroline had promised to throw her considerable public relations weight behind the breaking of her engagement to the Prince of Orange. If Charlotte was to be married, she was determined that it would be to the handsome and eligible Prince Leopold of Saxe-Coburg-Saalfeld, who she had met at a party in London.

Armed with Brougham's formidable eye for PR, the newspapers that supported the princess raised concerns about her fate should she marry into the House of Orange. Would she be allowed to stay in England, they asked, or might she be spirited away to the continent? The Prince Regent knew exactly what Caroline and Charlotte were up to and dug his heels in. Whatever the Whigs and the press said, he had promised his daughter to Orange and nothing would make him change his mind. Nothing except Charlotte's masterplan. She agreed to the marriage only on condition that her mother be allowed unrestricted access to her marital home, something that she knew Prince William of Orange could never agree to if he wanted to keep the Regent on side. When Orange said no, it gave Charlotte exactly what she wanted. She couldn't marry a man who intended to treat her mother like a lesser citizen, she declared, and if her fiancé was willing to do that, then how could he ever be the loving husband she was hoping for?

The Prince Regent was outmanoeuvred. He called off the wedding and agreed to meet Prince Leopold, to ascertain if he was a suitable husband for his daughter. Happily, the two men got on like old friends and Princess Charlotte of Wales was finally betrothed to the man she wanted. The couple were devoted to one another, but their marriage would be cut tragically short.

But the battles had wounded Caroline. When she was excluded from celebrations held in honour of a joint visit by the King of Prussia and the Russian Tsar in the summer of 1814, it was the final blow. The grand occasion was intended to celebrate the abdication of Napoleon and the restoration of order in Europe, and Caroline fully expected to play a part, especially since she was related to both of the visiting monarchs. When Queen Charlotte told her that her presence would not be required, Caroline was shaken. She took up her pen and issued a thinly-veiled threat to the queen.

> "Your Majesty is well acquainted with the affectionate regard with which the King was so kind as to honour me up to the period of his Majesty's indisposition, which no one of his Majesty's subjects has so much cause to lament as myself, and that his majesty was graciously pleased to bestow upon me the most unequivocal and gratifying proof of his attachment and approbation by his public reception of me at his Court, at a season of severe and unmerited affliction, when his protection was most necessary to me, where I have since uninterruptedly paid my respects to your Majesty.
>
> [...]
>
> I beseech your Majesty to do me an act of justice, to which, in the present circumstances, your Majesty is the only person competent, by acquainting those illustrious personages with the motives of personal consideration towards your Majesty which alone induce me to abstain from the exercise of my right to appear before your Majesty; and that I do now, as I have done at all times, defy the malice of my enemies to fix upon me the shadow of any one imputation which could render me unworthy of their society or regard.
>
> Your Majesty will, I am sure, not be displeased that I should relieve myself from a suspicion of disrespect towards your Majesty, by making public the cause of my absence from Court at a time when the duties of my station would otherwise peculiarly demand my attendance."[110]

---

110. Brougham, Henry (1871). *The Life and Times of Henry, Lord Brougham, Vol II*. Edinburgh: William Blackwood and Sons, pp.218-220.

It was an audacious ultimatum. If Caroline was excluded from the celebrations, she warned that the public would want to know why. To be more specific, *her* public would want to know, and she would be happy to tell them. The queen didn't relent, and Caroline was dealt a second blow when neither the tsar nor the king made any effort to see her during the visit. Caroline needed a change and with her daughter about to marry a man she loved and her horizons in England shrinking again, she began to dream of different shores.

When Charlotte found out that her mother was making plans to travel, she was heartbroken. Yet Caroline had no stomach for the battle in England anymore, worn down by years of struggle against her estranged husband and his family. She wrote a last letter to Lord Liverpool in which she set out her many complaints, but it was little more than a paper exercise. The Prince Regent would certainly not stand in Caroline's way if she wanted to leave. With her daughter soon to be married and starting out on her own life, the time had come to move on. When Caroline told Lady Charlotte Campbell Bury that, "I rejoice in the thought of so soon being far off from all of them," she meant it.

Parliament voted to grant Caroline an annual income of £50,000 but she played the PR game again and chose to take only £35,000. In a last nod of thanks to her attendants, she guaranteed her domestic staff board and wages for a maximum of one year, or until they found a new job, whichever came first. To those who had been in her loyal service for the longest periods, lifelong annuities were granted.

Caroline and Charlotte said their tearful goodbyes at Connaught House in July 1814, then the Princess of Wales travelled to Worthing with Edwardine Kent and William Austin, who had once been the cause of so much trouble. Though William remained at Caroline's side until her death, Edwardine was married off in short order upon their arrival in Brunswick. She had known the groom for less than a day, and even she didn't quite understand why Caroline had married her off in such haste.

The party sailed for the continent on the *Jason* on 8 August, under the experienced hand of Captain James King. As she waved goodbye to her adopted land, the Princess of Wales was ready to embark on the most scandalous chapter of her already eventful life. With her Caroline carried her insurance policy: a large box containing her tell-all memoirs. "There are some men, we suspect, as well as woman," wrote the *Examiner*, "who would give their ears (and no small gift, either!) to know what is inside of this mysterious receptacle."[111] And chief among them was the Prince Regent himself.

Whooping It Up

Joined by a party of her favourite friends and retainers including the ever-loyal Lady Charlotte Lindsay, Caroline of Brunswick, by then 46, greeted the rough seas through which *Jason* ploughed with a smile that even seasickness couldn't dim. There was music and dancing and a salute was fired in honour of the Prince Regent, to whom Caroline drank a toast. Brunswick was free from French occupation and she could not wait to be back there after 19 long years in England; where better to make her next new start than the place where it had all begun? Caroline's travelling party included physician Sir Henry Holland and classicist Sir William Gell, and at one point she was even joined by Captain Charles Hesse, whom you may recall she had once locked in the royal bedchamber with Princess Charlotte of Wales. What they had all reckoned without was being made to dress in tabards of Caroline's own design, which captured a certain Renaissance fair version of medieval pageantry. It was all very Caroline.

When she arrived in Brunswick Caroline was ecstatic to be home, but once the honeymoon period had passed, she discovered that very little had changed despite the years of tumult since her departure. She was in her homeland less than a week before she decided to head for the far more entertaining shores of Italy. After experiencing Brunswick for himself, Holland commented that, "some of [Caroline's] breaches of decorum might almost be regarded as a retaliation on the part of the Princess for those dull formalities of the Brunswick Palace in her youth."[112] How right he was.

As the procession travelled south towards Italy, travelling companions came and went, and the learned men of the party shook their heads in disbelief at their patron's lack of scholarly interest. Caroline wasn't there to enjoy the classical delights of the continent though, she was there to have fun. She danced on the shores of Europe with the most fashionable

---

111. *Examiner*, 14 August 1814; issue 346.
112. Holland, Henry (1872). *Recollections of Past Life*. New York: D. Appleton and Company, p.117.

friends she could find, free of her husband's spies and her thin-lipped attendants. The party tarried in France for a week then headed into Switzerland and a happy interlude with Marie Louise, the wife of the exiled Napoleon. The gentle company of the former empress was a marked contrast to the scenes in Geneva, where Caroline's entourage had to scour the city for people willing to attend a ball in honour of the notorious new arrival. Caroline loved her continental life, where she could dress as flamboyantly as she wished, pencilling in thick black eyebrows and donning showy wigs that did little to flatter her, but it wasn't always to the taste of her friends. When she attended the Genevan ball in her most outrageous costume to date, Lady Charlotte Campbell Bury was determined to get an invitation. "I really think she must be mad," she wrote, "And I should like to see her for an instant, to assure myself she is the same woman whom we remember – so agreeable and so well behaved, but a few years back at Kensington."[113]

But Caroline was done with being well behaved. When Lady Charlotte *did* see her, it was enough to send her scurrying for the exit.

> "What was my horror when I beheld the poor Princess enter, dressed *en Venus*, or rather not dressed, further than the waist. I was, as she used to say herself, "all over shock." A more injudicious choice of costume could not be adopted and when she began to waltz, the *terrae motus* was dreadful. [...] As I really entertained a friendship for the Princess, I was unfeignedly grieved to see her make herself so utterly ridiculous."[114]

Caroline's singular manner chased away some of her friends, including Lady Charlotte, but if she noticed, she didn't care. What Caroline really wanted was a companion, and the man of her dreams was about to stride into her life, "six feet high, a magnificent head of black hair, pale complexion, mustachios which reach from here to London."[115] The owner

---

113. Bury, Lady Charlotte Campbell (1838). *Diary Illustrative of the Times of George the Fourth: Vol I*. London: Henry Colburn, pp.228-229.

114. Bury, Lady Charlotte Campbell (1838). *Diary Illustrative of the Times of George the Fourth: Vol II*. London: Henry Colburn, p.59.

115. Ibid., p.195.

of that moustache was a man named Bartolomeo Pergami, and he was to play a leading role in the final years of Caroline of Brunswick.

Caroline travelled over the Alps into Italy, where she rested a short time before heading down to Milan. Here the party came to rest and Caroline put the word out that she was looking for a native Italian speaker to join her group and act as both attendant and guide. Interested candidates were to call at the Palazzo Borromeo for an audience with the Princess of Wales.

As strapping as he was handsome, former soldier Bartolomeo Pergami knew that it was the job for him. He dressed in his finest Hussar uniform and headed for the palazzo, where he found a lady trying to free her elaborate dress from where it had become entangled in the furniture. He gallantly dropped to one knee and freed the entrapped lady, then asked if she knew where he might find the Princess of Wales. In fact, the damsel in distress was no other than Princess Caroline, and she hired him on the spot. It was an unorthodox start to an enduring relationship.

From that moment on, 30-year-old Pergami became Caroline's favourite. Wherever she went, he was there, whether to an audience with the Pope or Prince Lucien Bonaparte. Prinny had hoped that his wife's decision to quit England would be the last he heard of her, instead it was quite the opposite. Reports of her escapades and happy new situation flooded in, but George saw a silver lining. The more openly Caroline partied, the more likely it was that she would give him the ammunition he needed for his divorce. With that in mind he established a network of spies who would report on Caroline's every move. At the top of the tree sat Baron Friedrich Ompteda, a former Hanoverian retainer who would join Caroline's party in Italy and become the Regent's eyes and ears.

Ompteda arrived in time to join the group during a visit to King Joachim Murat, Napoleon's brother-in-law. He swiftly set about fulfilling his mission, sending word to London of Caroline's happy domestic set up. Pergami was always at her side and when he and Caroline retired to bed, they took adjoining or even shared rooms, whilst they slept together beneath a tent on the deck of a boat when travelling by sea. The implication was clear: Pergami was far more than a servant. For a time Ompteda was thrown by rumours that Pergami, already a husband and father, had been rendered impotent by battle injuries, but he soon discovered that wasn't the case. If gossip was to be believed, Pergami was able to perform like a trouper. And so was his employer.

"The Princess danced [with] indescribable abandon. Her dress consisted of a single embroidered garment, fastened beneath the bosom, without the shadow of a corset and without sleeves. A shawl floating in the air did not succeed in making the costume decent even to the eyes of the Roman ladies, who were themselves not particularly scrupulous in the matter of dress."[116]

And so it went on. When Caroline heard rumours that George was looking into divorce she briefly considered returning to England, but the lure of Italy was too strong. By the time the winter of 1815 had passed she had long since abandoned any plans to head for London. Besides, when William Gell's ill health led to his resignation in Naples, Caroline was able to promote Pergami into the role of chamberlain, warmed by "his unlimited zeal for her person"[117]. Now they could be closer than ever.

Whenever Caroline rode out in her royal liveried coach, dressed in diaphanous gowns or even short skirts that flashed her legs, her whiskered soldier on her arm and William Austin at her side, she made her husband a laughing stock. Whether she was doing it on purpose was debateable, but it was certainly a happy by-product of her new life of leisure. Her English attendants did their best to make up for the dignity that she was perceived to lack, but the Princess of Wales was undoubtedly the star of the show.

Though Ompteda could observe to a point, as a Hanoverian newcomer to the entourage he wasn't anywhere near Caroline's inner circle. What he needed was a spy on the inside. He found one in stablemaster Maurice Credé, who was happy to delve into the princess' dirty linens.

As Caroline settled in her new home at the Villa d'Este on the shores of Lake Como, she learned that her brother, Frederick William, had been killed in battle. She received the news with stoicism and consoled herself with the presence of Pergami's young daughter, Victorine, and his mother, who cared for the little girl. His wife, quite understandably, preferred to remain in Milan with the couple's other child. Whilst Caroline mourned though, she little suspected that Credé had become her husband's spy. Credé furnished Ompteda with the most intimate comings and goings

---

116. Chapman, Frederic (trans.) (1897). *A Queen of Indiscretions, The Tragedy of Caroline of Brunswick, Queen of England*. London: John Lane, pp.55–56.
117. *Morning Post*. 30 August 1817; issue 14542.

of the household, yet to Ompteda's disappointment and the Regent's chagrin, the most intimate comings and goings were nothing to write home about. Ompteda kept up his surveillance as Caroline d'Este, as she occasionally signed herself, visited Tunis, where she purchased two lionesses as a gift for the Emperor of Austria. From there she travelled to Sicily then went on to Jerusalem and Turkey, where she dazzled in pantaloons and a turban, her travels keeping her entertained whilst renovations were carried out at the Villa d'Este. Yet on the personal side, there was nothing to report but rumour. If things continued like this, the Prince Regent might never get his divorce.

It wasn't until the princess returned to her palatial home on Lake Como that scandal erupted. Since Credé had been recruited by Pergami, she had assumed he was loyal, so when his subterfuge was discovered, it was devastating. He immediately pointed the finger at Ompteda, who had become a familiar face at the Villa d'Este, and the Regent's spies were banished from Caroline's household. Between them they had done some unexpected damage to the princess' spirits and reputation. Caroline's unconventional clothing and behaviour had already won her plenty of detractors and now the idea that she was doing something *worth* spying on further added to her woes. Openly cavorting with the chamberlain to whom she had awarded the ranks of Baron of Francina and Knight of Malta, did her no favours whatsoever.

Caroline could never sit still for long. Though the villa and its renovations had seriously depleted her coffers, she was soon off on her travels again, but this time she found that the most illustrious invitations no longer came her way. The indisposition of George III was well known amongst the ruling houses of Europe and it was whispered that he would not live long, meaning that the Prince Regent would soon reign as George IV. When that happened, a good relationship with the new monarch would be worth far more than a night spent partying with his estranged wife. Prinny knew it too and with the help of the Milan Commission, he intended to be rid of her once and for all.

The Milan Commission

Caroline had spent a fortune on the Villa d'Este, but by the summer of 1817 the house was on the market. She settled instead at Pesaro, where she and Pergami established a happy family household with

Caroline's home, the Villa Caprile, and she asked him what news he was carrying in his black-bordered message. When he told her that it was a report of her only child's death, the shocked princess fainted.

With Caroline shattered by grief, Prinny drove the knife in. Though Ompteda had no smoking gun, George had heard plenty of rumours from Italy of shared rooms and carriages, of rumpled bedsheets and baths big enough for two, and he was furious. Most sickening of all was the knowledge that Caroline was happy in her new life with Pergami, and her husband was determined to destroy that idyll. Queen Charlotte's death in 1818 meant that there was no longer anyone in the prince's life who could calm his worst excesses and without his mother, George was entirely ungoverned. His first move was to step up the Milan Commission, which was charged with cataloguing the intelligence gathered by his spies in Europe. Their evidence was stored in a notorious green bag, and the prince hoped that it would be enough to finally get him the divorce he longed for.

Brougham observed all of this with his usual watchfulness, ready to advise Caroline when the moment came. He wasn't driven to her defence by his belief in her innocence though, but by how useful she might prove to him and the Whigs in the future. By championing Caroline, who was the darling of the people, Brougham hoped for nothing less than the eventual embarrassment and downfall of the oppressive Tory government. In the plight of Caroline of Brunswick, he foresaw the fall of the Liverpool administration.

It looked as though things might go his way too, for the Milan Commission was not going as smoothly as George anticipated and the politicians who sifted through the evidence found little more than conjecture and hearsay. If anything, they feared that any move towards divorce might only strengthen public sympathy for the princess, especially coming so hot on the heels of Charlotte's death. The Prince Regent promised them compelling evidence and his spies in Italy set to work corralling witnesses who would be willing to spill the beans on the happy household in Pesaro. It was a lengthy and difficult task.

Gossip spread fast across Italy and soon Caroline had heard of her husband's efforts against her. Still grieving, she held her silence until Brougham's brother, James, arrived in Pesaro in 1819 for a summit at which Caroline's domestic and financial situations were the topics of conversation. Brougham found a comfortable and sociable household which was more domestic than grand, where visitors were welcome and there was little need to stand on ceremony. Pergami's mother and daughter lived openly with the couple and there was no doubt that the princess and Pergami were a couple. Brougham was impressed by Pergami though, who he found to be an intelligent, devoted, and solid sort of man. It seemed as if Caroline had at last found the kind of suitor that Malmesbury had imagined for her so long ago.

The finances of the Princess of Wales were less impressive than the character of her gentleman friend. She owed thousands to creditors in England and on the continent and as Brougham's visit drew to a close, the princess conceded that she would consent to a divorce if her husband made her an offer that she couldn't refuse. She was happy in Pesaro with Pergami and didn't want to come home to England if an arrangement could be reached. Brougham suggested a compromise in which Caroline would admit adultery and consent to a divorce in return for her royal title and an annual allowance of £50,000. Caroline refused point blank to admit to adultery and so began a stalemate that only a messy and embarrassing public battle would be able to break.

Mrs King

When George III died on 29 January 1820, the country was plunged into mourning. The Prince Regent succeeded to the throne as George IV and his estranged wife was his unwanted queen. Even the fact that she was in Italy in the arms of her Italian chamberlain wasn't enough to turn her supporters against her. By the time of the king's death, the Milan Commission had spent long months examining the evidence that had been laid before them and had decided, no doubt with some serious nudging from the Prince Regent, that there was enough evidence to bring charges of adultery. With the stakes higher than ever, Caroline set out for England and a final showdown.

Caroline's decision to come back to England went against everything the Brougham brothers had advised. They asked her to sit tight in Italy, promising that they would negotiate a formal separation which would guarantee Caroline an additional £15,000, whilst sparing her the potential embarrassment of the Milan Commission's evidence. Caroline was determined to have her moment, and she set out for England, sustained by the popular support that she knew awaited her. She had long enjoyed the support of the people, but now she added to that the loyalty of political radicals who hoped to use her as a rallying point against the established order.

The first indication that things might not go as Caroline had hoped came not from London, but from Rome. When Caroline arrived there as Queen of England she expected a full guard of honour and a papal audience, but she received neither. No sooner had she suffered that embarrassment than she heard that her husband had had her name stricken from the liturgy that called for heavenly blessings on the royal family. Queen Caroline was being written out of the picture. Her response was to hit back twice as hard. She courted her radical supporters and dismissed Brougham's desperate entreaties to stay in Europe without a second thought. The queen wanted her crown.

By the time Caroline and Pergami arrived in Saint-Omer, France, there was no going back. James Brougham met her there and urged her to go no further, but Caroline wouldn't hear of it. Brougham's promises that she would be recognised and treated as queen if she remained on foreign soil did nothing to dissuade her, nor did his warnings that she faced charges of adultery or treason if she returned to England. Caroline was intent on being crowned beside her husband and by the time she said goodbye to Pergami in Calais and sailed for her adopted land, there was nobody on earth who could talk her round.

Though Caroline would no doubt have preferred to have Pergami at her side when she returned to London, it would have been a recipe for disaster. Pergami's presence would only have further supported the claims of adultery and she fully expected to return to him once the sorry affair had been resolved. Instead, she would never see him again.

Caroline arrived in England on 5 June 1820, in the company of Sir Matthew Wood, Alderman of the City of London. They headed for the capital along roads crowded with her supporters. "She was everywhere received with the greatest enthusiasm," wrote Charles Greville. "Women waved pocket handkerchiefs, and men shouted wherever she passed."[120] Few voices were raised in support of the king, but his family stood at his shoulder. George's eldest sister, Charlotte, Dowager Queen of

---

120. Greville, Charles (1899). *A Journal of the Reign of King George IV, King William IV and Queen Victoria, Vol I*. London: Longmans, Green, and Co, p.29.

Württemberg, summed up the Hanoverian mood when she denounced "the very imprudent and ill-judged arrival of the Queen in England."[121] It was everything the king had dreaded.

Caroline took up residence in Brandenburg House, where she waited to hear of her husband's next move. Messages of support arrived by the sack load and the streets echoed with cries of solidarity for her. The new king had spent a lifetime making enemies, Caroline could simply sit back and make friends of his foes. As queen consort she requested an official residence and complained that no royal yacht had been dispatched to ferry her from Calais to England, but her position was muddied by the evidence contained in that green bag, especially allegations that she had committed treason when she slipped between the sheets with Pergami.

Henry Brougham spoke out on Caroline's behalf in Parliament, asking at what point she could expect her persecutors to rest. The debates raged on for days in the House of Commons and the mood on the streets was febrile. Crowds were gathering outside Brandenburg House in support of Caroline's cause and the king feared violence, but a compromise proved ever elusive. Every time a point was close to resolution, be it financial, practical or the matter of the liturgy, another reared up to take its place. The windows of Lady Hertford's home were smashed by opponents of the crown and with the mood blacker than ever before, the decision of the Milan Commission was handed down. Enough evidence existed to proceed against Caroline. She was about to face the biggest challenge of her life.

Pains and Penalties

The Pains and Penalties Bill was George IV's last chance to be rid of his wife and Caroline's last chance to cement her place in the hearts and minds of the people, as she had dreamed of doing since childhood. The bill was "An Act to deprive Her Majesty Caroline Amelia Elizabeth of the title, prerogatives, rights, privileges, and exemptions of Queen Consort of this Realm; and to dissolve the Marriage between His Majesty and the said Caroline Amelia Elizabeth." The House of Lords would decide

---

121. Georgian Papers Online (http://gpp.rct.uk, August 2020). RA GEO/MAIN/51819 Letter from Charlotte, Dowager Queen of Wurttemberg, to George IV, 16 June 1820.

whether the queen consort had committed adultery and if it decided that she had, her marriage would be over and her rank and privilege would be stripped from her. But Caroline didn't expect to lose. She came out fighting, with Henry Brougham, still determined to create his legacy and to bring down the Tory government, in her corner once more.

Fearing civil unrest as a peaceful but vast crowd gathered outside the Palace of Westminster, the House of Lords was prepared as though for battle. Rarely had there been more obvious evidence of the gulf between the peers and the people as there was then. Soldiers and constables patrolled the streets and encircled the Houses of Parliament to protect the arriving peers, whilst gunboats waited on the Thames, primed for trouble. The people who assembled at the barricades wore white cockades and waved white handkerchiefs in support of their queen, and they anxiously awaited her arrival. As Caroline's carriage carried her past Carlton House, cheers rang out for the public's favourite wronged woman, the princess who had been hitched to an oaf and betrayed time and time again. Under Brougham's guidance, Caroline penned an open letter to her husband that drove home the idea of the tormented wife with aplomb.

> "You have cast upon me every slur to which the female character is liable. Instead of loving, honouring, and cherishing me, [...] you have pursued me with hatred and scorn, and with all the means of destruction. You wrested from me my child, and with her my only comfort and consolation. You sent me sorrowing through the world, and even in my sorrows pursued me with unrelenting persecution. Having left me nothing but my innocence, you would now, by a mockery of justice, deprive me even of the reputation of possessing that. [...] If my life would have satisfied your Majesty, you should have had it on the sole condition of giving me a place in the same tomb with my child; but, since you would send me dishonored to the grave, I will resist the attempt with all the means that it shall please God to give me."

The letter set the tone for Caroline's defence and Solicitor General Sir John Copley was left to lead a prosecution that had no support in the vast majority of the country. It might be surprising, but whilst very

177

Victorine, surrounded by trusted servants and safely away from the prince's spies. As the princess was settling down, far away in England, Princess Charlotte was enjoying a happy domesticity all of her own. She had married Prince Leopold in May 1816 and in early 1817, the couple announced that Charlotte was pregnant. The succession of the crown was as good as assured. Caroline wrote to Charlotte to tell her that, 'I have gleaned so much real knowledge, and been gratified with such long-anticipated sights, that I feel well repaid for the trouble, and I shall be the more disposed hereafter to sit down contentedly wherever my destiny may fix me,'[118] and Charlotte no doubt felt much the same. It looked as though it was to be happy endings all round.

> "It is this day our melancholy duty to make known to our Readers, the demise of her Royal Highness the Princess CHARLOTTE. This young, beautiful, and interesting Princess survived the delivery of a still born child but a few hours."[119]

Princess Charlotte, Caroline's only child, delivered a stillborn boy on the evening of 5 November 1817. Exhausted by the traumatic labour, Charlotte died in the early hours of the following morning. Across the nation, people from every station of life reacted with stunned despair to the death of the 21-year-old princess, who had been more popular than her father could ever hope to be. Soon it seemed as though the only person who hadn't heard the reports was Caroline. Instead, she was waiting in Italy for news of her daughter's happy event, desperate to be a grandmother.

Reeling from the death of his beloved wife, Leopold was too shocked to write to his mother-in-law to tell her of the death of her only daughter. The Prince Regent, meanwhile, deliberately chose not to do so. Caroline was still anticipating good news when a messenger from the Regent passed through Pesaro en route to Rome. He stopped for refreshments at

---

118. Princess Charlotte of Wales and Caroline, Princess of Wales (1820). *Royal Correspondence, or, Letters between Her Late Royal Highness the Princess Charlotte, and Her Royal Mother, Queen Caroline.* London: Jones and Company, p.118.
119. *Morning Chronicle.* 7 November 1817; issue 15138.

few people actually believed that Caroline was innocent of adultery, nor did they hold it against her. Her apparently settled family life with Pergami was at odds with the reports of indecent dances and diaphanous costumes and it seemed as though the wildest thing the loving couple had done lately was adorn "their heads with the halves of a melon, as a resource against the piercing sun-beams"[122]. Hardly shocking by Georgian standards. In fact, the public rather liked the sound of their domestic idyll, and it was certainly preferable to the tumultuous love life and financial affairs of the debauched king.

When she appeared before the House of Lords, Caroline was the picture of cool composure. The scene was captured by Sir George Hayter in his immense canvas, *The Trial of Queen Caroline*, that shows the queen sitting calmly beside a dynamic and bewigged Brougham whilst the all-male members of the House of Lords decide her case. What the painting cannot capture is the noise of the crowd outside the chamber, which roared in support of the wronged queen.

As she sat placidly in the House of Lords, Caroline gave no indication that she fully appreciated the gravity of what was happening. She frequently nodded off or played card games in an anteroom, keen to get to the verdict and dispense with the troubling legalese. It wasn't that Caroline didn't care, it was simply that she liked to get things done. The trial began on 17 August 1820, when Attorney General Thomas Gifford summed up the evidence that Caroline and Pergami had unashamedly been adulterous lovers for half a decade. They slept in the same bedroom, dressed and undressed in front of one another and had shared baths, beds and even tents in scenes that Gifford told the House "must disgust every well-regulated mind." The newspapers lapped it up and the following week the headlines were united on one subject: the sex life of Caroline of Brunswick.

Yet there were few legal minds more able than Brougham. Whilst he told his friends privately that Caroline was less pure innocence, more "pure in-no-sense", when he took apart the witnesses for the prosecution there was not a flicker of doubt. He crushed those members of Caroline's household who had turned against her and systematically destroyed their statements, ably dismantling the prosecution case bit by bit. These were

---

122. *Lancaster Gazetter*. 7 October 1820.

her former servants, Brougham reminded the Lords, dishonourable and disloyal to a fault.

When the Lords heard testimony from witnesses who had peeped through keyholes or listened at doors, it simply made matters worse for the prosecution. Tales of stains on bedsheets were regarded as improper by the court of public opinion, whilst a coachman who claimed he had found the couple asleep in his carriage, Caroline's hand still tucked into Pergami's unfastened breeches, was scoffingly told that such a manoeuvre was a physical impossibility. Tellingly, one of the few witnesses who wasn't dismissed as a liar was an Englishman. Captain Thomas Briggs had been at the helm of *Leviathan*, on which Pergami and Caroline had explored the Mediterranean. Whilst his crew testified that the couple had shared a tent on the deck of the ship and had openly kissed and canoodled, Captain Briggs told a different story. He had seen nothing improper, he assured the Lords.

The Italian witnesses who came to speak against Caroline found themselves subject to abuse in the streets just as they were subject to Brougham's questioning in the chamber. He reduced their statements to nothing but backstairs gossip, casting doubt on their morality and honesty that was echoed in the press. Though loyalist publications such as *John Bull* went in hard on Caroline, they were the minority – she enjoyed a popular support that her husband could only dream of. Brougham reserved his particular disdain for Theodore Majocchi, once one of Caroline's most trusted servants and now the star witness for the prosecution. When he appeared in the dock, Caroline gasped his name and fled. Her opponents said it was the sign of a guilty conscience, but her supporters lamented her distress and lambasted her traitorous servant.

Majocchi had been personally recruited to Caroline's household by Pergami, but he became an enthusiastic witness for the prosecution. He had been able to recollect the smallest and seemingly most trivial details of tangled bedsheets or how many times he had found not one but two chamber pots in Caroline's bedroom, but faced with Brougham's intimidating interrogation, he crumbled. Each time Brougham challenged some piece of evidence, the whey-faced Majocchi replied nervously, "non mi ricordo" ("I don't remember"), which provided the trial with an unlikely catchphrase and haunted the unfortunate servant. Majocchi was nicknamed *Signor Non mi Ricordo* by the press, who delighted in his humiliation, and the line was screamed at him in the streets. It even inspired poems and ballads that mocked the Italian witnesses and accused them of accepting bribes to perjure themselves. Life became so difficult for Italian immigrants in London that some even wrote to the newspapers in an effort to show that, "not all Italians are alike, and that all have not suffered to be bribed by the gold of the enemies of the Queen of England"[123].

Whilst George IV still hoped that he might win the case against his wife, the scenes in the House of Lords suggested otherwise. Brougham's speech to the Lords was called by Greville, the "most magnificent display of argument and oratory that has been heard in years", and in it he promised to take no prisoners. Should he have to reveal secrets about the king in order to save the reputation of the queen, Brougham warned darkly, he would do so. He dismissed the witnesses as paid liars whose statements had been written by the prosecution and where there was muck to rake and throw at them, he was happy to fling it. "Save the country," he urged, "From the horror of this catastrophe – save yourselves from this situation – rescue that country, of which you are the ornament, but in which you could flourish no longer, when severed from the people, than the blossom when cut off from the root and the stem of the tree." By the time the defence and prosecution came to rest, things appeared to have gone very much Caroline's way.

The vote was held on 6 November 1820, the third anniversary of Princess Charlotte's death. One by one the peers rose to their feet and said *content* if they supported the bill, or *not content* if they opposed it. A win meant that the bill would move on to the House of Commons and divorce would be one step nearer, but a loss would be a messy and embarrassing defeat for the king. In the event an initial vote resulted in a majority of less than 30, which sent a shockwave through the king's camp. At the vote on 10 November, the Bill was passed by 108 votes to 99. It was a sure sign that it should go no further.

When Lord Liverpool rose to his feet in the House of Commons, he was ashen faced. He told the House that a decision had been taken not to proceed with the Bill in recognition of the division in the Lords and the tumultuous state of the country. Caroline had lost the vote, but in doing so she had somehow won the day.

---

123. *The Times*. 2 September 1820; issue 11028.

That night, London rang to the sound of cheers and breaking glass. The offices of newspapers who had supported the king were burned, whilst the homes of those who had opposed Caroline were ransacked. When the victorious queen attended a service of thanksgiving at St Paul's Cathedral at the end of November, tens of thousands of her loyal supporters turned out to greet her. It was likely the finest moment of a turbulent life.

An Injured Queen

As the cheers of Caroline's supporters and the embers of the bonfires died away in the capital, George IV reeled. Yet as her husband looked for someone to blame, Caroline was busy consolidating her position. She demanded that her name be restored to the liturgy and that her annuity be raised to a figure befitting a queen. She should have her own residence, she said, and she should be treated with the respect and deference due to the wife of the reigning sovereign. Yet Brougham had not succeeded in his own aims even as he had won the day for his client. The Liverpool government did not fall. Parliamentary reform was still a long way off, and Caroline was not the means by which it would be realised.

At Brandenburg House, Caroline focussed on the future. Now she had no more use of her radical sympathisers she abandoned them, determined instead to live the life that she believed a queen deserved. But it didn't all go her way. Although her annuity was increased to £50,000, her name remained absent from the liturgy and Caroline looked to her Whig friends for support. She was surprised to find that no one came running to her aid. With her aims now entirely personal and mostly centred around money and privilege, the politicians lost interest in their would-be patroness.

Caroline's focus now was on confirming her new rank and the key to that was the forthcoming coronation. As though her attendance was a forgone conclusion, Caroline wrote to the king asking him to provide her with an order of service, sufficiently ennobled attendants and even an idea of what he would like her to wear. Wisely, George didn't reply. Instead, he passed the letters on to Lord Liverpool and asked him to let Caroline know that, "the Queen can form no part of that ceremonial except in consequence of a distinct authority from the King; and that it is not his Majesty's intention under the present circumstances to give any such authority."[124] Simply put, Caroline was not welcome. She had long jested that "[George] will never be kink [sic]"[125], after a German fortune teller warned that she would never be queen. Only now did an alternative interpretation of that prophecy become painfully clear.

All that Liverpool's intervention achieved was to further incense Caroline and make her more determined than ever to be crowned. She wrote to the Archbishop of Canterbury and asked him to perform a coronation ceremony the day after the king's, but he regretfully informed her that it wouldn't be possible. What Caroline should have done at this point was to swallow her pride, take her victory, and go home to Pergami in Pesaro. Instead, she fatally misjudged the public mood and the affection of her subjects. The past few years had been punishing and the coming summer promised a new start. The coronation was going to be a national party and people wanted to enjoy it, whatever they thought of George IV. They'd had their fill of scandal and dissent, so any spectre at the feast would be far from welcome. Caroline seemed determined to make herself that spectre and despite the best efforts of Brougham to keep her away, she was set on being the star of the coronation.

At dawn on 19 July 1821, Caroline travelled to Westminster Abbey to attend the Coronation of her estranged husband. She told the doorkeeper, "Let me pass, I am your Queen," only to have the door slammed in her face. With the gentlemanly Lord Hood as her escort, Caroline went from door to door and every time, the response was the same: she wasn't welcome at the Abbey without a ticket. As the crowd that had once cheered her name began to jeer, Lord Hood offered his own ticket to Caroline. She turned it down and as she did, the doorkeepers sniggered at her predicament. Humiliated, Caroline fled for her carriage and returned to Brandenburg House. As Brougham so acutely recognised, "she flinched, for the first time in her life."[126]

124. Huish, Robert (1831). *Memoirs of George the Fourth: Vol II*. London: Thomas Kelly, p.310.

125. Stanhope, Lady Hester (1846). *Memoirs of the Lady Hester Stanhope, Vol I*. London: Henry Colburn, p.308.

126. Brougham, Henry (1871). *The Life and Times of Henry, Lord Brougham, Vol II*. Edinburgh: William Blackwood and Sons, p.422.

The End

As George IV partied long into the night, a subdued and teary Caroline hosted a small party of friends at Brandenburg House. She did her best to keep up appearances, but the humiliation she had been subjected to at Westminster Abbey laid her lower than ever before. On 30 July, Caroline made her last public appearance when she visited Drury Lane theatre, but when she returned home that evening she could barely stand. A team of doctors were summoned and they diagnosed Caroline with an obstruction of the bowel. Against their advice she opted to treat it with her own mixture of magnesium and laudanum, which she downed in huge quantities. Caroline feared that she had been poisoned but in fact, as she swallowed gulp after gulp of the potent cocktail, she was effectively poisoning herself.

Dr Matthew Baillie, a highly respected royal physician, came to the bedside of the stricken queen consort and advised solemnly that the prognosis was not good. His patient understood and drew up her last will and testament, in which William Austin was the main benefactor. Also contained in that document was her wish that she be buried in Brunswick and that her tomb be inscribed simply, "Here lies Caroline, the Injured Queen of England." At her final meeting with Brougham, Caroline told him, "I am much better dead, for I be tired of this life."[127] Soon afterwards, she slipped into unconsciousness.

> "Yesterday evening, at twenty-five minutes after ten o'clock, the QUEEN departed this life after a short but painful illness, at Brandenburgh [sic] House, at Hammersmith."[128]

Caroline of Brunswick died at 10.25 pm on 7 August 1821, aged 53. Those who saw her body claimed that Caroline had begun to decompose almost immediately upon her death. In accordance with her wishes, no visitors were allowed to pay their respects to her open coffin. Instead, she was placed in a sealed coffin with little delay.

As King George IV reluctantly ordered the minimum period of mourning for his late wife, Caroline's coffin set off through London

---

127. Ibid., p.423.
128. *The Morning Post*, 9 August 1821; issue 15725.

on the first stage of its route to Brunswick, accompanied by an armed escort. A huge crowd walked behind the late queen and unrest broke out, resulting in the death of two men. When the procession came to rest for the night at Colchester, Stephen Lushington, Caroline's executor, screwed an engraved plate onto the coffin which carried Caroline's desired epitaph of "Injured Queen." It was promptly removed before the coffin was loaded onto the boat for Brunswick.

Even in death Queen Caroline knew how to grab the headlines, and in her last act, she had once again proven that the public loved her still. The crowds who turned out to watch her solemn journey home didn't do so simply to gawp at the spectacle, but to mourn. The Injured Queen was loved to the end.

Afterword

Maria Fitzherbert and Caroline of Brunswick never met, but their lives were irrevocably intertwined thanks to the man that one certainly loved and one might have done, given the chance. Though George IV bestrides this book like a corseted Colossus, he was a supporting player in the lives of two women from very different worlds who, for a brief time, occupied a shared space of sorts.

Maria and Caroline deserve to be recognised as more than two in the long list of women who shared the bed of Byron's *Leviathan of the haut ton*. They were fascinating characters in their own right and their stories were part of the fabric of Georgian Britain. That Maria and Caroline came to prominence via George IV is undeniable, but there was so much more to them than Prinny. From the lot of a Catholic widow to that of a royal daughter, their stories offer us a glimpse into the lives of two very different women, who happened to share one undeserving husband.

Bibliography

Abbot, Charles, Lord Colchester. *The Diary and Correspondence of Charles Abbot, Lord Colchester: Vol I*. London: John Murray, 1861.

Adolphus, John (ed.). *A Correct, Full and Impartial Report, of the Trial of Her Majesty, Caroline, Queen Consort of Great Britain, Before the House of Peers*. London: Jones and Co, 1820.

Anonymous. *The Dublin Review Part 2*. London: Burns and Oates, 1854.

Anonymous. *The Edinburgh Review: Vol CXLIII*. Edinburgh: Longman, Green, Reader, and Dyer, 1876.

Anonymous. *The Important and Eventful Trial of Queen Caroline, Consort of George IV*. London: Geo Smeeton, 1820.

Anonymous (ed.). *Letters of his Royal Highness the Prince of Wales, and the Right Honourable William Pitt*. London: B McMillan, 1810.

Anonymous. *Nemesis, or a Letter to Alfred*. London: Privately published, 1789.

Anonymous. *The Universal Magazine of Knowledge and Pleasure, Vols 84-85*. London: Privately published, 1789.

Aspinall, Arthur (ed.). *The Correspondence of George, Prince of Wales, Vol I*. London: Cassell, 1963.

Aspinall, Arthur (ed.). *The Correspondence of George, Prince of Wales, Vol II*. London: Cassell, 1963.

Aspinall, Arthur (ed.). *The Correspondence of George, Prince of Wales, Vol III*. London: Cassell, 1965.

Aspinall, Arthur (ed.). *The Correspondence of George, Prince of Wales, Vol IV*. London: Cassell, 1965.

Aspinall, Arthur (ed.). *The Correspondence of George, Prince of Wales, Vol V*. London: Cassell, 1965.

Aspinall, Arthur (ed.). *The Correspondence of George, Prince of Wales, Vol VI*. London: Cassell, 1965.

Aspinall, Arthur. *The Later Correspondence of George III, Vol I*. Cambridge: Cambridge University Press, 1962.

Aspinall, Arthur. *The Later Correspondence of George III, Vol II.* Cambridge: Cambridge University Press, 1962.

Aspinall, Arthur. *The Later Correspondence of George III, Vol III.* Cambridge: Cambridge University Press, 1962.

Aspinall, Arthur. *The Later Correspondence of George III, Vol IV.* Cambridge: Cambridge University Press, 1962.

Aspinall, Arthur. *The Later Correspondence of George III, Vol V.* Cambridge: Cambridge University Press, 1962.

Aspinall, Arthur. *Letters of the Princess Charlotte 1811–1817.* London: Home and Van Thal, 1949.

Atkinson, Charles Milnes and Mitchell, John Edwin. *An Account of the Life and Principles of Sir Samuel Romilly.* London: Hobson & Son, 1920.

Beacock Fryer, Mary, Bousfield, Arthur and Toffoli, Garry. *Lives of the Princesses of Wales.* Toronto: Dundurn Press, 1983.

Bell, Robert. *The Life of the Rt. Hon. George Canning.* London: Harper, 1955.

Belsham, William. *Memoirs of the Reign of George III to the Session of Parliament Ending AD 1793, Vol III.* London: GG and J Robinson, 1801.

Bessborough, Earl of (ed.). *Georgiana: Extracts from the Correspondence of Georgiana, Duchess of Devonshire.* London: John Murray, 1955.

Bickley, Francis (ed.). *The Diaries of Sylvester Douglas (Lord Glenbervie), Vol I.* London: Constable & Co, 1928.

Bickley, Francis (ed.). *The Diaries of Sylvester Douglas (Lord Glenbervie), Vol II.* London: Constable & Co, 1928.

Black, Jeremy. *The Hanoverians: The History of a Dynasty.* London: Hambledon and London, 2007.

Brougham, Henry. *The Critical and Miscellaneous Writings of Henry Lord Brougham.* London: Lea & Blanchard, 1841.

Brougham, Henry. *The Life and Times of Henry, Lord Brougham, Vol II.* Edinburgh: William Blackwood and Sons, 1871.

Brougham, Henry. *Opinions of Lord Brougham on Politics, Theology, Law, Science, Education, Literature, &c. &c. Vol* I. Philadelphia: Lea & Blanchard, 1839.

Browning, Oscar. *The Political Memoranda of Francis Fifth Duke of Leeds.* London: The Camden Society, 1884.

Buckingham and Chandos, Duke of. *Memoirs of the Court of George IV, Vol I.* London: Hurst and Blackett, 1859.

Bury, Lady Charlotte Campbell. *Diary Illustrative of the Times of George the Fourth: Vol I.* London: Henry Colburn, 1838.

Bury, Lady Charlotte Campbell. *Diary Illustrative of the Times of George the Fourth: Vol II*. London: Carey, Lea and Blanchard, 1838.

Chapman, Frederic (trans.). *A Queen of Indiscretions, The Tragedy of Caroline of Brunswick, Queen of England*. London: John Lane, 1897.

Cobbett, William (ed.) (1813) *Cobbett's Political Register, Vol XXIII*. London: Richard Bagshaw, 1813.

Craig, William Marshall. *Memoir of Her Majesty Sophia Charlotte of Mecklenburg Strelitz, Queen of Great Britain*. Liverpool: Henry Fisher, 1818.

Croly, George. *The Life and Times of His Late Majesty, George the Fourth*. London: James Duncan, 1830.

Curzon, Catherine. *Kings of Georgian Britain*. Barnsley: Pen & Sword History, 2017.

Curzon, Catherine. *Queens of Georgian Britain*. Barnsley: Pen & Sword History, 2017.

Curzon, Catherine. *The Scandal of George III's Court*. Barnsley: Pen & Sword History, 2018.

David, Saul. *Prince of Pleasure*. New York: Grove Press, 2000.

Donne, Bodham W (ed.). *The Correspondence of King George the Third With Lord North from 1768 to 1783: Vol I*. London: John Murray, 1867.

Fitzgerald, Percy Hetherington. *The Life of George the Fourth*. London: Tinsley Brothers, 1881.

Fox, Charles James. *Speeches of the Right Honourable Charles James Fox in the House of Commons, Vol III*. London: Longman, Hurst, Orme, and Brown, 1815.

Fox, Charles James. *Speeches of the Right Honourable Charles James Fox, Vol V*. London: Longman, 1845.

Fraser, Flora. The *Unruly Queen: The Life of Queen Caroline*. Edinburgh: A&C Black, 2012.

Gore-Browne, Robert. *Chancellor Thurlow*. London: Hamilton, 1953.

Gray, Denis. *Spencer Perceval: The Evangelical Prime Minister, 1762–1812*. Manchester: Manchester University Press, 1963.

Greville, Charles. *A Journal of the Reign of King George IV, King William IV and Queen Victoria, Vol I*. London: Longmans, Green, and Co, 1899.

Hadlow, Janice. *The Strangest Family: The Private Lives of George III, Queen Charlotte and the Hanoverians*. London: William Collins, 2014.

Hamilton, Lady Anne. *Secret History of the Court of England*. London: William Henry Stevenson, 1832.

Hayward, A (ed.). *Diaries of a Lady of Quality from 1797 to 1844*. London: Longman, Green, Longman, Egberts & Green, 1864.

Hibbert, Christopher. *George III: A Personal History*. London: Viking, 1998.

Hibbert, Christopher. *George IV*. London: Penguin, 1998.

Hibbert, Christopher. *George IV: Prince of Wales*. New York: Harper & Rowe, 1974.

Holland, Lord. *Memoirs of the Whig Party During My Time: Vol II*. London: Longman, Brown, Green and Longmans, 1854.

Holland, Henry. *Recollections of Past Life*. New York: D. Appleton and Company, 1872.

Holt, Edward. *The Public and Domestic Life of His Late Most Gracious Majesty, George the Third, Vol I*. London: Sherwood, Neely and Jones, 1820.

Holt, Edward. *The Public and Domestic Life of His Late Most Gracious Majesty, George the Third, Vol II*. London: Sherwood, Neely and Jones, 1820.

Horne Tooke, John. *A Letter to a Friend on the Reported Marriage of His Royal Highness the Prince of Wales*. Dublin: P. Byrne, 1787.

Huish, Robert. *Memoirs of George the Fourth: Vol I*. London: Thomas Kelly, 1830.

Huish, Robert. *Memoirs of George the Fourth: Vol II*. London: Thomas Kelly, 1831.

Huish, Robert. *Memoirs of Her Late Majesty Caroline, Queen of Great Britain, Vol I*. London: T Kelly, 1821.

Irvine, Valerie. *The King's Wife: George IV and Mrs Fitzherbert*. London: Hambledon, 2007.

Jefferys, Nathaniel. *A Review of the Conduct of His Royal Highness the Prince of Wales*. London: Privately published, 1806.

Jenkinson, Robert Banks. *The Speech of the Right Hon. The Earl of Liverpool in the House of Lords*. London: John Hatchard and Son, 1820.

Jesse, John Heneage. *Memoirs of the Life and Reign of King George the Third, Vol II*. London: Tinsley Brothers, 1867.

Jesse, John Heneage. *Memoirs of the Life and Reign of King George the Third, Vol III*. London: Richard Bentley, 1843.

Klercker, Cecilia (ed.). *Hedvig Elisabeth Charlottas Dagbok.* Stockholm: PA Norstedt & Söners, 1927.

Langdale, Charles. *Memoirs of Mrs. Fitzherbert.* London: Richard Bentley, 1856.

Laquer, Thomas W. The Queen Caroline Affair: Politics as Art in the Reign of George IV. *The Journal of Modern History.* Vol. 54, No. 3 (Sep., 1982), pp. 417–466

Lehman, H Eugene. *Lives of England's Reigning and Consort Queens.* Bloomington: AuthorHouse, 2011.

Leslie, Anita. *Mrs Fitzherbert: A Biography.* York: Scribner, 1960.

Leslie, Shane. *The Letters of Mrs. Fitzherbert.* London: Burns Oates, 1940.

Leslie, Shane. *Mrs. Fitzherbert: A Life Chiefly from Unpublished Sources.* New York: Benziger Brothers, 1939.

Littell, E. *Littell's Living Age, Volume IV.* Boston: TH Carter and Company, 1845.

Lloyd, Hannibal Evans. *George IV: Memoirs of His Life and Reign, Interspersed with Numerous Personal Anecdotes.* London: Treuttel and Würtz, 1830.

Malmesbury, 3rd Earl of (ed.). *Diaries and Correspondence of James Harris, First Earl of Malmesbury, Vol III.* London: Richard Bentley, 1844.

Melville, Lewis. *An Injured Queen, Caroline of Brunswick: Vol I.* London: Hutchinson & Co, 1912.

Melville, Lewis. *The First Gentleman of Europe, Vol II.* London: Hutchinson & Co, 1906.

Miles, William Augustus. *A Letter to the Prince of Wales.* London: J Owen, 1795.

Minto, Countess of (ed.). *Life and Letters of Sir Gilbert Elliot, First Earl of Minto, Vol I.* London: Longmans, Green and Co., 1874.

Minto, Countess of (ed.). *Life and Letters of Sir Gilbert Elliot, First Earl of Minto, Vol III.* London: Longmans, Green and Co., 1874.

Munson, James. *Maria Fitzherbert: The Secret Wife of George IV.* New York: Carroll & Graf, 2002.

Nightingale, Joseph. *Memoirs of Her Late Majesty Queen Caroline.* London: J Robins and Company, 1821.

Nightingale, Joseph. *Memoirs of the Last Days of Her Late Most Gracious Majesty Caroline, Queen of Great Britain, and Consort of King George the Fourth.* London: J Robins and Company, 1822.

Nightingale, Joseph. *Memoirs of the Public and Private Life of Her Most Gracious Majesty Caroline, Queen of Great Britain*. London: J Robins & Co, 1820.

Oulton, CW. *Authentic and Impartial Memoirs of Her Late Majesty: Charlotte Queen of Great Britain and Ireland*. London: Kinnersley, 1819.

Perceval, Spencer. *The Book, Complete*. London: Sherwood, Neely, & Jones, 1813.

Pergami, Bartolomeo. *Tales of the Baroni, or, Scenes in Italy*. London: J Bailey, 1820.

Plowden, Alison. *Caroline and Charlotte*. Stroud: The History Press, 2011.

Princess Charlotte of Wales and Caroline, Princess of Wales. *Royal Correspondence, or, Letters between Her Late Royal Highness the Princess Charlotte, and Her Royal Mother, Queen Caroline*. London: Jones and Company, 1820.

Reeve, Henry (ed.). *A Journal of the Reigns of King George IV and King William IV, Vol II*. London: Longmans, Green, and Co, 1874.

Richardson, Joanne. *The Disastrous Marriage*. London: Jonathan Cape, 1960.

Robins, Jane. *The Trial of Queen Caroline: The Scandalous Affair that Nearly Ended a Monarchy*. New York: Simon and Schuster, 2006.

Robinson, Mary. *Memoirs of the Late Mrs Robinson*. London: Hunt and Clarke, 1827.

Russell, Lord John. *The Life and Times of Charles James Fox: Volume II*. London: Richard Bentley, 1859.

Rutland, Charles Manners. *The Manuscripts of His Grace the Duke of Rutland: Vol. III*. London: Her Majesty's Stationery Office, 1894.

Smith, EA. *George IV*. New Haven: Yale University Press, 1999.

Stanhope, Lady Hester. *Memoirs of the Lady Hester Stanhope Vol I*. London: Henry Colburn, 1846.

Stanhope, Lady Hester. *Memoirs of the Lady Hester Stanhope Vol II*. London: Henry Colburn, 1846.

Stanhope, Philip Henry, 4th Earl Stanhope. *Life of the Right Honourable William Pitt, With Extracts from His Papers, Vol II*. London: John Murray, 1879.

Stott, Anne. *The Lost Queen*. Barnsley: Pen & Sword History, 2020.

Taylor, Stephen. *Defiance: The Life and Choices of Lady Anne Barnard*. London: Faber & Faber, 2016.

Tillyard, Stella. *A Royal Affair: George III and his Troublesome Siblings*. London: Vintage, 2007.

Urban, Sylvanus. *The Gentleman's Magazine: Volume LXXXIII*. London: Nichols, Son, and Bentley, 1813.

Wallace, William. *Memoirs of the Life and Reign of George IV, Vol I*. London: Longman, Rees, Orme, Brown, and Green. 1831.

Wallace, William. *History of the Life and Reign of George IV, Vol II*. London: Longman, Rees, Orme, Brown, and Green. 1832.

Wallace, William. *Memoirs of the Life and Reign of George IV, Vol III*. London: Longman, Rees, Orme, Brown, Green, & Longman. 1832.

Walpole, Horace. *The Last Journals of Horace Walpole During the Reign of George III from 1771–1783*. London: John Lane, 1910.

Watkins, John. *Memoirs of Her Most Excellent Majesty Sophia-Charlotte, Queen of Great Britain*. London: Henry Colburn, 1819.

Weigall, Lady Rose. *A Brief Memoir of the Princess Charlotte of Wales*. London: John Murray, 1874.

Wheatley, Henry B (ed.). *The Historical and Posthumous Memoirs of Sir Nathaniel William Wraxall*. London: Bickers & Son, 1884.

Wilkins, William Henry. *Mrs Fitzherbert and George IV*. London: Longmans, Green, and Co, 1905.

Wilks, John. *Memoirs of Her Majesty Queen Caroline Amelia Eliz, Vol. I*. London: Sherwood, Neely and Jones, 1822.

Williams, Thomas. *Memoirs of Her Late Majesty Queen Charlotte*. London: W Simpkin and R Marshall, 1819.

Williams, Thomas. *Memoirs of His Late Majesty George III*. London: W Simpkin and R Marshall, 1820.

Newspapers Cited

All newspaper clippings are reproduced © The British Library Board; in addition to those cited, innumerable newspapers were consulted.

Websites Consulted

19th Century UK Periodicals (https://www.gale.com/intl/primary-sources/19th-century-uk-periodicals)

British and Irish Women's Letters and Diaries (www.bwl2.alexanderstreet.com)

British History Online (http://www.british-history.ac.uk)

British Library Newspapers (https://www.gale.com/intl/primary-sources/british-library-newspapers)

The Georgian Papers Online, Royal Archives, Windsor (https://gpp.rct.uk)

Hansard (http://hansard.millbanksystems.com/index.html)

Historical Texts (http://historicaltexts.jisc.ac.uk)

House of Commons Parliamentary Papers (http://parlipapers.chadwyck.co.uk/marketing/index.jsp)

JSTOR (www.jstor.org)

The National Archives (http://www.nationalarchives.gov.uk)

Oxford Dictionary of National Biography (http://www.oxforddnb.com)

Seventeenth and Eighteenth Century Burney Newspapers Collection (https://www.gale.com/intl/c/17th-and-eighteenth-century-burney-newspapers-collection)

The Times Digital Archive (https://www.gale.com/intl/c/the-times-digital-archive)

Index